DIFFERENCE, DIALOGUE, AND DEVELOPMENT

Difference, Dialogue, and Development is an in-depth exploration of the collected works of Mikhail Bakhtin to find relevance of key concepts of dialogism for understanding various aspects of human development. Taking the reality of differences in the world as a given, Bandlamudi argues that such a reality necessitates dialogue, and actively responding to that necessity leads to development. The varied works of Bakhtin that span several decades passing through the most tumultuous period in Russian history, are brought under one banner of three D's—Difference, Dialogue and Development—and the composite features of the three D's emerge as leitmotifs in every chapter.

Dr. Lakshmi Bandlamudi is a Professor of Psychology at LaGuardia Community College, City University of New York. She is the author of *Dialogics of Self, The Mahabharata and Culture: The History of Understanding and Understanding of History*, and several other papers focusing on dialogic consciousness.

"In an ocean of Bakhtiniana, this is a fresh voice. Lakshmi Bandlamudi brings together the disparate works Bakhtin wrote over a long lifetime in a reading that adds 'Development' to the usual 'Ds' (Dialogue, Difference) in Bakhtin studies. In so doing, she adds another dimension to the heteronomy called 'Bakhtin.'"

—Michael Holquist, Professor Emeritus,
Comparative Literature, Yale University

"Lakshmi Bandlamudi's *Difference, Dialogue, and Development* has to rank among the very best, certainly the clearest, most astute expositions of Bakhtin's writings. Her aim is not simply to explicate the Russian thinker's wide-ranging, at times seemingly contradictory, essays but to depict his worldview and the ethical implications that derive from his commitment to the ever-shifting dialogical dimensions of human life—to encounters that resist definition, as definition is demanded. Bandlamudi accepts, indeed elaborates, the challenges to the staid visions of the human sciences that Bakhtin poses. As such, she challenges those same staid assumptions that govern so much of our lives. Her work is transformative."

—Vincent Crapanzano, Distinguished Professor,
Anthropology and Comparative Literature.
Graduate Center, City University of New York

DIFFERENCE, DIALOGUE, AND DEVELOPMENT

A Bakhtinian World

Lakshmi Bandlamudi

NEW YORK AND LONDON

First published 2016
by Routledge
711 Third Avenue, New York, NY 10017

and by Routledge
2 Park Square, Milton Park, Abingdon, Oxon OX14 4RN

Routledge is an imprint of the Taylor & Francis Group, an informa business.

© 2016 Taylor & Francis

The right of Lakshmi Bandlamudi to be identified as author of this work has been asserted by her in accordance with sections 77 and 78 of the Copyright, Designs and Patents Act 1988.

All rights reserved. No part of this book may be reprinted or reproduced or utilized in any form or by any electronic, mechanical, or other means, now known or hereafter invented, including photocopying and recording, or in any information storage or retrieval system, without permission in writing from the publishers.

Trademark notice: Product or corporate names may be trademarks or registered trademarks, and are used only for identification and explanation without intent to infringe.

Library of Congress Cataloging-in-Publication Data
Bandlamudi, Lakshmi.
  Difference, dialogue & development : a Bakhtinian world / by Lakshmi Bandlamudi.
     pages cm
  Includes bibliographical references and index.
  1. Bakhtin, M. M. (Mikhail Mikhailovich), 1895–1975—Criticism and interpretation.   I. Title.
  PG2947.B3B39 2016
  801'.95092—dc23
  2015020078

ISBN: 978-1-138-80592-7 (hbk)
ISBN: 978-1-138-80593-4 (pbk)
ISBN: 978-1-315-66933-5 (ebk)

Typeset in Bembo
by Apex CoVantage, LLC

In Dedication

To

Mikhail Bakhtin

for showing an open-ended world with innumerable possibilities. . . .

This, [in the beginning], was only the Lord of the universe. His Word was with him. This Word was his second. He contemplated. He said, "I will deliver this Word so that she will produce and bring into being all this world."

Tandya Maha Brahmana XX, 14, 2

The Word is infinite, immense, beyond all this. . . . All the Gods, the celestial spirits, men and animals, live in the Word. In the Word all the worlds find their support.

Taittiriya Brahmana II, 8, 8, 4

To study the word as such, ignoring the impulse that reaches out beyond it, it is just as senseless as to study psychological experience outside the context of that real life toward which it was directed and by which it is determined.

Mikhail Bakhtin, DN. P. 292

CONTENTS

Preface   *viii*
Acknowledgments   *x*
Abbreviations   *xii*

1   Introduction: Dialogue = Development   1

2   The Novel and the Hero: Developmental Narrative and the Developing Subject   14

3   Creative Living and Aesthetic Vision: Cultivating Finer Sensibilities   40

4   Carnivalization of Consciousness: A Catalyst for Development   63

5   Authoring the Self—Answering the Other: Epistemological Necessities and Ethical Obligations   87

6   Dialogic Method for Human Sciences: Between the Message Giver—Message—Messenger—and Message Receiver   105

7   Differences as the Will to Power and Freedom to Choose   121

References   *137*
Index   *141*

PREFACE

> **World of Differences . . . Dialogic Possibilities . . . Developmental Gains . . .**
>
> Out of a still Immensity we came!
> These million universes were to it
> The poor light-bubbles of a trivial game,
> A fragile glimmer in the Infinite.
>
> It could not find its soul in all that vast:
> It drew itself into a little speck
> Infinitesimal, ignobly cast
> Out of earth's mud and slime strangely awake,—
>
> A tiny plasm upon a casual globe
> In the small system of a dwarflike sun,
> A little life wearing the flesh for robe,
> A little mind winged through wide space to run!
>
> It lives, it knew, it saw its self sublime,
> Deathless, outmeasuring Space, outlasting Time.
>
> *Sri Aurobindo,* The Infinitesimal Infinite

This book emerges from an ongoing conceptual delight and anguish. First, about the delight: when a book falls in your lap and you meet a thinker, it does change your life. It opens up new possibilities, allows you to make sense of your intuitions, and awakens valuable dormant thoughts. Ever since I encountered Mikhail Bakhtin's works as a graduate student in the mid-1980s, I have been wandering in the Bakhtinian world. This wandering pushed me into other improbable journeys, and the most significant one was a delightful excursion into a timeless past—deep into my cultural past—the great epic past of The Mahabharata, which had greater immediate presence in my lived life. In a systematic study that became a book—*Dialogics of Self, The Mahabharata and Culture: The History of Understanding and Understanding of History*—I discovered ways in which individuals engage with the text; for many the text is fixed, distant, and antiquated and there is an impenetrable barrier between the self and the text, while a few others take delight in entering the fluid text and they are able to discover new semantic possibilities about their lives and life around them. In short, lived life entered into a dialogue with the living text. While the monologic reader was not able to discover anything new, the dialogic reader displayed incredible dynamism, keeping wonder and curiosity alive, and not only found comfort in the world of differences and ambiguities, but also seemed skillful in orchestrating divergent viewpoints.

My wandering in the Bakhtinian world took me on other adventures as well, but for the sake of brevity I shall not go into those details. But the important point is that a persistent idea—an idea of dialogic development—occupied my mind.

When I examine the incredible progress made in various areas of science, I see, despite my limited knowledge, the full force of dialogic principles operating in creativity and innovation. Einstein tells us that space and time are not absolutes and that they are infinitely baffling, and Heisenberg's principle tells us that at a subatomic level, the principle of causality does not hold. Cosmology tells us that the expanding universe is made of billions of galaxies that are unending. Raised as a Hindu, I was told that the universe moves according to the rhythms emanating from the drums of Lord Shiva—the Cosmic Dancer—and his drums produce inexhaustible sounds. Feeling captivated by this idea, I made a pilgrimage twice to what is considered the abode of Shiva—Mount Kailash, in the Himalayas—and walking on the Tibetan Plateau, my soul recorded incredible variations in the Silence that pervades the region. Who ever thought that sound and silence could have so many variations? Science, astronomy, cosmology, and many more disciplines seem to suggest that the world of differences keeps you on the move, ever exploring, learning, and realizing new things.

Now, the part about anguish: our notions of progress and our theories on development don't seem to consider the potential for multidirectional and multidimensional development in a diverse world. It seems stuck with linear models that are unidirectional with some endpoint. But reality presents another picture.

My wandering in the Bakhtinian world tells me that there is a way of addressing our epistemological questions and accounting for ethical obligations and understanding emotional responsiveness in a world of differences. It is with this promise that I once again entered the Bakhtinian world, and what emerged from that voyage is this book on *Differences, Dialogue, and Development*.

ACKNOWLEDGMENTS

Ideas do not emerge in a vacuum—they are the result of ongoing dialogues with innumerable thinkers of the past from so many regions in the globe and countless people in various walks of life; therefore, it would be impossible to acknowledge the debt owed to so many. That said, it is still my duty and obligation to express gratitude to a select few who have directly or indirectly contributed to this project.

The thematic organization of this book took shape in 2013, when I spent six months at the Advanced Research Collaborative at the Graduate Center, City University of New York as a CUNY Distinguished Fellow. Meaningful conversations I had with other Fellows were priceless. I thank Donald Robotham for making this possible.

I am grateful for the consistent and unwavering support that Joseph Glick has given to each and every one of my academic projects. Without him as an interlocutor, many ideas would not have taken shape.

John Dore introduced me to the Bakhtinian world in the late 1980s, and ever since he has been a great partner in an ongoing dialogue. I thank him for his critical reading of a few of my chapters.

I am grateful to Vincent Crapanzano, who has been my role model in doing interdisciplinary work. He gave valuable advice in early stages of formulating this work.

It is indeed encouraging and validating when an eminent Bakhtin scholar like Caryl Emerson gives a generous review of a book proposal and offers new directions. I am so grateful that her works provide clarity and force to my thinking.

I wish to extend heartfelt thanks to fellow Bakhtin enthusiasts—James Cresswell and Paul Sullivan—for their critical reading of a few of my chapters. Their works have found their proper place in this work.

Acknowledgments **xi**

A very special thanks to my dear friend and colleague Lily Shohat, who has supported me on so many levels. She has been my unwavering cheerleader. It is touching and humbling to receive that kind of support.

Thanks are due to Sara Zarem, Linda Mayers, Eduardo Vianna, Lorraine Cohen, Mark Zuss, and Joanne Reitano. Without their encouraging words, I could not have brought this project to fruition.

I must express my gratitude to President Gail Mellow and Provost Paul Arcario of LaGuardia Community College, City University of New York—my institution—for their support in my scholarly pursuits.

My mother, *Saraswati Bandlamudi*, who lives up to her name—the goddess of knowledge—always finds ways to make sure that I pursue my scholarly activities. Immeasurable is her support.

My late father, *Visweswariah Bandlamudi*, has always been my super addressee. Without his early introduction to Dostoevsky's works during my teenage years, I could not have developed the same degree of passion for Bakhtin's ideas. I hope from above I get his approving nod.

Interestingly and paradoxically, many principles of dialogism and aspects of Bakhtin's life played out while I was writing this book. Many chapters in this book were written while I was coping with a sudden onset of a debilitating condition—the autoimmune condition of rheumatoid arthritis. Several months went by when I could barely turn a page, let alone hold a pen to write. As I was dealing with my corporeal woes, I felt such a strong connection and sympathy for Bakhtin and even identification, as he himself struggled with osteomyelitis all his life. So my hero was no stranger to problems with movement and flexibility—the very same issues I was dealing with. Because I opted for alternative medicine to reset my body, rather than suppress the immune system, I had to rely on principles of dialogicality to get the cells in my body to engage with each other with regard, rather than attack each other indiscriminately. Dialogicality penetrated deep into my body, at a cellular level. I am much better now, and this would not have been possible without my caring team of healers—Dr. Lance Li, who gave acupuncture and Chinese massage at pressure points and herbs; and my Ayurvedic clinicians who provided their comprehensive treatment, Dr. Ambika Nair, Dr. Shyla Matthew, Dr. Priya Balamurugen and Mr. Gary Grewal. These ancient healing methods do have a way of getting the cells in your body to live in harmony. These healers made it their business to ensure that I would resume writing. I am eternally grateful to them for their skill, professionalism, kindness, and commitment.

I am, of course, thankful to Georgette Enriquez of Routledge for believing in my project and for the consideration she has shown for unavoidable delays in the project as I was coping with health issues.

Without the Guiding Presence of Universal Parents—Lord Shiva and Devi Parvati—thoughts would not have ripened into words. Their power of healing Silence was felt and realized as never before in the process of writing this book.

ABBREVIATIONS

AA   *Art and Answerability* in Bakhtin, M. M. (1990) *Art and Answerability: Early Philosophical Essays by M.M. Bakhtin* (V. Liapunov, Trans.) M. Holquist and V. Liapunov (Eds.) Austin: University of Texas Press.

AHAA   *Author and Hero in Aesthetic Activity* in Bakhtin, M. M. (1990) *Art and Answerability: Early Philosophical Essays by M.M. Bakhtin* (V. Liapunov, Trans.) M. Holquist and V. Liapunov (Eds.) Austin: University of Texas Press.

CMFVA   *Content, Material, and Form in Verbal Art* in Bakhtin, M. M. (1990) *Art and Answerability: Early Philosophical Essays by M.M. Bakhtin* (V. Liapunov, Trans.) M. Holquist and V. Liapunov (Eds.) Austin: University of Texas Press.

DN   *Discourse in the Novel* in Bakhtin, M. M. (1981) *The Dialogic Imagination: Four Essays* (C. Emerson and M. Holquist, Trans.) M. Holquist (Ed.) Austin: University of Texas Press.

EN   *Epic and Novel* in Bakhtin, M. M. (1981) *The Dialogic Imagination: Four Essays* (C. Emerson and M. Holquist, Trans.) M. Holquist. (Ed.) Austin: University of Texas Press.

FM   Bakhtin, M. M. and Medvedev, P. N. (1985) *The Formal Method in Literary Scholarship: A Critical Introduction to Sociological Poetics* (A. J. Wehrle, Trans.) Cambridge: Harvard University Press.

FNM 70–71 *From Notes Made in 1970–71* in Bakhtin, M. M. (1986) *Speech Genres & Other Late Essays* (V. W. McGee, Trans.) C. Emerson and M. Holquist (Eds.) Austin: University of Texas Press.

FTCN   *Forms of Time and Chronotope in the Novel* in Bakhtin, M. M. (1981) *The Dialogic Imagination: Four Essays* (C. Emerson and M.

	Holquist, Trans.) M. Holquist (Ed.) Austin: University of Texas Press.
PDP	Bakhtin, M. M. (1984b) *Problems of Dostoevsky's Poetics* (C. Emerson, Trans. and Ed.) Minneapolis: University of Minnesota Press.
PND	*From the Prehistory of Novelistic Discourse* in Bakhtin, M. M. (1981) *The Dialogic Imagination: Four Essays* (C. Emerson and M. Holquist, Trans.) M. Holquist. (Ed.) Austin: University of Texas Press.
PSG	*Problems of Speech Genres* in Bakhtin, M. M. (1986) *Speech Genres & Other Late Essays* (V. W. McGee, Trans.) C. Emerson and M. Holquist (Eds.) Austin: University of Texas Press.
RAW	Bakhtin, M. M. (1984a) *Rabelais and His World* (H. Iswolsky, Trans.) Bloomington: Indiana University Press.
RQNM	*Response to a Question from Novy Mir* in Bakhtin, M. M. (1986) *Speech Genres & Other Late Essays* (V. W. McGee, Trans.) C. Emerson and M. Holquist (Eds.) Austin: University of Texas Press.
TMHS	*Toward a Methodology for the Human Sciences* in Bakhtin, M. M. (1986) *Speech Genres & Other Late Essays* (V. W. McGee, Trans.) C. Emerson and M. Holquist (Eds.) Austin: University of Texas Press.
TPA	Bakhtin, M. M. (1993) *Toward a Philosophy of the Act* (V. Liapunov, Trans.) V. Liapunov and M. Holquist (Eds.) Austin: University of Texas Press.
TPT	*The Problem of the Text* in Bakhtin, M. M. (1986) *Speech Genres & Other Late Essays* (V. W. McGee, Trans.) C. Emerson and M. Holquist (Eds.) Austin: University of Texas Press.

1
INTRODUCTION
Dialogue = Development

> Life can be consciously comprehended only as an ongoing event, and not as Being *qua* a given. A life that has fallen away from answerability cannot have a philosophy: it is, in its very principle fortuitous and incapable of being rooted.
>
> *Mikhail Bakhtin,* Toward a Philosophy of the Act, *1993, p. 56*

This brief excerpt from Mikhail Bakhtin's early writings on the philosophy of the act says so much about so many aspects of human development—what constitutes development, how development might be understood, and why certain modes of consciousness and being in the world qualify as comprehensive developmental achievement. At the same time, Bakhtin also cautions forcefully about the dangers of assuming development to be an individual affair. First and foremost, every domain of human activity within the overarching framework of life is given the dynamic thrust of movement, when Bakhtin insists that it be comprehended as an "ongoing event" and not as a given being. This living subject in a changing world is held accountable by what Bakhtin calls the "unity of answerability" to practically every entity in culture and history, including the self, and failure to fulfill this obligation of answering the other results in growth that happens to be a chance occurrence. More importantly, it becomes a rootless existence. From these few sentences in Bakhtin's early works, we can extract the very essence of human development. But Bakhtin did not set out to theorize about human development.

For that matter, it is difficult to situate Bakhtin within the strict confines of academic disciplines. Although largely recognized as a literary theorist, Bakhtin pursued interests that went way beyond literary texts. In their authoritative biography, Clark and Holquist (1984) claim that Bakhtin really considered himself a philosophical anthropologist at heart, probing into the interconnections between texts, cultures, and histories. While his works that span several decades passing through the most tumultuous period in Russian history display incredible insights into the diversity of the world, he was not necessarily driven by a single question or an overriding concern. He was not out there to solve a philosophical riddle once and for all, nor was he an intellectual "hedgehog" digging deeper and deeper to discover some stable structures. Instead, in Bakhtin's works, one finds a free, open-ended play of ideas going in multiple directions, expressed in a myriad of ways. This does not mean that there is no unity in the collection of his works. The unity is a "non-monologic" one—one that does not erase other voices. As Morson and Emerson (1990) point out, Bakhtin was interested in that kind of unity in which concepts or entities are connected loosely, not in a way that results in amorphousness, but the kind of connection that allows ample movement for the creative processes to emerge. If one theme unifies his works in their stages of development, in Bakhtin's (1986) own words, it is the "internal open-endedness" of many of his ideas. In his "Notes made in 1970–71" toward the end of his life, he reflected on the seeming inconsistencies in his works and their potential for misunderstanding and says, "The unity of emerging (developing) idea. Hence a certain open-endedness of many of my ideas" (p. 155). It is very instructive for anyone interested in studying developmental processes—be it of an idea or an individual or any domain of human functioning—that Bakhtin sees open-endedness as a necessity. He further clarifies that it is "an open-endedness not of the thought itself but its expression and exposition" (p. 155). Bakhtin on top of that personalizes his methods in an almost confessional tone. "My love for variations and for diversity of terms for a single phenomenon. The multiplicity of focuses. Bringing distant things closer without indicating the intermediate links" (p. 155). In many ways this open-endedness, which in his view was the requirement for the development of an idea, in a paradoxical manner, was also an entry point for the misappropriation and misreading of his works. Those notes made toward the end of his life, although rather spotty, are profound to our concerns about development. If our focus is on the product of development and we see it as teleological and assume the path to be unidirectional, then we are left with a non-contradictory, single-voiced, and unified view of development, whereas when our concerns are with the processes of development, then we have to consider the unfinalized and unpredictable nature of developmental pathways.

In addition to open-endedness, Bakhtin had a deep fascination with differences—variations in tone, subtleties in voices, changes in time periods—in short, nothing else seemed to impress him as much as the varying shades in cultural landscapes and distinctive tones in individual voices. Perhaps few thinkers have celebrated the cornucopia of differences in the world as much as Bakhtin did. It is this fascination with variety that makes his works appealing to so many disciplines—from Slavic studies to literary criticism to anthropology to linguistics and, to a limited degree, to psychology. It may be that Bakhtin's name is mentioned in the classrooms and corridors of every discipline in the humanities and social sciences, even if it is limited to some of his selected works, particularly his later works. It is not surprising, given that words like "plurality," "diversity," and "dialogue" have become fashionable even in popular discourses. Bakhtin's appeal goes beyond disciplines—it has been absorbed by various schools of thought, often with competing ideologies, as Caryl Emerson, one of the foremost authorities on Bakhtin, observes:

> Bakhtin offers something to every camp. Neo-humanists detect in him a liberal spirit and a patron saint of the new plurality and *tolerantnost'*; philosophers of religion have discovered a "vertical hierarchy" in his thought and a commitment to absolute values; Russian nationalists locate his roots in Orthodox spirituality.
>
> *(1997, p. 17)*

Clearly, Bakhtin's open-ended ideas invite various schools of thought to appropriate him as their own. His works are capacious enough to accommodate every angle in an idea, and every voice, however feeble, gets a fair hearing. This appeal to everyone also leaves Bakhtin in a deeply ironic situation; none understands him, at least in a comprehensive manner. He did not exactly start a "movement" or a "school of thought," and neither did he come up with easy, analyzable tools, and, in the intellectual world, although prominent, as I. N. Fridman observes, "Bakhtin remains homeless and unattached" (cited by Caryl Emerson, 1997, in *The First Hundred Years of Mikhail Bakhtin*). In fact, everything about Bakhtin is contentious—his intellectual roots, his personal life, his academic life (his doctoral dissertation on Rabelais caused furor then and continues to generate controversy to this day), and even his identity is in dispute, for there is considerable debate on whether Volosinov and Medvedev were separate individuals or if they were indeed Bakhtin. I draw attention to the complexities and the contradictions in Bakhtin's works and the controversies about his works and his life, only to establish at the very outset the challenges in hearing those profound voices relevant to various aspects of human development in his incredibly insightful works that often seem repetitive and yet so highly nuanced. In giving a feel for the man, his style, and his mind, Caryl Emerson's observations are revealing:

> In place of God, Bakhtin deified the everyday interlocutor. A creature made neither for prayer nor parenting, he reigned in a world of philosophical conversations carried out over endless tea and cigarettes in small rooms in the dead of night. Bakhtin was a *mezhdusoboinik* (a "just-between-you-and-me-nik"). For him, the intimate voice and the chamber space was all.
>
> *(1997, p. 5)*

Given this characterization of Bakhtin's world, one must then enter the chamber space with a preparation and willingness to listen, listen to the voices in the texts that Bakhtin is engaging with, listen to the conversations that Bakhtin has with those voices, and listen to Bakhtin's voice while he is ruminating about the deep meanings of the text. In all his works, Bakhtin recommends the auditory over the visual—his preferred method to grasp the nuances of culture and text. Bakhtin asks us to fine-tune our ears not only to hear the contents of the voice but also the fluctuations in tone. For a thinker who insisted on the unsystematizability of culture and the unfinalizability of meaning-making ventures, it is only understandable that his works demand an unorthodox approach. It is with this not so clearly defined method that I approach his collected works, which despite their internal differences could be brought under one banner of three D's—Difference, Dialogue, and Development. The composite features of these three D's will emerge as leitmotifs in every chapter in this book.

Differences Necessitate Dialogue

In both popular and academic cultures, there has been a great deal of emphasis on similarities—in the former it is to achieve the ideal of unity and harmony in society with the motto being, "let us focus on what is common among all of us" to affirm our collective humanity, and in the academic world it is the call of "Universalism" that tries to search for the "deep truth"—the abstract points of similarities—while treating differences as trivial surface manifestations. Differences are seen as irrelevant and unimportant and considered a distraction that pulls one away from constructing an ideal society, or they are treated as interferences in our search for "truth" that is considered stable, rational, and objective. What is ignored in the ideal and rational world is the main focus for Bakhtin—the variations in the world. A merger of voices and an obliteration of identities to make a homogeneous whole, for Bakhtin, is epistemologically flawed, leading to false consciousness. To him, differences are an immediate reality that cannot be transcended, but they create the necessity for the other, making individuals truly interdependent. That's what makes us social animals. Bakhtin (1990) asks, "What would I have to gain if another were to *fuse* with me?" It is the "other" with its distinct voice occupying a unique position in time and space that serves as a mirror to reflect and reveal the uniqueness of my voice and my special position in time and space. This distinction between self and other cannot be erased in an attempt to gain a roving perspective on reality, which, in Bakhtin's view, is really a myth. Bakhtin insists that one needs the other only because each one gets only a partial glimpse of reality and hence needs the "other" to offer another perspective. For Bakhtin, heterogeneity cannot be subordinated to homogeneity and uniformity cannot be a sought-after ideal. Differences to him are not surface disturbances to be ignored in search of deep, stable structures; instead, they are rich, real, and necessary for developing not only the rudimentary cognitive functions but also the finer sensibilities to develop an aesthetic vision.

Bakhtin's fascination with variety and plurality must not be construed as a kind of philosophical relativism. If anything, he probed into how "one" can become "many"—one word and its ability to convey a whole range of meanings when strung together with other words; one action or experience that takes on different meanings and significance in the course of life; one private thought that assumes different meanings when expressed for public consumption depending on the listeners. How can a "word" or an "utterance" have different meanings? For Bakhtin, the answer lies in the purpose and context of their usage and their contact with other words and utterances and who the interlocutor is at a given moment. Not only is the variety enjoyed by words, but also the absence of words—those pauses, occasional stammers, and stutters also enjoy the same privilege of variety in interpretation. Think about all the meanings that "silence" may assume—a necessity when deep thoughts are being churned, a screen while searching for the right word or phrase, an interval for mining the ore of ideas in order to resume their public display, a mask for ignorance, a sign of wisdom, a consent, or a snub, a form of tyranny or a strategy for defiance, a remedy for raging temper, an exercise to develop a steady mind, a symptom of dumbness, or an indication of a contemplative soul in search of its Creator. Silence may be a place for the exhausted word to retire, but the meaning of silence remains inexhaustible in an unfinalized form. It is this variety that fascinated Bakhtin and thus, to understand the meaning of words and utterances or actions, one needs to be extra sensitive to the social context, the historical climate, and the correspondence or the dis-correspondence between the speaker and the listener.

Thus, what we see here is Bakhtin's emphasis on the plenitude of differences in the world—voices, customs, meanings, and so on are not merely meant for empty celebration, which so often is the case in our globalized existence, where every institution is keen on celebrating the multicultural world without grasping the philosophical depth of differences in the world and their loose interconnections. For Bakhtin, differences are an ontological reality and must be taken seriously in theorizing every branch of human activity, be it epistemology, ethics, or aesthetics. As diverse as Bakhtin's writings are, they are built primarily on the fundamental reality of differences—the one in many and many in one—so that difference is not at the expense of unity. It is the difference that necessitates a dialogue.

Dialogue Leads to Development

Development as a theme or as a topic seldom appears in Bakhtin's works; in fact, the very word is rarely used. But we can hear him hint at it in his celebration of Dostoevsky's novels and Goethe's works, or when he traces the life of a novelistic hero, or in his philosophical essays on architectonics—a study of how entities relate to each other—or in the nature of the relationship between the author and the hero that could create an aesthetic vision. In all these seemingly disparate bodies of works, Bakhtin does come across as a patron saint of dialogue, because in every topic he probed into he saw the versatility of dialogic relations—their ability to create innumerable potentialities, and their vitality in social relations without subordinating one voice to the other, and their unique capacity to mate the individual with the surrounding environment—all these findings clearly suggest an immense developmental potential in dialogic consciousness. But how, then, does one sift out some concepts of development from his works that did not set out to do that? Can we pull out some metaphors from his works to examine how the idea of development plays out in his thinking? The approach clearly has to be unconventional: one must simply accept Bakhtin's invitation to enter his world to hear the voices of consciousness that he plays from the texts that he is engaging with, only to hear them slowly emerge from ordinary impressions of the world to artistic thinking to aesthetic vision. This movement is by no means linear; it is full of zigzags and coils. In Bakhtin's early works on architectonics and the philosophy of the act, he makes a more than compelling case for what constitutes aesthetic vision, even while pointing out the factors that inhibit the achievement of this heightened consciousness. About differences and dialogue, Bakhtin had much to say, but only through a circuitous route can one link them to human development. One must be willing to look in the most unusual of places in Bakhtin's world to find something precious to our concerns in developmental psychology.

Bakhtin saw dialogic relations as both a feature of fundamental awareness of self and other in society and as a mark of exceptionally creative thinking. It is only through the encounter with the other that one comes to recognize oneself in full depth—one's position in the world, the unwritten script that culture has provided to conduct oneself in the world, and the unseen history one has inherited, and this heightened awareness is not possible unless one is face to face with the other (Bakhtin, 1986; RQNM). The revelation that occurs during this encounter may have a different impact on individuals. In one case, the individual could feel exposed because the invisible aspects of self and culture are revealed and might even feel threatened by the other, and hence the individual begins to cope with this anxiety by constructing a very rigid view of culture. The individual may construct "imaginary homelands" and unambiguous cultural practices or use culture as an excuse for all his or her actions. In short, the forces of culture and history, which by their very nature are dynamic and changing, are treated as rigid and frozen by individuals, which results in a monologic view of themselves and their surrounding world. In Bakhtin's view, it would be pernicious to claim that you are the way you are because your culture and history have showcased you in a certain fashion. Bakhtin was not a cultural determinist. But what impressed him was that the revelation that occurs during the dialogic encounter has the potential to produce a deeper understanding of self, operating in an ever-changing cultural and historical process. This awareness creates a unique opportunity for the self to be creative in picking and choosing aspects of culture and history. This allows individuals to release themselves from the trappings of culture and history. The individual is neither disembodied from the cultural soil nor is lost in the cultural flux. Likewise, he or she feels neither uprooted from history nor burdened by the errors of the past. Herein lays the potential for growth and development in dialogic relations.

Narratives on Development and Tales about Children

The central trope in the narratives about growth and development is that the movement is systematic, sequential, linear, and unidirectional, and, in order to trace this trajectory—assumed to be universal—we write stories about where we came from or what we started out with and how far we have come. We designate "the child"—not actual children living in a specific culture at a unique historic moment—but "the child" the "epistemic child"—as the principal character and construct the plot around various domains of development—cognitive, emotional, social, and so forth. The core assumption in the vast majority of developmental narratives is that all of humanity proceeds in the same direction and differences are only in the ranking. Thus, developmental psychologists tell us stories, grand stories, about children, with claims of scientific verifiability. That being so, we take "the child" as a starting point to trace our own history, our developmental pathway, ignoring the fact that childhood itself has had a very long history in presenting different images of childhood. Throughout history the image of the "child" has never been stable: it changed from a "miniature adult" during medieval times to an absolute nothingness—a *tabula rasa* in the hands of John Locke, only to be shaped by the world. The world has a tendency to put you in shackles, says romantic philosopher Jean Jacques Rousseau, and as a challenge to the Lockean subject, he created *Emile* as an emblem of a child born free, and who is naturally self-sufficient and curious and bound to develop according to nature's plan and timetable. While Rousseau created a fictional character to impress upon the world the natural path of development, the psychologists of the twentieth century claimed to have discovered the "laws of development" in their children. Jean Piaget told us the story of the *epistemic child*, citing detailed observations he made with his children's behavior. He told us that the world is wide open for this ever-inquisitive child to explore, only to construct the laws governing the world in his mind. This heroic epistemic child of Piaget is forever laboring at the construction site called "the mind," facing challenges from the world to slowly ascend from an ignorant state where primitive sensory impressions dominate to the intuitive operations in early childhood to finally reach the pinnacle of cognitive development—the formal operational stage—governed by abstract, scientific, and rational thought.

The father of evolutionary theory, Charles Darwin, claimed that he detected "emotions" in his infant son that set the stage for drawing parallels between ontogeny and phylogeny. The idea that individual growth recapitulates species evolution came to be the dominant principle in developmental theories that followed. Since then, we started looking into our long, evolutionary history for some hints or explanations for children's behavior. This trend of using one's child as a site for constructing theories of development—regardless of the approach—made developmental psychology distinctly child-centered. Almost every major theorist contributed to this trend. Sigmund Freud said he identified "desire" in his daughter, and James Watson presented his son as a proof of classical conditioning, and James Baldwin claimed that he detected "thought" in his young daughter. All of them claimed that universal laws of thought and behavior were at work *in* their children, and none of them speculated on how "my child" became "the child." How did the subjective experience of a parent–child relationship mutate into an objective, universal truth about children? In the annals of developmental psychology, the parent and the researcher switched roles almost unreflectively, and their children became the *heroes* of the developmental tales that they were eager to convey. Note that their tales were restricted to their children's early years, and after that, the theory took on a life of its own to support their philosophical leaning. As authors of developmental stories, these psychologists, along with innumerable contemporary researchers, sketched out an *image* of "the child" to fit their ideology. Never so innocent and pure, these narratives were couched in the language of science and objectivity to present their version of innocence and purity of the child. In his landmark essay, William Kessen (1979) aptly observed that "the child" and the developmental narratives are in fact cultural inventions.

Taking Kessen's observation seriously, we then have to acknowledge that "the child" in the developmental narratives is more than a concrete child; the child becomes an idea, a concept, and a metaphor to write commentaries on cultural conditions. These developmental narratives surely have some partial truths, but missing is how the child has become a site to explore our origins, our evolution, and our desire in the open-ended future.

Theories about human development, more than any other subfield in psychology, have a powerful impact on our everyday lives and ways of thinking about ourselves. When I say theories, I am going beyond what professional philosophers and psychologists put forth; I am referring to theories that all humans, particularly since the Industrial Revolution, have been developing. Ideas about progress, change, and development began to emerge with the Industrial Revolution because technological advances created real-life possibilities to improve living conditions. Implicit in childrearing practices is a theory on the preferred and desirable path that must be charted out for the growing child. Even if we set aside the child, simple questions we ask ourselves—"how am I doing," "where am I going," "why am I stuck"—and questions others ask of us—"why are you not married," "when are you going to be a parent," and so on—are loaded with assumptions on progress, success, and development. And yet they are fundamental to our existence. In raising such contemplative questions, we either have an already formed template or trajectory that we have imbibed from the world around us, or we want to reject the given trajectory in search of a new direction.

In short, individually and collectively, we are constantly building and rebuilding theories on what constitutes childhood, progress, success, intelligence, maturity, and so on, and this exercise is fundamental to human existence.

Development as an idea is very complex; it is complicated because there are no neat universal pathways, although many theorists would like us to believe in such pathways; it is controversial because it is so value-laden, and yet it is an idea that we desperately need to make sense of the surrounding world and ourselves. We could raise many questions about each of the theoretical models. How capacious is the theory to be able to account for various domains of development? What is the explanatory capability? Who is included? Who is excluded? The questions can go on. My point is that ideas about development are so fundamental to human life and human interactions that it would be impossible to reflect on the path we have taken, reassess the goals we have set for ourselves, reevaluate the abstract ideals we hold on to, and so on without some explicit and/or implicit theory about development.

My question for the current project comes from the immediate cultural reality we live in. Unarguably, we live in a very rapidly changing, diverse world. Existing theories, each in their own way, present a very tidy picture of a developmental pathway, but the realities we observe in the social world remain unaccounted for. How, then, do we make sense of the world of differences and how can we manage to grow and develop in such a world with due regard for others without losing personal integrity? With these questions in mind, I approach the collected works of Mikhail Bakhtin to find some insights. After all, very few thinkers in recent times have shown the kind of fascination that Bakhtin had with the plenitude of differences in the world.

Does a Theory of Development Exist in Bakhtin's World of Differences?

A straightforward answer to this question is a simple "no" and a complicated "yes." First, why the simple "no"—because Bakhtin did not set out to theorize about human development or any one specific aspect of human development, be it cognition, emotion, morality, or any other domain. Even if Bakhtin did not intend to give an account of human development, do we hear him hint at any systematic developmental processes? The answer would be no. In psychology, development is typically understood as teleological; Piaget concentrated on abstraction and generalization with a clear stage theory, while Vygotsky spoke about higher mental functions without a stage theory, and Werner and Kaplan explained the orthogenetic principle, where development is characterized by the dual processes of differentiation and hierarchic integration. Therefore, by the criteria of these existing models, Bakhtin certainly has no developmental theory.

Now, coming to the complicated "yes"—Bakhtin's works do not allow us to see human development as a generic process along some universal dimension, nor is there any indication of a domain-specific, context-dependent account of development; but if we are willing to consider a radically different understanding of development—that is, processes of becoming a person amidst the incredible diversity of the world, a living aesthetic, ethical, and emotional responsiveness to a life lived with different others—then we are bound to find valuable insights in his collected works.

I enter the Bakhtinian world to release myself from monologic positions that have only led me to dead ends, and enter the dialogic world to see and discover what others see about how humans interact with fellow humans and with cultural and historical processes, and how and why many hold fixed views, and how and why some manage to feel at home and grow in a very fluid and diverse world. As a developmental psychologist, the latter interests me.

This book is an in-depth exploration of the Bakhtinian oeuvre or, better, it is a wandering, an intense, purposeful wandering in the Bakhtinian world in search of what his favorite writer, Dostoevsky, famously said—to find the "man in man," or rather to figure out how to find the "man in man."

The chapters follow Bakhtin's writings closely, not necessarily in the same sequence they were written in, but based on topical relevance to psychology. Thus, the chapters could be read as stand-alone or as an integral part of the dialogic world.

The novel as a genre is emblematic of consciousness for Bakhtin, and the novelistic hero is forever in search of meanings to develop his identity amidst cultural-historical forces. The idea of "development" and the image of a "developing subject" find their direct and clearest expression in Bakhtin's writings on the novelistic genre, which to him was a break from the epic genre. While the epic is an already developed genre, the novel is a developing genre, and if the epic hero is a developed subject, the novelistic hero is a developing subject. In Chapter 2, I build a case for treating various novelistic genres as developmental narratives and extend Bakhtin's analytical tool—chronotope, the spatiotemporal configuration in the narrative that he deploys to show the image of the hero and his relationship to the surrounding world—to various models of development in psychology. This exercise, I argue, allows us to theorize human development in all its dimension and scope. Engaging in chronotopic analysis, Bakhtin identifies various types of novels in three broad categories—(a) novels of non-emergence that present a static image of a hero against the backdrop of an immobile world; (b) novels of emergence that present a developing hero in a static world; and (c) novels of historical emergence that present a developing hero in a changing world. I extend Bakhtin's typology of novels to identify various images of developing subjects. The sections in the chapter are—(a) the Greek romance marked by life tested by fate; (b) the adventure novel, where crisis changes self and the change is not necessarily developmental; (c) the travel novel that presents self as a passive traveler in a static world; (d) the biographical novel that holds on to the idea of an ideal life; (e) the *Platonic* hero as an epistemic self in search of authentic knowledge that is verifiable by abstract mathematical principles; (f) the rhetorical biography that presents a staged self; I draw parallels between narratives on self constructed in the public square in ancient times and the staging of self in the modern-day digital square; (g) the Roman autobiography that presents a clan self; and last (h) the sociohistorical novel that presents a dialogical self, where the individual develops alongside a changing world.

In the chapter that follows—Chapter 3—I delve into Bakhtin's early philosophical work on the author–hero relationship to understand the psychological dimensions of creativity and aesthetic vision. Based on Bakhtin's discussion on *architectonics*—the nature of relationship between art and life, author and hero, experienced life and narrated tale, and so on and how these myriad forms are brought together to form a consummated whole—I explore the psychological dynamics of cultivating finer sensibilities and sensitivities. I argue that creativity emerges in the process of achieving the ideal of unity in the infinite show of variety in the world.

The chapter sets up a dialogue between Bakhtin's architectonics and Lev Vygotsky's work on the psychology of art to explore a suitable methodology for studying creativity and to critique Sigmund Freud's take on artistic activity. The chapter proceeds to engage in a Bakhtinian/Vygotskian critique of the works of John Dewey, Mihaly Csikzentmihalyi, Howard Gardner, and others on creative acts.

The chapter does not restrict creativity to works of art alone, but explores creative composition of self and life, based on Bakhtin's early philosophical works. I argue that creativity is dialogic through and through because only in the full play of competing ideas and intermingling of diverse voices do the possibilities for novel forms and meanings to emerge exist.

In Chapter 4, I explore the topic of "Carnivalization of Consciousness" as a catalyst for development. The world of the carnival with its uninhibited laughter, coarse language, grotesque body images, and excessive indulgence in food and liquor, according to Bakhtin, brings wholesomeness to our cultural life. This chapter is an attempt to extend these ideas to the realm of consciousness, so that we may begin to see how carnivalization at a psychological level functions as a catalyst for development. The chapter begins with a discussion of the philosophical dimensions and the liberating potential of carnival, addressing questions such as: is it liberation *from* the world or *in* the world, and is it mockery, rebellion, or revelation? I argue that laughter reveals hidden truths and some truths reveal themselves only to laughter. I discuss the linguistic sophistication in jokes that demand mental quickness and alertness, where utopias are not created but the utopian element is retained in order to affirm freedom. The chapter continues with a discussion of the virtue of street talk with bawdy voices and body images to argue that the principles of the lower stratum of the body are an inevitable part of the birthing process to produce newer forms of knowledge.

I argue that carnivalized consciousness is faithful to the universal and the local, and is primarily concerned with raw truth. The colorful masks at a carnival externalize the layers of psychological masking to expose the imposter in each of us. Carnivalization is a call to drop all pretensions of uniqueness and superiority and blend into the collective.

From his early philosophical works to his later works on speech genres, Bakhtin was concerned with the nature of selfhood, in both art and life. In Chapter 5, I address the topic of "Authoring the Self" as necessarily and ideally conjoined with "Answering the Other" to fulfill ethical obligations and to respond emotionally with regard, to both self and the other. Bakhtin situates the identity formation at the intersection of three lines—*I-for-myself* (how self appears to its consciousness), *I-for-others* (how self appears to others), and *Others-for-me* (how others appear to self). The central argument in this chapter is the presence and necessity of the other in authoring the self. The chapter proposes a metalinguistic model of selfhood; that is, a dialogical relationship between the lived life and the narrated self. The chapter addresses an important aspect of self–other relations: how do we acknowledge the need for the other even while resisting the oppressive other? Among the most remarkable aspects of Bakhtin's early philosophical works on author–hero and self–other relationships is the sophistication he displays in articulating emotional responsiveness, and I point out that these insightful ideas have direct relevance to psychology in dealing with empathy, sympathy, pain, and healing. For Bakhtin, the very essence of self-development is in the relationship between the spirit and the soul—the free spirit always in search of loopholes and the stable soul that sets the rhythm for momentary closure. I argue that this movement between spirit and soul is valuable in examining social relations in our complex, globalized world.

In Chapter 6, I argue that dialogue is not only an ontological reality and an epistemological necessity, but also an inevitable methodology for human sciences. I point out the dialogic exchange and transition between the message giver, the message, the messenger, and the message receiver. The prevalent investigative practices, by their very nature, are resistant to dialogicality in psychology, and this comes right from the time of its birth, when it established itself as a scientific discipline. I argue that dialogic method is neither anti-science nor unscientific, but in fact it is the only way to retain scientific integrity in studying the human world. Questions must be framed in such a way that they open up new possibilities for understanding the complex and changing psychological functioning, so that we may hear the voices of the mind in all their fluctuations in tone and shifts in meanings. The sharp analytical categories like genres and chronotopes enable us to make sense of the narratives generated in the research. I make a case for dialogic method as an alternative to positivist science.

In the final, concluding Chapter 7, the goal is to affirm the power of dialogue. We have grown accustomed to building the ideal of unity on sameness—deep down, we are the same—and in this motto we turn the other into an alibi, and Bakhtin insists on non-alibi for Being; therefore, we need to reexamine this motto and find comfort and advance the "deep down, we are different" motto as there is much to gain in the world of differences. Erasing differences is a clever ploy for the powerful as it allows them to pull other groups into their orbit and define unity according to their agenda. Furthermore, it is also a timid act, as one need not take the trouble to find the real reasons behind social disharmony and the artificial unity gives an illusory comfort. Dogmas come in many guises, appearing in religion, philosophy, politics, theory, and method; in fact, no area in the human world is immune to it. Our ability to engage with the different other is the best bet against extremism and militancy. Truth is disembodied, impersonal, decontextualized, and de-historicized in a monologic world, and Bakhtin was more than forceful in displaying his impatience with such a world; instead, he celebrated the open, dialogic world that has the capacity to find unified truths and enable the development of a well-integrated individual, and, more important, it can build institutions that promote innovation. Besides, freedom is sanctioned to all in a world of differences. There is no compromise on that front. That seems more human and humane.

The open-ended world of differences is full of vigor and vitality, and the direction one wants to freely move in has incredible potential to teach one something new. Closed worlds, strict formulas, and fixed trajectories only suffocate the individual and make no room for innovation and awareness. In short, there is no scope for development. Bakhtin tells us that "Quests for my own word are in fact quests for a word that is not my own" (FNM 70–71, p. 149), which means—without the different word and different other—there is no frame of reference to assess my word and my self.

Dialogism (I use this term reluctantly) is not another "ism" and not another theory with a standard set of principles; in fact, I like to push the argument further—it is not a theory at all; it is a way of looking at the world, a method to make sense of the diverse world we live in. Therefore, the theoretical lens must allow us to see, make sense of, and, if needed, change aspects of the world we live in. Unless one recognizes the value of living in a world of differences, how would anyone learn how to navigate in such a world fearlessly, without the need to negate the other to affirm the self or not put the self at risk and expose it to indiscriminate attacks in an open world? After all, the world of differences cannot lead us to a clash of civilizations, but, despite the murkiness, it must make room for a healthy dialogue between competing ideas. Impelled by these pressing concerns of our time, I invite the reader to a "Bakhtinian World"—perhaps, we will find new ways of thinking about *Dialogic Development* in a world of *Differences* that forever renews itself and continues.

2

THE NOVEL AND THE HERO

Developmental Narrative and
the Developing Subject

> Goethe's novels cannot give us a complete statement of Goethe, but they show his preference of mind as plainly as an intimate diary could do. For it is not in our diaries but in our books that we record ourselves, our true selves.
>
> Marcel Proust, On Art and Literature, *1997, p. 364*

The rupture between lived experiences (with all the concrete events, observations, thoughts, and feelings) and their narration is fundamental, but it is at the link between the two that the author leaves his signature. Like Marcel Proust, Mikhail Bakhtin claims that "Pure everyday life is fiction" (FNM 70–71, p. 154), as it entails a ritualistic shaping of segments from inner and outer life. In this shaping process of the narrative, the image of the author and the characters develops. The nature of this construction and the image of the author/hero are varied and they move in multiple directions. Shaping entails choice: choosing from the superabundance of socio-ideological languages and the materials chosen to construct the novel and the hero hints at the nature of the developmental narrative and the developing subject. Bakhtin asserts that "Consciousness finds itself inevitably facing the necessity of *having to choose a language*" (1981, p. 295). Thus, in this chapter, I want to examine closely the language of developmental theories to identify the varied images of developing subjects.

Experiences acquire meaning and gain significance through their narration. Narratives, in turn, do not mechanically signify experiences. Instead, in the very process of narrating, individuals select segments from their lives, highlight a few events, narrate some in a matter-of-fact manner, and carefully guard others by evading persistent questions to make up life stories with their interlocutors. As in any field of knowledge construction, the psychologists studying human development also select certain aspects of human functioning that they consider of significance to development and convey their observations through select genres. The chosen genre configures the events to present unique images of the subjects and their relationship to the world around them. A genre must not be treated as a conveyor belt of impressions about our experiences or observations of the world around us. Bakhtin envisaged genres as necessary conceptual lens that evolve over time—absorbing new dimensions and branching out in diverse forms—to aid the speaker and the writer. Interestingly, Bakhtin observes that the manner in which the ordinary speaker/writer uses genres is different from the ways talented orators and writers deploy them, as explained in his later works:

> Genres (of literature and speech) throughout the centuries of their life accumulate forms of seeing and interpreting particular aspects of the world. For the writer-craftsman the genre serves as an external template, but the great artist awakens the semantic possibilities that lie within it.
> *(RQNM, p. 5)*

Bakhtin's distinction between the craftsman and the artist represents the distinction between fixed monologic discourses and fluid dialogic discourses. The former are built with a fixed template—a specific worldview that is sealed off, with predictable utterances and phrases and fixed positioning of characters—whereas the dialogic discourses are characterized by open-endedness with immense potentialities, and hence they are unpredictable. Monologic visualization is keen on picking up stable features of the world and consistent actions of individuals, and therefore the language may very well be stylized, but the genre appears sterile because it rejects contradictory and incompatible elements. Bakhtin points out that from the standpoint of monologism, Dostoevsky's world might appear too chaotic and his language too inconsistent. When we are dealing with culture in a state of flux, murkiness is inevitable. Bakhtin avers that Dostoevsky's polyphonic novel is characterized by "*independent and unmerged voices and consciousnesses*" (PDP, p. 6), and these features are necessary to show growth, development, and creativity.

If genre is the lens for visualizing, conceptualizing, and narrating reality, is it then a linguistic device? Bakhtin's answer is a firm no. Human activity cannot be conducted without language, and our activities are diverse, and hence the manner in which language is used is also going to vary. Bakhtin explains that "Language is realized in the form of individual concrete utterances" (PSG, p. 60), which are constitutive of their content (what is said), style (how it is said), and compositional structure (the manner in which words, phrases, and grammar are put together to form a whole). These elements forming an inseparable unit, according to Bakhtin, become genres. The forces of history bring about changes in cultural climate, and in each time period genres set the tone for everyday communication and for literary art forms. The unity between theme, content, and compositional structure is neither mechanical, as if they are strung together by some external device, nor does the genre lend itself to purely linguistic analysis.

Bakhtin, along with Medvedev, explains that "the reality of the genre and the reality accessible to the genre are organically interrelated" (FM, p. 135), and for this reason, they say that one must move back and forth between linguistics and metalinguistics and between language and society to understand their reciprocal relationship. Bakhtin and Medvedev explain that each genre—drama, poetry, epic, novel, and so on—is differentiated not just by its volume or style, but the manner in which it guides you to see reality. Genres draw the parameters within which selected aspects of reality are showcased to orient one's attention to their scope and depth. Furthermore, genre and reality create each other: "Genre appraises reality and reality clarifies genre" (FM, p. 136). Because genre and reality are related bilaterally, the artist must exercise judgment in choosing the appropriate genre to convey the message in the most effective manner. For example, the unofficial truth lends itself best to a carnival genre. Each genre addresses a particular type of audience, and it thrives in a particular environment. A musical genre that may be well suited for a church recital may not work in a concert hall, or a play that is effective on a live stage might fail on screen. Bakhtin and Medvedev assert:

> Each genre is only able to control certain definite aspects of reality. Each genre possesses definite principles of selection, definite forms for seeing and conceptualizing reality, and a definite scope and depth of penetration.
> *(FM, p. 131)*

If each genre is equipped with a unique capacity to capture only some aspects of reality, how, then, do we detect variations within each genre that tell the story of various characters and the world around them? For any narrative to achieve meaning, Bakhtin insists, we must identify the nature of spatial and temporal configurations. The intrinsic connectedness of time and space in the narrative is what he refers to as the *chronotope*. Bakhtin borrows the concept from Einstein's Theory of Relativity to point out the shifting nature of meanings, as narratives occupy different positions in culture and in history. Bakhtin explains that chronotopes are the "organizing centers" for the events in a tale to unfold, and they are also "the basis for distinguishing generic types"—like travelogues, suspense, biographies, and so forth—and for detecting "specific varieties of the novel genre" (FTCN, pp. 250, 251).

Bakhtin's detailed explanation of various chronotopic motifs guides those of us in the social sciences interested in studying and analyzing narratives. As an analytical tool, chronotope is sharp in its ability to draw subtle differences in narratives, and it is also comprehensive enough to account for the cognitive, social, emotional, and ethical stances of the characters. About the versatility of this analytical tool, Bakhtin argues:

> It can even be said that it is precisely the chronotope that defines genre and generic distinctions, for in literature the primary category in the

chronotope is time. The chronotope as a formally constitutive category determines to a significant degree the image of man in literature as well. The image of a man is always intrinsically chronotopic.

(FTCN, p. 85)

The nature of spatial and temporal formations in specific narrative genres sketches out the image of the person and the world around him, and this enables us to understand the situatedness of the subject in culture and his or her relationship to various cultural entities. The manner in which time and space are fused varies from narrative to narrative—thus offering different images of the individual. For Bakhtin, chronotopes explicitly served a typological function, and they enabled him to classify various types of novels. For social scientists and psychologists in particular, chronotopes address other questions—the relationship between human behavior and the cultural context. Is the cultural context a passive backdrop, or is it controlling human actions, or is the context mediating behavior, or is the cultural setting used as a lame excuse for irresponsible actions? In other words, when, where, and why do individuals use their culture as a justification for their conduct? Similar questions may be posed about temporality. How do we determine historical necessities? How is history used and abused? How do individuals release themselves from the trappings of history? How do forces of history mediate our development? More important, is time open and flexible or closed and fixed? In the narrative, does time appear to be singular or plural? Gayatri Spivak argues that "Time" is referring to a fixed "Law," whereas "Timing" is indicative of changing "History"; as she asserts, "Time often emerges as an implicit Graph only miscaught by those immersed in the process of timing" (1991, p. 99). When Bakhtin classified various types of novels, he was essentially examining how time operates—weak and static temporal categories offer an image of an unchanging subject against the backdrop of a fixed world, whereas strong temporal categories show the changing subject in a dynamic world.

Epic and Novel: The Developed and the Developing Subject

The idea of "development" and the image of a "developing subject" find their most direct and clearest expression in Bakhtin's writings on the novelistic genre, which to him was a break from the epic genre. Bakhtin saw the novel as the "sole genre that continues to develop" (EN, p. 3), whereas we inherit epic as a "completely finished" text and as "a congealed and half-moribund genre" (EN, p. 14). Bakhtin saw the epic as an ossified genre, and therefore not available for any further reshaping, whereas the novel, like a growing child, is malleable, and, as a result, the various shapes it will take and the multiple directions it is likely to move in are open-ended and unpredictable. Bakhtin observes, "We encounter the epic as a genre that has not only long since completed its development, but one that is already antiquated" (EN, p. 3). Everything about the novel, in Bakhtin's view, is associated with "youngness"—open and incomplete with innumerable potentialities and plastic possibilities. Bakhtin says that the novel is younger than the "written language" and "the book"—and hence organically connected to the living present, unlike the epic that is associated with the dead past. Like the parents who pass on some traits and attributes to their newborn infant, the authors of a novel also endow the hero with some traits: but neither the parents nor the authors can fully determine the course of their creation. The child/hero develops in the "full light of historical day" (EN, p. 3), in close contact with the "multi-languaged world."

A close examination of Bakhtin's fascination with the novel as a genre can help theorize human development in all its dimension and scope. First and foremost, the study of the novel, for Bakhtin, is a simultaneous study of the text operating in cultural systems that are pulled by contradictory forces of history. A detailed study of Bakhtin's take on the life of a novel reveals some interesting insights into the development of its hero. The hero as an unfinished character in search of meaning and identity could very well be an emblem of the developing subject. Unlike the epic hero whose life is complete and personality set, the novelistic hero is yet to develop. The hero operating and transacting with the cast of characters both inside and outside the text struggles to build his identity. Bakhtin asserts, "The novel is the only developing genre and therefore reflects more deeply, more essentially, more sensitively and rapidly, reality itself in the process of its unfolding" (EN, p. 7). For Bakhtin, any given moment in the life of the novel is always heteroglot—representing the voices of various groups, epochs, and generations and the necessities of the "day" or even the "hour"—thus displaying the contentious nature of a living culture. In Bakhtin's view, meanings are never contained in the text and the author never seals the hero's fate. It is Bakhtin's call to move beyond the "text" into "extra-textual" materials and from "linguistics" to "metalinguistics" to track the movement of the hero inside and outside the novel that is profoundly instructive to developmental psychologists. Like the emerging hero of the novel, the developing child is neither independent of his or her creators (parents, genetic inheritance, etc.) nor entirely determined by them.

According to Bakhtin, the epic is characterized by "prophesy," and its realization occurs within the bounds of the text or the epoch it covers, whereas the novel aspires to prediction, but its fulfillment is never guaranteed because of its openness for reexamination and reevaluation. Like the developing individual who seeks a developmental pathway to ascend, but is invariably subjected to extraneous conditions and must consider alternative pathways, the novel must come to terms with its compelling wish to predict the future and the discrepancies in its realization. The *telos* must confront reality. The epic genre as an already developed product demands reverence and worship. It is an emblem of the glories of a culture's collective past—the "world of fathers and of founders of families" (EN, p. 13)—and hence meant to be showcased, but not open to be touched by the present. The novel is a developing genre that needs to be touched and retouched by the present in all its myriad forms.

Any genre that is absolute, conclusive, and closed cannot lend itself to the study of development—be it in the realm of culture, text, or individual. Thus, the study of the novel, because of its inconclusiveness and openness, occasions the study of development. Keep in mind that while the novel as a genre is flexible and open, specific novels are not necessarily so. The novelistic genre is differentiated, and Bakhtin's system of classifying novels based on spatiotemporal configurations gives us a clear picture of novels characterized by stasis in every realm, the novels in which we see the growth of the hero against the backdrop of a static world, and the novels that present the developing hero in the changing world. In short, a close examination of the novel is a study of modes of consciousness.

The Greek Romance: Life Tested by Fate

Bakhtin identifies the Greek romance as one of the ancient types of novels that is built on the specific theme of characters caught in the clutches of events beyond their control. The worldview these novels present is very clear and straightforward—fate, destiny, gods, and other unknown forces play cruel tricks on individuals, who in turn simply *endure*—not necessarily *transform*. In fact, nothing changes; the social structure remains stable and social arrangements are neither altered nor specific to cultural location and historical time. Everything remains static. The characters may even be afflicted with some incurable disease, which they may either endure or perish from (usually these tales have happy endings). Whatever the nature of the adversity that thickens the plot, the emotions of the characters—love between the hero and the heroine, the chastity of the characters, and how they relate to each other—everything remains stable and intact. Fate slaps the subjects with its cruel hands, but their stoicism, chastity, or bravery eventually triumphs over these unpredictable and powerful forces. After being put through some tough testing in life, the characters, as in a fairy tale, live happily ever after.

The story at the very outset endows the characters with admirable qualities, and, as the story proceeds, there are chance encounters and flare-ups of instantaneous passions, as if relationships were preordained and because of the all-powerful force of destiny the lovers are bound to face obstacles and separation. The novel offers no details about the characters' lineage or which sect they belong to or the social hierarchies or classifications that prevail at that time. In fact, the story itself remains untouched by actual time and place. The characters do set out on adventures and visit faraway places and the author documents various aspects of the land—their customs, their superstitions—in great detail. But what is important here is that the characters remain untouched and unaffected even by the adversities they face; as Bakhtin puts it, they "leave no trace, and therefore, one may have as many of them as one likes" (FTCN, p. 94).

What is instructive about the Greek romance to psychological study? For one thing, it is clear that the image of the person in the novel is passive. Things, particularly bad things, happen *to* the characters—it is chance, fate, or natural disasters. All forces are seen as beyond their control, and the novel gives no indication whether the characters by way of their choices or poor judgment could have contributed to the crisis. One might be abducted by villains and held in captivity for a considerable period and when the eventual reunion with the lover occurs, the character remains the same. In psychological parlance, we see an external locus of control in its extreme form. We see the lives and worldviews of individuals who take no initiative or ownership *of* their actions or responsibility *for* the consequences. Consciousness is consistently guided by fatalism.

In this type of ancient novel, the author puts the hero and the heroine through a variety of tests—fate strikes at the most unexpected moments in the most unusual places—and through these numerous tests, the characters' innocence is verified and established. The narrative is filled with "suddenlys" and "at just that moments" to show how dramatically events change. The plots are built on a "can do no wrong" hero struggling with an "always doing wrong" villain, denoting a clear-cut division between good and evil. The Greek romance does not entertain real growth and becoming. Dangers and adversities are the trials that characters face—only to come out pure and tested. Their identities or emotions do not undergo any transformation. It is precisely the absence of becoming that makes this a non-developmental narrative.

To account for real development, in Bakhtin's view, one must consider the real cultural atmosphere in which one is operating in real time, for disregarding the cultural air that one inhales or selectively resisting it is to write the tale of an alienated subject. To live in a world detached from the "laws governing the sociopolitical and everyday life" amounts to perceiving the world as "indefinite," "unknown," and "foreign" (FTCN, p. 101). Without the organic connection to the cultural soil, all one is left with is to experience "random contingency" (ibid.). Life guided by fatalism is to surrender agency, and without agency there is neither self-awareness nor a grasp of the world around you, and without an in-depth knowledge of self/other there can be no development.

The Adventure Novel of Everyday Life: Crisis Changes Self

If the hero of the Greek romance endures adversities, the hero of the adventure novel is selectively transformed by crisis. The transformation is not necessarily developmental; in other words, the novel does not show the hero slowly ascending to higher modes of consciousness; instead, it shows a contrasting image of the hero *before* and *after* a crisis. Bakhtin observes that this type of novel must be credited "for showing *how an individual becomes other than what he was*" (FTCN, p. 115), and hence does not trace "evolution in the strict sense of the word" (ibid.), but instead we see a causal link between "crisis and rebirth" (ibid.).

Bakhtin observes that this type of ancient novel, although few in number, has been extremely influential. According to Bakhtin, only two novels, in the strict sense, show a unique kind of spatiotemporal configurations that blend adventure time with everyday time. Bakhtin identifies fragments of *Satyricon* of Petronius that have survived as *The Golden Ass* of Apuleius, which has been handed down in its entirety as the other, and these two works show the quintessence of adventure novels. These two works depicting unique chronotopes have been extremely influential in producing satires in the Hellenistic period and, more important, numerous works on Christian hagiographies—depicting lives of saints filled with desires of the flesh and temptations of all sorts and put to an end by crisis resulting in rebirth.

Bakhtin's detailed discussion of various types of novels from ancient times to the nineteenth century is in reality a rigorous approach to account for the image of a person and the conceptualization of the world in each type of novel, and to systematically trace the gradual progression of the hero's identity and the world around him from a static to a dynamic form. If the ancient novel shows no progression in the hero's outlook, the nineteenth-century novels of historical emergence show the hero developing along with the world—changing *in* the world, changing *with* the world, and changing *the* world. If the ancient novel shows a complete disconnect between the hero and his social milieu, the hero of the modern novel is invariably bound to cultural and historical forces, and as a result the former shows barely any temporal categories, while the latter operates in the fullness of historical time.

In discussing the adventure novel right after the Greek romance, Bakhtin shows the gradual entry of temporality in the former, while the latter is completely devoid of it. The presence of time in the narrative enables the author to depict movement, sanction some agency to the hero, and document changes in the hero. While the events in the Greek romance are sudden and unexpected and the hero simply endures the ordeal, the hero of the adventure novel plays an active role. There is nothing magical about it; adventures happen because the individual willfully ventures out. Bakhtin explains that the adventure novel draws its philosophy of metamorphosis to a great extent from folklore, which was concerned with human transformation and identity. On the nature of wholesale transformation of all entities that the adventure novel incorporated from folklore, Bakhtin observes, "The motifs of transformation and identity, which began as matters of concern for the individual, are transferred to the entire human world, and to nature, and to those things that man himself has created" (FTCN, p. 112).

Bakhtin's main interest in studying the adventure novel is to examine the philosophy and logic of metamorphosis, built on the principle of bringing about change in individual lives and in cultural history. Therefore, in sharp contrast to the Greek romance, the adventure novel indicates that change is real, irreversible, and varied. Identity is merely tested in the Greek romance, while it undergoes real change in the adventure novel. The hero of the Greek romance reverts back to his original identity, even after enduring a series of ordeals; his identity is considered chaste and desirable at the outset, and the story demonstrates that these lofty traits remain intact, whereas the hero of the adventure novel is inevitably reborn. The nature of the crisis is irrelevant in Greek romance because it brings about no change, whereas in the adventure novel the nature and sequence of the crisis are not definitive or predictable and the course that the character takes as a result of the crisis is not necessarily unidirectional. Bakhtin discovers the "idea of development" in its nascent stage in the adventure novel and observes that the movement takes a very complex route:

> Metamorphosis or transformation is a mythological sheath for the idea of development—but one that unfolds not so much in a straight line as spasmodically, a line with "knots" in it, one that therefore constitutes a distinctive type of *temporal sequence*. The makeup of this idea is extraordinarily complex, which is why the types of temporal sequences that develop out of it are extremely varied.
>
> (FTCN, p. 113)

Even while pointing out modest developmental gains in the adventure novel compared to the Greek romance, Bakhtin is quick to point out that these gains are purely personal. Both these types of ancient novels present the hero's tale as separate from the rest of the society. He is neither affected by the society nor does he leave any mark on the society. The hero might experience guilt as a result of his sinful deeds, pay retribution, sincerely repent and cleanse himself, but these emotional changes are purely private. When change is so personal and life is so sundered, metamorphosis is somewhat "unproductive," says Bakhtin, and he explains that "Such an individual's potential for initiating actions is, however, not creative; it is realized only negatively, in rash and hasty acts, in mistakes, in guilt" (FTCN, p. 119).

A close study of Bakhtin's analyses of these types of ancient novels presents us with a clear picture of developmental milestones reached in each type of novel and the limitations or the goals yet to be achieved in the realm of human consciousness. Based on our discussion of the Greek romance and the adventure novel, it is clear that Bakhtin sees development as uniquely individualistic and yet unarguably collective and inescapably localized in historical time. First, about individuality, Bakhtin gives sufficient weight to individual traits, their personality, and, above all, he is sensitive to the place they occupy at a given time in the cultural field. In short, each life is unique and unrepeatable, and yet one does not operate in a vacuum—social and historical forces are real and they invariably pull the growing individual in multiple directions. The individual may resist some forces and yield to others. But, to account for this tug-of-war between the individual and culture and history, one must consider their complex interactions.

The Greek romance and the adventure novel present the fate of the hero "cut off from both the cosmic and the historical whole" (FTCN, p. 114), and as such we only see the hero enduring crisis after crisis or being selectively changed by crisis.

Moreover, Bakhtin is also cautioning against equating crisis endurance with developmental gain and rebirth as presented in the adventure novel with developmental achievement. A simple survivor's tale, regardless of how horrific the adversity is, does not constitute a developmental tale. In Bakhtin's view, the survivor might deserve our sympathy, but the stoic endurance must reach higher levels to incorporate various social and historical strands to be credited with developmental gains. With respect to the minimal personal gains, by way of change or rebirth as a result of crisis, Bakhtin would argue that waiting for an externally imposed tragedy or tension to change is not necessarily a mark of development. Crisis does change life and Bakhtin would not dispute that, but letting only a cataclysmic event bring transformation renders the life far too passive. Besides, if the upheaval fails to broaden the consciousness to produce a deeper understanding of self located in a broader episteme, then the change that is so personal is limited. Bakhtin explains that in the adventure novel, time appears in an isolated and fragmented manner, and thus fails to show any cogency in temporal sequences; therefore, what we are left with are snapshots of the hero at different points—mainly before and after a crisis—with no organic connection between the hero and his world. Unlike the nineteenth-century novels of historical emergence that are steeped in historical time, the ancient novel tends to be anachronistic, as it fails to link the individual with appropriate temporality. In sum, without temporality there is no development and a narrative that does not show the strong traces of temporality fails to provide an adequate account of development.

The Travel Novel: Self as a Traveler

In his essay on the *Bildungsroman*, Bakhtin identifies the travel novel as the foremost in the broad category of "novels without emergence" that depict a static view of both the hero and the world around him. It would be instructive to consider the sense in which Bakhtin addresses the notion of travel, because although as a novelistic genre the discussion is brief and somewhat insignificant, this type of genre dominates psychological studies, particularly positivist psychology. Let us consider modern-day travel in which one hops onto a plane to visit a foreign land, where detailed observations are made about the "static social diversity of the world (country, city, culture, nationality, various social groups and specific conditions of their lives)" (1986, p. 10) in a very undifferentiated manner and the observations are communicated in a presumably neutral fashion, and this is what characterizes the travel novel. This kind of demographic account gives no indication whether the wandering had any effect on the traveler. In contrast to passive travel, adventure shows some degree of agency and change. The nature of the wandering in a pilgrimage is markedly different from travel or adventure because the pilgrim undertakes the arduous journey seeking rebirth, and the pilgrimage region is saturated with myth and history and held sacred. Therefore, both the individual and the geographic location are charged with temporal categories in a pilgrimage, while the travel narrative is devoid of temporality in depicting both the hero and the world around him.

The travel novel genre finds expression in various theoretical and methodological approaches in psychology. The positivist paradigm dominates most APA-accredited journals, and in this paradigm the image of a subject or subjects is virtually invisible because various psychological factors are weighed according to some psychometrics and sociological factors are reduced to a set of variables—race, class, gender, age, and so forth—and the emphasis is placed on differences and contrasts. Bakhtin says that in the travel novel, "The hero is a point moving in space. He has no essential distinguishing characteristics, and he himself is not at the center of the novelist's artistic attention" (1986, p. 10). We see parallels in positivist psychology that favor experimental methods and psychometric measures, and as Kurt Danziger (1990) observes, psychology, in its zeal to be an "exact science," has been relentless in "numerizing" and "serializing" behavior, thereby legitimizing quantitative knowledge. When the focus is on statistical significance, we are neither able to see subjects' images nor hear their voices. The researcher assumes a neutral position and reports the findings, disregarding the fact that all data are theory-laden and theories are value-laden, very much akin to the manner in which the author of a travel novel reports about the "world" through his created hero.

The nature of the discourse in both the travel novel and empirical psychology illuminates the position of the author/researcher in relation to his or her created/studied subjects, and both operate through a "direct referentially oriented discourse" (Bakhtin, 1984b, p. 187) in which the task is to name, represent, and express their impressions and observations in a detached manner. Such a discourse with clear-cut boundaries between author/researcher and hero/subject, Bakhtin says, is intended for an "equally un-mediated, object oriented understanding" (1984b, p. 186), and it is precisely these claims of neutrality that trouble Danziger (1990) because they constitute a "new kind of priesthood" that covertly exerts complete semantic authority.

In an earlier work on the narratives on self and the cultural epic text—The Mahabharata (Bandlamudi, 2010)—I demonstrated that the greater the claims of objectivity and neutrality that individuals make, the less is the responsibility and accountability in their interpretive act and the judgments they pass. Bakhtin says that the world of a traveler is "a spatial contiguity of differences and contrasts, and life is an alternation of various contrasting conditions: success/failure, happiness/unhappiness, victory and defeat" (1986, p. 11), and these categories are treated as fixed and bound and hence assumed to be identifiable through scientific methods. But the reality is, humans operate in zones of ambiguity and to assume that categories of interpretation are black and white renders the observations fundamentally unscientific. Bakhtin explains that the "scientific character of natural sciences" is defined in terms of its "relation to the empirical and its relation to mathematics," whereas "the scientific character of human sciences" is defined by "their relation to meaning and purpose" (2001, p. 206), and hence dialogicality, in its open-ended and unfinalized form, is the very essence of human sciences. Because the image of the person is indistinguishable in the travel novel and empirical psychology, tracing human emergence and development becomes practically impossible.

The Biographical Novel: Idea of the Ideal of Life

Forms of sketching the image of a character and presenting various attributes of a character have varied, and that is why Bakhtin (1986) points out that there has never been a pure form of biographical novel, and therefore our focus must be on the biographical principle—the mechanics of configuring a character—and the configuration says something about the nature of the relationship between the character and his surrounding world. If one form of ancient biography was based on Aristotle's notion of *energia*, the other form was *analytic*, based on the normative course of life—a template in which biographical information was distributed. The prescribed rubric of the classical era paved the way for newer forms of constructing biographies—the kind based on the "idea of life"—an abstract concept of the course of life. Bakhtin discusses the features of this type of biographical narratives in many of his works, for instance, contrasting the plot of a biographical novel with that of Dostoevsky's works (1984b) and briefly in his essay on chronotope (FTCN, 1981) and in his later essay on the *Bildungsroman* (1986), and he observes that the distinctness of this form lies in the image of the character built on the normative course of life, enumerating the "successes and failures in life" (1986, p. 17).

More importantly, the narrative is based on a definitive "idea of life" and, through the fixed idea, the character's objectives in life, his works, deeds, relationships, achievements, failures, and so on are communicated. Furthermore, the idea of life is built on a certain notion of the *ideal* of life, assuming that this ideal is universal and time-honored. In an earlier work, I argued that the "humanist" school of thought in psychology that attempts to trace life span development based on the fulfillment of life's tasks while adhering to some time-honored virtues is a psychological version of a biographical novel (Bandlamudi, 1999). Bakhtin observes that, although the biographical novel very clearly depicts the life course of the hero, it still "lacks any true process of becoming or development" (1986, p. 17) because the character is already given and the passage through various seasons of life, the given, or the potential, is realized and revealed. Let us consider Abraham Maslow's (1976) discussion of personal growth: he says self-actualization—the pinnacle of human growth—is the realization of the deepest potentials in human beings, and to reach this peak, Maslow says, the individual must persevere and be honest, self-aware, and tenacious. Therefore, the ideal must guide real life, and if they are far apart, Carl Rogers (1969) recommends therapeutic intervention to close the gap. Erik Erikson (1959) also charts out the entire course of life—from birth to death—into eight distinct stages and argues that in each stage the individual faces a set of societal demands and in the process of resolving them identity develops.

In humanism, as in the biographical novel, life itself is a "track" built on some ideals considered applicable to all of humanity, and therefore the task set for the individual is to stay on the "right track" and take the necessary steps to avoid derailment. So, what then is problematic when an ideal guides and evaluates life? For Bakhtin (1993), lived life is unique, unrepeatable, open-ended, and unpredictable because it operates in complex cultural systems, and when some "abstract idea of life" is used as a measuring rod, we are left with no dialogue between *what ought to be in life* and *what has been in life*. In Bakhtin's dialogic system, if the "ought to" has the authority to judge life, life has an equal right to confront the "ought to" and only at this juncture we might find something that is socially, psychologically, and/or ethically valid. If the ideal can appraise reality, reality in turn can clarify and modify the ideal. George Lukács asserts, "The 'should be' kills life" (1971, p. 48), and therefore he would like to retain the inevitable paradox, because life not only exposes the ideals that have been unrealized, but also shows how some are perhaps unrealizable under certain conditions. Lukács writes about the built-in paradox of biographies:

> The fluctuation between a conceptual system which can never completely capture life and a life which can never attain completeness because completeness is immanently utopian, can be objectivized only in that organic quality which is the aim of biography.
>
> *(1971, p. 77)*

Real life subordinated to an abstract idea and phantom ideals fails to capture the life of real individuals, developing in real space and time with all the contingencies, complexities, and indeterminacies, and therein is the limitation of the biographical novel and humanism.

Ancient Biography and Autobiography

Bakhtin identifies biography and autobiography in ancient times not as a genre that we recognize in modern times as life stories, but as an antiquated form of life story that had an immense influence on the biographical novel as we know it today. This early form, according to Bakhtin, must be credited for giving birth to a "new type of *biographical time* and a human image constructed to new specifications, that of an individual who passes the course of a whole life" (FTCN, p. 130). Thus a new chronotope came into being in which temporality was able to display not only a new image of the person, but also track the movement of this image through various stages of life. Although the earliest form cannot display too many works in this category, it had profound influence not only on later literary genres but also on philosophical questions about self. It set the stage for posing questions on those aspects of self that are worthy of philosophical speculation—drawing clear distinctions between authentic and real self as opposed to the ordinary and the quotidian aspects of life. With respect to temporality, the ancient biography and autobiography were a significant improvement in comparison to the other two types of ancient novels. The Greek romance, built on chance and fate, only showed "extra temporal hiatus" in life, while the adventure novel presented a "before" and "after" image of the person to indicate a selective and limited metamorphosis. The ancient biography and autobiography for the first time was able to portray real biographical time, and hence proved a significant turning point in literary and intellectual histories.

Bakhtin identifies two types of life stories in the classical era, one—the *Platonic*—that tells the tale of emerging self-consciousness, beginning with ignorance or sensory knowledge and slowly ascending to higher forms of knowledge characterized by abstract theoretical principles. The second type is the *rhetorical autobiography and biography*—characterized by "encomium"—a grand narrative of life events in the public square.

The Platonic *Hero: The Seeker—the Epistemic Self*

The first type, *Platonic*, needless to say, includes works of Plato, such as the *Apology* of Socrates and the *Phaedo*—and true to its philosophy—this is not a tale of concrete life events in the traditional sense but the story of the emerging self-consciousness. The narrative traces "the Seeker's Path," beginning from "self-confident ignorance, through self-critical skepticism, to self-knowledge and ultimately to authentic knowing (mathematics and music)" (FTCN, p. 130). For the seeker, the world itself is a school, and hence he is always seeking analytical tools to comprehend lawful relationships in the world around him. Indeed, the world around him is constantly changing, but the task is to discover stable forms that are deep and lend themselves to rigorous scientific scrutiny. In Plato's world, authentic knowledge is governed by logic and mathematical principles, and arriving at that stage is the mark of development in life. In this type of narrative, the movement of the hero is through the intellectual stages. The journey is not smooth; it is full of upheavals, self-doubt, and constant experimentation with various schools of thought. Thus, it is a tale about "the course of soul's ascent toward perception of Forms" (FTCN, p. 131).

The *Platonic* novel is devoid of "real biographical time"—the concrete events become irrelevant and they defer to the "ideal" and the "abstract" time. It is important to take note of the nature and the role of crisis in the *Platonic* novel, which is distinctly different from the adventure novel. Crisis of a personal psychological nature results only in the rebirth of the hero albeit by developmental gains, whereas in the *Platonic* novel crisis is markedly intellectual, which forges the construction of superior structures of the mind. In my earlier work, I argued that Jean Piaget's *epistemic* child is a *Platonic* hero, who takes the genetic inheritance as the starting point to construct necessary structures of the mind through alternating processes of assimilation and accommodation (Bandlamudi, 1999). The challenge from the world is a permanent feature of life, giving rise to periodic intellectual crisis, to which the growing child responds by constructing the necessary tools of the mind, called *schemas*, to regain intellectual balance on a higher plane.

The *seeker* in the *Platonic* novel and the *epistemic* child in Piaget's narrative embody the enlightenment maxim that the human mind is fundamentally rational and scientific, and hence the dictates of reason are unarguably binding for all humans regardless of time, space, and individual disposition. In a lapidary formulation, the enlightenment thinkers declare objective reasoning as the only method for uncovering the deep structures that hold universal truths, and therefore surface matter is to be disregarded as insignificant. The individual in this school of thought is driven by intrinsic curiosity to discover lawful relationships that govern the world, in order to successfully navigate. If reason is the universally applicable standard for judging the validity of various phenomena in the world, do all individuals acquire this tool? The school of enlightenment recognizes the failure of individuals to understand proper canons of correct reasoning; they may be limited by purely sensory perception, as is the case with Piaget's epistemic child in his early years, or be misguided by intuition or blinded by passions and irrational motives; nonetheless, by virtue of being human and equipped with a valuable asset called the mind, the enlightenment school says, one naturally strives toward reason and even manages to reason about his reasons. Recognizing the power of logical, scientific, and mathematical thinking in producing an accurate account of the world around, the individual yields to reason and corrects his misapprehensions. However, failure to do so results in remaining in an underdeveloped state.

If we can trace the systematic and sequential progression of the hero in his developmental ascent, why is the *Platonic* novel "*Bildungsroman* in a narrow sense" in Bakhtin's view? As a sole seeker and builder of knowledge, the hero is forever constructing mental tools that are logical and mathematical in order to accurately gauge the world around him. Therefore, the seeker emerges against the backdrop of an immobile world. One gets a clear picture of the child's construction of the world with virtually no focus on the world's construction of the child. Treating growth and development as solely an individual affair is problematic for Bakhtin, and he insists that the individual grows along with the world and his growth "reflects the historical emergence of the world itself" (1986, p. 23). The ontological status of Jean Piaget's epistemic child indeed is disconnected from the cultural and historical forces. The world is wide open for exploration and experimentation, and the growing child steadily acquires tools of science to study the world. The process of man's *becoming* is multi-determined and multidirectional for Bakhtin, and therefore to account for the hero's emergence while ignoring the cultural input amounts to telling only half the story.

What form does "time"—the most important category that is capable of accounting for movement—take in Jean Piaget's genetic epistemology? Interestingly, time assumes two forms; at an ontogenetic level, time operates in a linear manner in accounting the systematic, sequential, and stage-like development of the child, but at a universal level, time becomes cyclical; that is, every generation across cultures must pass through the same sequence. Variations may occur in the hierarchical positioning of subjects, but the horizontal plane is anathema to this rationalist/objectivist epistemology.

What, then, is problematic with this universalist view of time? Gayatri Spivak's (1991) critique of Hegel's account of the philosophy of history is instructive, as she argues that Hegel's theory is not "epistemology" at all, but "an epistemography"—"a graduated diagram of how knowledge (an adequate fit between sign and varieties of meaning) comes into being." Thus, the graph lays out what is considered normative and universal, and any "misfits" along the way either lie outside the theoretical focus or take a position on the lower rung. In Hegel's universal teleological principle, the histories and art forms of various ancient civilizations—Persia, India, and Egypt—are not seen as produced *by* the *Spirit*. He states with a great deal of certitude that the Hindu Pantheon produced only an immature "idealism of Imagination" (1857/2010, p. 94) and could never reach the "idealism of Thought" (p. 95) that is capable of producing the universal and hence proclaimed that Hindus "have no History" (p. 108).

The trend in Piagetian studies was similar. Piaget took chunks of time and formulated a stage theory—in Gayatri Spivak's (1991) terms, an *epistemograph*—and the telltale themes of the highest stage—the formal operational—are universal, rational, and scientific. Taking Piaget's graph as the objective measuring rod of intellect, developmental psychologists traveled to remote parts of the world to see how children in various cultures and tribes fare. In a very Hegelian spirit, the cross-cultural Piagetian studies also proclaimed that in the vast majority of cultures, children rarely reach the pinnacle of cognitive developmental stages. Time in this "graph" model serves as only a milestone—by this time x, y, z ought to be accomplished—making the theory distinctly product oriented. Furthermore, time gets spatialized, and thus one is not able to account for the processes of development, which could very well be multidimensional and multidirectional. For Bakhtin, the absence of a complex web of chronotopes that highlights real historical time makes this *Bildungsroman* limited.

The Staged Self

The second type of ancient biography that Bakhtin identifies is "rhetorical" in nature, characteristic of "civic funeral and memorial speech" (FTCN, p. 131)—the *"encomium"*—the public oration extolling select virtues of a specific individual considered an important public figure. Encomia were early forms of self-accounting or accounting of the other, and these accounts yielded to the demands of the occasion and the décor of the public square. While the *Platonic* novel presented an image of a seeking self (in search of knowledge), the "advocatory speech" of the rhetorical biographies presented a *staged* self, which was a well-crafted image of a usually prominent individual. This event-based characterization of self is dominated by an "exterior real-life chronotope in which the representation of one's own or someone else's life is realized as verbal praise of a civic-political act or as an account of the self" (FTCN, p. 131), and this narrative is for the exclusive purpose of publicity, and hence what is missing is the "internal chronotope"—the actual time-space of the individual's lived and/or represented life. In this type of ancient narrative, there was nothing private about self-consciousness, for the events in one's life were "laid bare and shaped in the public square" (ibid.). The trigonal formulation—*I-for-myself, I-for-others*, and *Others-for-me*—that Bakhtin insists on for achieving a wholesome image of self is devoid of two of its major stems. Because the stamp of approval in the public square is the driving force, the *I-for-others* erases the other two variables in the theorem for selfhood.

This ancient and classical form of representing self or the other is not necessarily "literary" or "bookish" in nature; instead, these forms were exclusively determined by events that enabled real individuals immersed in real social and political situations to give public accounts of themselves or others. Bakhtin contends that this "real-life chronotope" constituted *in* and *by* the public square is markedly different from the novels discussed thus far—the Greek romance, the adventure novel, and the *Platonic* novel—for these novels, being literary in nature, present a more comprehensive image of a character, whereas the rhetorical biographies and autobiographies present snapshots of a character's image while illuminating select traits, anecdotes, and so forth in all their specificity. Bakhtin explains that the public square in which the narratives took shape was not the kind Pushkin had in mind, where the "common people" congregated in "bazaars," "puppet theaters," or "taverns" (1981, p. 132); instead, the public square referred to the "entire state apparatus, with all its official organs" (ibid.) that gave its "stamp of approval" to the narrative.

Interestingly, the ancient form of sketching an outline of an individual for public display—the "exterior real-life chronotope"—seems to find expression, although selectively, in the public digital square of the modern day. Consider Facebook, the most densely populated digital public square that creates innumerable opportunities for self-expression, where individuals post various aspects of their selfhood in a fragmented form—the activities they have engaged in, the Web sites they have browsed, the opinions they have on any subject matter—all in an attempt to gradually draw a profile of themselves for public display. We find interesting parallels between ancient rhetorical autobiographies and biographies and the modern-day digitally mediated forms of self-representation. The most obvious similarity is in the sheer exteriority of human image, as Bakhtin says, "the individual is open on all sides, he is all surface" (1981, p. 132), and the key words here are "all sides" and "all surface" because Facebook postings, no matter how inane they are, demand that they be considered, commented on, shared, and liked. Like the early Greek period that permitted self-glorification, the digital square provides a platform for tacit and/or blatant forms of self-glorification. Note that there is only a "thumbs up" sign and no "thumbs down" sign; therefore, the platform is set up so that there are only cheerleaders.

The chronotopes of ancient rhetorical autobiography and the modern-day digital square share few common features: both are shaped from their nascent stage to their clearly visible form in the full glare of the public, and in this very open image of a person, there is nothing "intimate or private, secret or personal, anything relating solely to the individual himself" (FTCN, p. 132), because the validity is established with a stamp of approval from the state or the digital apparatus and, more important, from the spectators. However, it is important to note a significant difference: while the chronotope of the public square of ancient times entailed verbal praise of specific political actions or personal deeds of prominent individuals, the digital square is open to all, and the chronotope here erases all distinctions between the prominent and the ordinary. If anything, with enticing polytexts linked with spectacular visual narratives, the ordinary quotidian events of everyday life morph into the glamorous.

The staged self of the digital public square is more than a doppelganger; it is a new and peculiar phenomenon of constructing models of self from digitally mediated relationships, in the vastness of cyberspace where a simulacrum of self must be periodically updated. The narratives of the public square in ancient times were modeled after *encomia*, and therefore the verbal praise had a loose connection to the select events of life or aspects of self, whereas in the simulations of the staged self, all bets are off with regard to the connection between self and representation; as Jean Baudrillard (1994) reminds us, simulation is not about the double or the mirror image, or the concept, but it is a hyper-real map of the self, with postings of vacation photographs or intended places for vacation and links to articles and videos, that creates an extravagant multimedia map to invite spectators into the incredible landscapes, mindscapes, and dreamscapes of the subject. The self in cyberspace has an incredibly dynamic spatiality—postings get responses at a supersonic speed and the spectators in this digital square are led through a sprawling psychological geography—constructed both methodically and spontaneously to invite comments and cheers. In the digital square, the self is always on display, and to draw attention, it must recast itself periodically, and, more important, in the words of Zygmunt Bauman, individuals become simultaneously "*promoters of commodities* and the *commodities they promote*" (2007, p. 6). Curiously, companies and individuals are often unabashed in reminding their connections to hit the "Like" button. Compliments are no longer treated as a gift from others, but they are demanded regardless of the interior feeling or reality to enhance the exterior image of the self.

The surface visibility and audibility of the individual in the digital square must not be confused with the frankness and coarseness of the folk world. There is certainly an irrepressible quality to folk narratives, and, unlike the fragmented presentations of self in the digital world, folklore presents a more comprehensive and clearer picture of the individual, revealing considerably the interior self and also hinting at real possibilities for growth and transformation. Forms of knowledge in the digital world are marked by an abundance of information and a scarcity of insight (Weinberger, 2007), and self is also subjected to the same trend, and therefore the image of a person emerges as an informational entity in this chronotope. Bakhtin says that the "Folkloric man demands space and time for his full realization" (FTCN, p. 150), whereas the staged self of the digital world demands space and time for attention and affirmation.

It is also interesting to note that if the advocatory speech of the public square set the stage for later forms of autobiography and biography, the staged self of the digital square also has heralded new forms of self-representation. It is already evident in the popularity of talk shows, where participants loudly discuss matters most personal and intimate in a very public forum that sensationalizes even pain and tragedy. In the world of the media, nothing despite its short life is muted or made invisible and all subtleties of human existence are oversimplified and the boundaries between outer and inner self are erased. In a very proverbial sense, life is a *three-day festival*.

Bakhtin discusses the *rhetorical* autobiography and biography as a brief but a somewhat significant intermediary phase in the development of the biographical novel in literary history. Why, then, must we pay so much attention to the avatar of this ancient chronotope in our contemporary period? We need to be vigilant for built-in dangers in this type of space-time configuration. When Jean Baudrillard published *Simulacra and Simulation*, it was a significant moment in theorizing the postmodern, in which he saw the digital world characterized by a series of simulations—the copy without an original, or "substituting the signs of real for the real" (1994, p. 2)—and therefore one does not see the contours of space and the transformative function of time. He is rather persuasive in arguing that the communication technology has been successful in creating the myth of enabling meaningful social relations, when in reality it has only redefined the meaning of socialization. "Everywhere socialization is measured by the exposure to media messages. Whoever is underexposed to the media is desocialized or virtually asocial" (p. 80). Baudrillard argues that the information overload "devours its own content" (ibid.) and "devours communication and the social" (ibid.) because "*it exhausts itself in the act of staging communication*" (ibid.), and, instead of "producing meaning, it exhausts itself in the staging of meaning" (ibid.). Extending Baudrillard's argument, we could very well say that the self exhausts itself in staging the self with inexhaustible minutiae, and that is a good enough reason for social scientists to watch for these dangers.

Roman Autobiography: The Clan Self

If the presentation of self in the Greek public square was based on *encomium*, the Roman public square celebrated the glory of the clan, and in this "family-clan soil," "autobiographical self-consciousness" (FTCN, p. 137) affirmed its collective identity by tracing its pedigree. In this public square, the story is not about the self at all, but about the ancestors, and it is no ordinary tale, but about the grandeur of their lives, their mighty deeds, their charitable nature, and the mark they left behind for several generations to come. Unlike the Greek public square that showcased the actions and traits of the self, the Roman square rendered the self virtually invisible, focusing exclusively on the history of the clan, and inferences could be drawn about living individuals based on the clan history. However, both the Greek and Roman autobiographies and biographies retained a deeply public character. The advocatory speech in the Greek type selected specific traits and deeds of usually prominent individuals, whereas the Roman type focused on a "particularized memory" of ancestors to show their prominence in history.

What is so instructive for psychologists and other social scientists in these ancient forms of public self-accounting, be it the Greek or the Roman type? First of all, these ancient forms and their manifestations in modern narratives that depict the *"public self-consciousness of a man"* (FTCN, p. 140) fail to record any genuine *becoming* in the character. Thus, what we get is a very static image of the individual against a backdrop of an equally immobile image of the world.

Bakhtin observes that even as biographical forms matured in the Roman-Hellenistic period and improved further with Aristotelian influence, they still failed to record the *becoming* or the growth of a character. An early year of a character's life is simply seen as the beginning and hence an incomplete disclosure of a character, and as biographical time progresses the character is "filled in" to show his essence. Even Plutarch, who built his biographical forms on Aristotle's concept of *energia*, showed movement of time only in disclosing an already predetermined character and not a character that changes and develops. In this model of biography, the image of a character only unfolds—very much akin to the models of *nativism* or *maturation theory* in explaining human development—where development is conceived as a matter of unfolding of genetically determined patterns.

Modifications in Ancient Autobiographical and Biographical Expressions

In the evolution of ancient forms of public accounting of self and other, Bakhtin (1981) identifies three kinds of distinct modifications that gradually led to more subtle forms of hinting at the interior self as narratives slowly became more suggestive and the volume more toned down.

In the first type of modification, the inner self was couched in "satirico-ironic" language. Parodying the public and often glorified image of the self suggested another interior truth about the individual. When matters deeply personal and private were "clothed in *irony* and *humor*" (p. 143), one was able to both reveal and conceal the inner self because these tropes are open to multiple interpretations.

The second modification brought about a shift from the public square rhetoric to "*drawing-room rhetoric*" (ibid.) because as the former reached its extreme form the human image became too stereotypical and bombastic. As human activity acquired more breadth and depth, a more private and interior self began to emerge, and it found expression in the "*familiar letter*"—a classic case being Cicero's letters to Atticus—and thus an "inner landscape" of the self with its own unique forms of spatiality and temporality was born.

The third modification that Bakhtin identifies is the "*stoic* type of autobiography" (1981, p. 144). While the letters were a form of conversation with others on matters most personal, the stoic type were "soliloquys"—solitary philosophical conversations with oneself. In this contemplative, reflective, and melancholic state, the philosophy of the consoler encounters the reality of the consoled, and hence the self plays the dual role of the consoling and the consoled subject in the absence of any witnesses—real or imaginary—for they are viewed as forces that diminish the power of self-evaluation. Hence the *I-for-myself* dominates because the turmoil of personal nature has no significance to others. Bakhtin, however, cautions that solitude at this stage in literary and cultural history is still "relative" and "naïve" (p. 145), but nonetheless exerted significant influence on the development of the novel.

These modifications in ancient forms of narratives of self heralded later forms of self-reflection and self-criticism and, more important, a permeable barrier between the private and public self emerged.

What, then, is the significance of displaying a porous partition between private thoughts and public expression of the heroes and showing the movement between these two spheres in the history of the novel, and in what way is this development in literary history relevant to human development? This issue is at the very heart of the sociohistorical epistemology of Lev Vygotsky. The relationship between thinking and speech, according to Vygotsky, is at the very nucleus of cognitive development. About the genesis of thinking and speech, Vygotsky explains that they have different roots both in phylogenesis and ontogenesis, and up to a certain point they run in parallel lines; we can identify a "pre-speech" stage in the development of thought and a "pre-intellectual stage" in the development of speech. During the early stages of language development, there is virtually no barrier between thinking and speech. Like the ancient autobiography everything is public and loud. But in the course of further development something significant happens in the ontogenetic process where the two lines intersect, and thus "thinking becomes verbal and speech intellectual" (1987, p. 112). Vygotsky sees this as a significant turning point in the "historical development of human consciousness" (1987, p. 243) because the porous screen is now established between deep-crystallized private thought and audible-fluid-public speech, and the transition and transformation from thought to speech is a developmental achievement and the process is complex and dynamic. The process transforms the thinking/speaking subject and the very nature of thought and speech. Vygotsky explains, "Speech does not merely serve as the expression of developed thought. Thought is restructured as it is transformed into speech. It is not expressed but completed in the word" (1987, p. 251). So if the depiction of the interior and exterior self is a significant turning point in the history of the novel, the partitioning of and the movement between thinking and speech is significant in the development of human consciousness.

In developing his wholesome theory of novelistic selfhood, Bakhtin is primarily concerned with the intra-psychic dialogue of competing ideas that the self engages in and also how the very same self enters into inter-psychic dialogue with others, and it is precisely the dialogue on these two planes that leads to growth. Novelistic discourse that can depict how the self that is unique and irreplaceable manages to enter into dialogic relations with the multifarious world presents a highly differentiated and nuanced picture of the individual and his surrounding world. Therefore, when Bakhtin identifies the modifications to ancient biography and autobiography as seeds sown for the emergence of full-fledged dialogic selves, he is directing our attention to how these modifications eventually produced novels of historical emergence. Lev Vygotsky's discussion of the development of thinking and speech is that in both the phylogenetic and ontogenetic processes the concerns are similar—to show the dialogicality between inner speech and outer words.

Sociohistorical Novel: The Dialogical Self

How is the "man in man" revealed to both the self and others? This question preoccupied much of Bakhtin's thinking. Through the *seeing eye* of Goethe and the *hearing ear* of Dostoevsky, Bakhtin was able to detect the emergence of "man in man" "with all of its necessity, its fullness, its future and its profoundly chronotopic nature" (1986, p. 23). Identifying and understanding the emergence of real individuals in real living cultural spaces and real historical time that concerned Bakhtin must also be the serious concerns of developmental psychology. A genuine sociohistorical epistemology demands that we understand the developing individual in a rapidly changing world, with all the advances and modifications in material tools and conditions, and the shifts in cultural practices and values that accompany them.

In the typologies of novels and the corresponding psychological developmental models discussed thus far, the image of a person is either static against the backdrop of an equally static world or we see the emergence of a person in an immobile world, whereas in the novel of historical emergence, growth of an individual is never solely a private affair; instead, the individual "emerges *along with the world*" and he reflects the historical emergence of the world itself" (Bakhtin, 1986, p. 23).

What, then, are the telltale themes of the novels of historical emergence that developmental psychologists need to be attentive to? First and foremost, it is the decentered self, occupying a unique place in time and space in dialogue with equally independent others, and hence what we sense is a "plurality of consciousness" (Bakhtin, 1984b, p. 6), with each voice having its unique philosophy. Even the heroes created by the author are not mechanical mouthpieces for the author to transmit his "authorial discourse" and philosophical views; instead, the created heroes are characters and philosophers in their own right. Bakhtin's observations about the artistic visualization of Dostoevsky's works are incredibly germane to researchers and theorists interested in studying the development of various psychological domains. Understanding development and change requires consideration of processes and the links to various psychological and sociological factors. Bakhtin writes that Dostoevsky "discovered personality and the self-developing logic of personality" (1984b, p. 286) because he was able to keenly observe the shifting positions of his characters even as they held on to big questions about the nature of the universe, without omitting the "intervening links" (ibid.) and the "most intimate and ordinary links" (ibid.). The various factors that contribute to the emergence of a new developing self are not presented in a neat sequential flow chart on a monologic plane—which often is the case in psychological studies—but Dostoevsky managed to display and analyze the interactions between many consciousnesses.

Bakhtin directs our attention to at least three facets of Dostoevsky's artistic imagination: first, the image of a human being "is not inserted into the *finalizing* frame of reality" (1984b, p. 284) because even death does not finalize the image of a person. Second, a developing idea is never separated from the developing "human event" (ibid.) because an idea is never presented as a purely abstract philosophical system. Third, it is the discovery of "dialogicality as a special form of interaction among autonomous and equally signifying consciousness" (ibid.). Approaching artistic activity in such a multidimensional manner, Bakhtin says, allows one to see transformation in everything—consciousnesses change, abstract ideas change, and even the content of dialogues change—and thus the microgenesis of developmental events is made visible and accounted for.

If Bakhtin's obsession was with the "novel of historical emergence" because it showed how characters evolve alongside a changing world, his contemporary and fellow Russian Lev Vygotsky was similarly obsessed with finding a suitable method that not only has the capacity to observe a developing subject, but also creates possibilities for development. Unarguably, Vygotsky was a polymath and rightly referred to as "the Mozart of Psychology" (Toulmin, 1978) because he approached the topic of human development from various angles. He orchestrated insights from literature, art, neurology, and defectology to propose a theoretical model that would take into account the flexibility and negotiability of the individual operating in an ambiguous and open-ended world to study the development of higher mental processes. If Bakhtin appreciated and celebrated

Goethe's ability "to *see* time" and "to read time" (1986, p. 25), Vygotsky (1978) also demands that human thinking and behavior be approached and understood as the history of thinking and behavior and hence the call to see and read time. In fact, time is not singular but plural, as Sylvia Scribner (1985) observes that in Vygotsky's scheme multiple lines of histories intersect in developmental events—that of the species, specific societies, individual history, and the very history of the psychological system under study—such that at the nexus all these histories create new futures.

Although it would seem axiomatic that Bakhtin's Dostoevskian model of dialogue of competing ideas and the Vygotskian model of the social formation of mind place similar and equal thrust on temporality, it would be instructive to take note of important differences between them, and these differences do not necessarily alter their shared overarching framework. Bakhtin saw the novel as an emblem of consciousness, and it was in Dostoevsky's works he detected the processes of developing consciousness in the hero, while Vygotsky equated psychology to drama, and therefore his preferred literary texts were works of Shakespeare. On that account, Vygotsky (1978) was far more sensitive to body language, gestures, grimaces, and mime and the "scene" in general, to account for the shifts that occur during developmental events. The scene he had in mind was the learning and developing scene—the chronotopes operating in and exchanges that occur between the expert and the novice in the "Zone of Proximal Development"—where the pull and push of the teacher and pupil, respectively, are played out. The chronotopes that constitute and function in the Vygotskian worldview with pedagogy and development as its central concern are capable of detecting modest advances and drastic changes that occur in the learning zones without losing track of the intermediary links. It is interesting to note that while Bakhtin's ideas on dialogue have had a far greater interdisciplinary reach despite their discipline-bound approach of dealing strictly with literary texts, Vygotsky addressed a disciplinary concern—human development from a wide range of disciplines—neurological studies, literary studies and its neighboring disciplines like theater and drama, in addition to pedagogical studies, and as such maintained the rigor of a scientist in studying a phenomenon microscopically without compromising the artistic sophistication in drawing the big picture. Thus, the particulars were always placed in a broad episteme.

Unlike Piaget, who set out to tell the story of an *epistemic* child, Vygotsky told stories not about a child, but different children—each with their unique genetic endowment using different sets of material and cultural tools, having varying levels of access to educational institutions, where they enter unique learning spaces with tutors with different pedagogical styles and philosophies—which leads to a complex web of interweaving chronotopes that produce a nonlinear, multidirectional, and context-dependent account of human development. There is no known account of Bakhtin and Vygotsky ever meeting or making

Typologies of Novels as Models of Human Development

Bakhtin's study of various types of novels is at its core a commentary on the perceptions of the human condition. He preferred to hear human voices with varying senses of present-ness and past-ness living alongside differing rhythms of a social clock with complex and circuitous links to specific cultural spaces. Bakhtin clearly rejected disembodied thinking that insists on closure because the range of meanings is restricted to fit some all-embracing system. The monological languages that characterize novels of non-emergence and selective emergence seek to impose limits upon the free-flowing languages that cannot be pulled into their orbit. Worldviews that are presented through unitary and fixed language feel threatened by the sheer diversity of other languages. The monologic worldview would rather restrict the spread of dialogics than make any attempt to expand itself.

Bakhtin's call for multiplicity does not translate into smug relativism: in fact, he shunned relativism as much as he despised dogma. Bakhtin inhabits a mixed world of neo-Kantianism and the wisdom and compassion of the Russian Orthodox Church and a selective world of Marxism to present a bold and novel worldview where answerability is the unifying link in the incredibly pluralistic world. Bakhtin (see the essay "Grounded Peace," 2001) goes even further to say that even in the realm of religion, its task is more than codifying conduct, but understanding how "prayer, ritual, hope" (p. 207) gain meaning and validity in the practice of faith and pose "dogma itself as a problem" in a non-dogmatic manner. Prayer, ritual, hope—these are all relational terms, embodied and open—such that they allow one to see the *ever-becoming* nature of humanity.

Developmental psychology has been for too long preoccupied with closure and definition in order to trace a neat linear trajectory with an endpoint, and if these demands continue to prevail, it is unlikely to find any comfort in the ever-open Bakhtinian world. Bakhtin calls for a radically new understanding of development. In the history of the novel, Bakhtin detects early forms of the "idea of development" (1981, p. 113) in the adventure novel in the form of "a line" with "knots in it" (ibid.), and hence has a clear "temporal sequence" (ibid.)—a before and after image of a hero, but as the novelistic genre developed, "knots in a straight line" and "temporal sequence" were replaced by focus on the very conditions that created "knots" and how and why they were unknotted at different times in different places. Thus, temporal sequence in accounting for the growth of the hero seemed inadequate, and the focus shifted to a complex web of chronotopic motifs that characterize sociohistorical novels to understand the emergence of hero alongside a changing world.

If developmental psychology can shift its focus from "straight lines" and "simple knots" to complex zigzags and coils in the developmental pathways—marked by polymodal, polyphonic, and polychronic aspects of human life—then there is much to gain from Bakhtin's world with its strong commitment to *becoming*. This call is neither an injunction nor a directive, rather an invitation to detect development amidst dialogical relations that happen anyway. Perhaps if we notice them, we may be able to tell more compelling and captivating stories about evolving individuals in real world in real time.

3

CREATIVE LIVING AND AESTHETIC VISION

Cultivating Finer Sensibilities

> Forms are many, forms are different, each of them having its limits. But if this were absolute, if all forms remained obstinately separate, then there would be a fearful loneliness of multitude. But the varied forms, in their very separateness, must carry something which indicates the paradox of their ultimate unity, otherwise there would be no creation.
>
> *Rabindranath Tagore,* The Creative Ideal, *2002b, p. 31*

In the infinite show of variety in the world, if we can achieve the ideal of unity, the act then becomes creative. Variety is not at the expense of unity or vice versa; instead one sees the centrifugal and centripetal forces at play in the incredible multitude of the world. How do heterogeneous entities relate to each other and how do we shape them into a provisionally conclusive ensemble? In his early works, Bakhtin was preoccupied with these questions. The nature of the relationship between entities—be it between art and life, author and hero, experienced life and narrated tale, and so forth—was his main concern, and it fell into the category of "architectonics" while its subcategory "aesthetics" dealt with the problem of bringing together a myriad of forms to make a consummated whole.

At the very outset, Bakhtin lays out the foundation for aesthetic activity by stating the relationship between created works and lived lives. "Art and life are not one, but they must become united in myself—in the unity of my answerability" (AA, p. 2). Bakhtin takes particular caution to point out that any random grouping of elements does not constitute wholesomeness of art, nor should the links be mechanical. A precariously glued relationship between art and life in which the individual leaves in desperation the "fretful cares of everyday life" to enter the world of art for "inspiration, sweet sounds and prayers" leads only to a split life. Art bears no responsibility toward life and life remains prosaic, untouched by the vitality of art. Both remain alien to each other because the "mechanical connection" between them only touches at a surface level. Bakhtin insists that only mutual answerability in which art and life converge within the individual—not as a synthesized whole but as partners in a dialogue—could set the stage for aesthetic vision. The humble prose of life must challenge the "audaciously self-confident" world of art to assume some blame and guilt. Art cannot inspire by taking possession of life because all that one would be left with is one dominant voice—that of the art. Any state of possession eliminates the very possibility of a dialogue for Bakhtin. Art cannot be mechanically sliced out of life either; it needs to be outside and has the right to demand some ornamentation to make it high-flown and grand. About the bidirectional and dynamic nature of *answerability* Bakhtin explains:

> I have to answer with my own life for what I have experienced and understood in art, so that everything I have experienced and understood would not remain ineffectual in my life. But answerability entails guilt, or liability to blame. It is not only mutual answerability that art and life must assume, but also mutual liability to blame.
>
> (AA, p. 1)

This push and pull in the relationship is crucial for Bakhtin; art cannot enjoy the exalted status and not do its duty to pull life to a higher plane, and life must push itself to ascend to a higher mode of consciousness in order to gain better perspective on its experiences. Life must also exercise its right to pull art to the "plains"—to the earthly level—so that it doesn't act with impunity and indifference toward all that is prosaic in life.

The genesis of art is certainly in life, but it is not life, nor can it be a mechanical mouthpiece for life to voice its concerns. But art has the ability to express life's concerns with greater clarity in a profound manner, so much so that the concern and its possible remedies are locked in, and with this dual capacity art answers to life. There is nothing magical about creativity and it does not necessarily burst out like a *flash*; it requires effort, and I want to argue that the product of this effort is a developmental achievement. It is convenient to live life without the answerability factor, as Bakhtin aptly points out. "For it is certainly easier to create without answering for life, and easier to live without any consideration for art" (AA, p. 2). In this kind of answerability alone can there be a creative, productive, and meaningful relationship between the creator and the created—the author and the hero—forming the very basis of architectonics.

In order to understand the psychological dimensions of Bakhtin's architectonics, it is befitting to bring Lev Vygotsky's extraordinary, but rarely cited work on *The Psychology of Art* (1971). In his introductory remarks to this work, A. N. Leontiev aptly recommends that this brilliant work be read on two levels—as the "psychology of *art*" and as the "*psychology* of art" (Vygotsky, 1971, p. vi)—so that neither art nor psychology is subordinated to one another. In this unique work, Vygotsky explored various forms of literature from fables to novels with particular emphasis on Shakespeare's tragedies. Like Bakhtin, Vygotsky found Formalism extremely inadequate in covering all the dimensions of aesthetics. The fundamental problem, Vygotsky says, lies in splitting the psychology of *art* from the *psychology* of art—the "aesthetics from above" derived from laws governing the soul—as if the soul had some grand undeniable existential features, and as such this approach did not lend itself to any meaningful scientific investigation, whereas the "aesthetics from below" caught up in the rigors of experimentation with exclusive focus on the forms in the art work could not yield anything more than "primordial and fundamentally meaningless facts" (p. 10). With its fact-obsessed methods, this approach was incapable of elevating the art, the artist, or the consumer of art to a higher plane. Vygotsky explains that works of art are unquestionably constituted by human feelings, sensations, passions, and so forth, and these very feelings that contribute to art are also transformed by the art. They are both suppliers for art and beneficiaries of art. Vygotsky argues that art should not be seen as a conveyor belt of the author's emotions. That sort of mechanical transmission of emotions would be very tragic for art, says Vygotsky. For instance, in Shakespeare's *Hamlet*, not only is the movement of tragic events conveyed, but it also transforms tragedy itself in a way to draw readers to grasp it on a higher plane of truth. Thus, we see the transformation of all the parties involved—the author, the text, the reader, and also the culture, along with the concepts of human emotions. For Vygotsky, the "aesthetics from above" and the "aesthetics from below"—the extreme subjective or objective exploration of the psychology of art—eliminates the voices of multiple parties and, more important, ignores the metamorphosis of emotions and concepts. Failure to recognize this transfiguration during the interaction between art and life, according to Vygotsky, in Shakespeare's tragedy would be tragic only for aesthetics.

Art seen exclusively as an expression of the author's feelings or as a reception by the reader would be impoverishing, says Bakhtin, and he gives his reasons:

> "Expressive" aesthetic theory is but one of many philosophical theories (ethical, philosophico-historical, metaphysical, religious) that we could call "impoverishing" theories, because they seek to explain the creatively productive event by reducing its full amplitude. And they do so, first of all, by reducing the number of participants: for purposes of explanation, the event is transposed in all its constituents to the unitary plane of a single consciousness, and it is within the unity of this single consciousness that the event is to be understood and deduced in all its constituents.
>
> (AHAA, p. 87)

When all the voices are placed on a single plane of consciousness, all we are left with is repetition or a "theoretical transcription of an already accomplished event" (AHAA, p. 87), whereas when multiple voices intermingle and interanimate there is the freshness of creativity.

Both Bakhtin and Vygotsky were equally frustrated with the dominance of Formalism in approaching the works of art. Both would argue that the essence and function of art are not contained in the works of art as inherent forms as if they have an independent existence, and the audience of the artistic work does not just discover those forms for its delight. Aesthetics is more than recognition or discovery of forms; if anything one plays an active role—as a co-participant to construct form during the interaction with the work of art. For Bakhtin, this extraordinary engagement is a serious event in which the work of art is transposed to another "axiological plane" to bestow "the gift of *form* upon it" (AHAA, p. 87), and transmute it formally. Bakhtin goes on to assert, "And this formal enrichment is impossible if a *merging* with the object so treated occurs" (AHAA, p. 87). Bakhtin often repeats, almost like a mantra, that there is no gain in merger. Without the contribution of multiple parties, aesthetics becomes a study of forms that are "atomized and insipid" and reduced to "positivist empirical data, which are lost in a wilderness of senseless detail" (Bakhtin and Medvedev, 1985, p. 4).

Vygotsky identifies at least three fundamental errors in experimental aesthetics that have dominated the psychology of art. The first problem is the introspective method, which Vygotsky argues is "starting from the wrong end" because its focus is mainly on individual feelings, responses, and appraisals, and these may very well be "arbitrary, secondary or even irrelevant features of aesthetic behavior" (1971, p. 18). Immediate responses, feelings, and impressions are far too simple and elementary; they do not necessarily constitute aesthetic experiences. Besides, aesthetic feeling is something that evolves as one reflects on immediate impressions and brings other experiences, texts, and voices to make sense of those instantaneous and unreflective responses. With the help of other extratextual materials, the immediate response may be strengthened, rationalized, and understood at a deeper level or might even undergo change. This slow evolutionary process cannot be captured by experimental methods.

The second problem that Vygotsky points out is the inability of experimental aesthetics to distinguish between ordinary and aesthetic experience. If the sublime cannot be set apart from the mundane, then the topic we are dealing with is not aesthetics at all. Vygotsky acknowledges that colors, sounds, lines, musical notes, or movements of the body are of course an integral part of artistic forms, but they are rudimentary and the perception and evaluation of these simple features do not authentically qualify as an aesthetic experience.

Third, the experimental aesthetics erroneously treats "a complex aesthetic experience" as "the sum of individual minor aesthetic pleasures" (p. 18), and this for Vygotsky is the biggest blunder. Stringing together each minor experience with mechanical links does not add up to a wholesome aesthetic experience; it does not show the interpenetration of experiences and impressions to transform each one of them to create a whole new awareness. In a very gestalt sense, the whole is larger than the sum of parts.

As a corrective measure to these problems, Vygotsky proposes an "objective—analytical method"—a term he borrowed from Müller-Freienfels—to address his twin concerns, the psychological aspects of art and the artistic aspects of psychology. According to Vygotsky, psychology for too long has been focusing exclusively on the artist or the audience for the purpose of analysis and has completely disregarded the work of art. Note that he wrote this work in the early 1920s, and almost a century later we still face the same problem. Trapped in rigid disciplinary boundaries, we think that the work of art is the exclusive business of literary critics or art historians or any other discipline specific to a particular art form. But then consciousness is the business of psychologists, and higher modes of consciousness and understanding finer sensibilities and sensitivities is the business of developmental psychologists in particular, and if we want to understand aesthetic experiences, we cannot disregard the work of art. Such an error, Vygotsky says, is akin to a judge passing a sentence based on the testimonies of the defendant or the plaintiff without considering what the case is. While the two parties' statements are crucial, they are only a few pieces of the puzzle. Psychologists concentrating mainly on the artist or the audience commit the same error, says Vygotsky. This shortcoming stems from taking things all too literally—that only individuals have a psyche, a voice, and a personality and hence qualify as worthy subjects for psychological study. Vygotsky reminds us that even works of art do possess these attributes. Like individual personalities, they invite certain kind of responses, stir certain thoughts and emotions, voice realities in a certain tone, encode messages in a certain manner, and although Vygotsky did not use the term "dialogue" or "voice" in this specific context, he clearly implies that one must address aesthetics as a living dialogue between the artist, the art, and the audience.

The essentialist approach with its experimental methods has failed to adequately address the phenomenon of psychology of art in a comprehensive manner, as Vygotsky has pointed out rather convincingly. These methods concentrate mainly on what is readily available—those that are visible and analyzable—all that occurs at a conscious level. But then, art, at both the creating and the receiving end, has been associated with something so inexplicable, mysterious, and magical and hence inaccessible to the conscious mind. It can only be felt and that feeling is beyond words. Normally, this is how most of us respond to art or express our sense of awe and wonderment when we feel captivated by works of art. There is no language to express the hypnotic trance we enter into. That being so, perhaps the secret of aesthetic experience lies in that mysterious zone of one's being—the subconscious or the unconscious level—and Freud emphatically said that one must plumb that bewildering region to gather fragments from our past buried there long ago as a way of coping with powerful dark forces of the psyche. These fragments provide clues to the negative and forbidden emotions that have been sublimated to find expression in an artistic form. Vygotsky acknowledges the workings of the subconscious in our engagement with art and recognizes that words may not be exacting and faithful in expressing our feelings for and about art. Vygotsky accepts that even artists cannot offer clear-cut methods or formulas they deploy for their creative work. With due consideration to all these factors, Vygotsky makes a compelling argument against the fundamental tenets of psychoanalysis.

First and foremost, Vygotsky avers that some well-fortified wall does not separate the conscious and the subconscious zones. "Processes generated in the subconscious frequently continue into our consciousness; conversely, many a conscious fact is pushed into the subconscious. In our minds there exists a continuous, lively, and dynamic connection between the two areas" (1971, p. 72). Vygotsky goes on to make an even more interesting observation: he says the subconscious does not passively reveal itself in the works of art, but is also transformed in the works of art. This simultaneous revelation and transformation makes clear that we cannot make any claims of unveiling the hidden zones of our unconscious world in some pure unmixed form. Any conscious interpretation or impressions of the art we offer with some links to the subconscious itself is a work of art, according to Vygotsky. He says this reflection "must be regarded as a subsequent rationalization, as a self-deception, a justification before one's own intellect, or an explanation devised post factum" (p. 72).

Vygotsky, like Bakhtin, clearly invites us to look into the ambiguous zone to appreciate the development of aesthetic sensibilities. Without the mystification, art would not retain the aura of grandeur—as something above and beyond the realm of consciousness—and without the demystification there would be no understanding of art. The former says a lot about the psychology of art and the latter speaks about the art of psychology.

For Freud, the psychical mechanisms explain all forms of social activity and organization. Because his theory is built on essential pathos of human nature, he sees art as a cover for our infantile fantasies, aggression, and forbidden desires. The shortcoming of the psychosexual theory of development is its failure to adequately explain the changing faces of art in history. What qualifies as a work of art has changed over time, and even those great works of art that have survived the test of time have been cast in a different light. Vygotsky points out that psychoanalysis operates as if it "had a catalogue of sex symbols and these symbols remained the same at all times, for all peoples, and that it were enough to find corresponding symbols in the artistic creativity of an artist to determine that he is suffering from an Oedipus complex, voyeurism and so on" (1971, p. 81). If emotions shown in works of art are treated as coded messages, then art loses its rightful place in our lives. Every emotion gets a negative twist: tender feelings of yearning become some sort of compensation for feelings of deprivation or as a wish-fulfillment, and if the topic is murder or some form of violent aggression it could get a pathological spin of necrophilia and so forth. The real danger in this unconscious-driven view of art is that the *remedy* for the ailment is mistaken as a *symptom* of neurosis. In concluding his critique of psychoanalysis, Vygotsky judiciously says, "Art as the subconscious is a problem: art as the social solution for the subconscious is its likely solution" (p. 85).

Psychology has had an incredible fascination with the idea of art as an individual affair, be it as a creator or as a recipient. John Dewey insists in his famous work *Art as Experience* that "the uniquely distinguishing feature of aesthetic experience is exactly the fact that no such distinction of self and object exists in it" (1958, p. 249), and thus claims that there is total absorption of the self in the art form. For Dewey, this self-surrender is crucial not only in experiencing art but in any activity that we undertake, particularly the ones that demand serious attention. Dewey sees this as a mark of maturity, when all the mental energy flows into the activity that one is engaged in.

In a similar vein, Mihaly Csikszentmihalyi recommends what he calls the "flow" to reach the pinnacle of human experience. This intense experience, he says, is critical for our overall growth. According to him, this necessary "flow" is characterized by clear goals, decisive action, merger of action and awareness, concentration, loss of self-awareness, altered sense of time, and finally the experience becoming "autotelic"—meaning an activity "worth doing for its own sake" (1993, pp. 178, 179). He cites examples from athletes, musicians, dancers, scientists, and even spiritual aspirants to convince us that "flow" is an essential trait of highly talented individuals. Furthermore, Csikszentmihalyi argues that "flow" has a therapeutic value and it can be cultivated; in other words, if one feels stagnated in life, one can learn to unblock the flow to break through inhibitions, so that creative activity may begin or resume. Csikszentmihalyi, on one hand, does not say, at least on a theoretical level, that creativity emanates exclusively from the individual. He says it is a combination of individual talent, the artistic domain, and the institutions that validate, reward, or reject. But when we read his account, clearly the focus is on the individual. Drawing inspiration from Csikszentmihalyi's works, Howard Gardner (1993) studied the lives of seven influential individuals—Freud, Einstein, Picasso, Stravinsky, Eliot, Graham, and Gandhi—in his influential book *Creating Minds*, to present what he calls in the subtitle of his book "An Anatomy of Creativity." The very word "anatomy" is indicative of his approach; it is precisely that—an attempt to dissect the lives of these individuals to identify some common attributes all of them share, like childishness, childlikeness, incredible powers of concentration and tenacity, and so forth. Gardner clearly and emphatically states that he has approached creativity from a "great man/great woman" perspective to perhaps identify the elements of Csikszentmihalyi's "flow" and in some way to track its course.

While the idea of "flow" is appealing and on some level is certainly desirable—after all, who could argue against building a steady mind and developing a focused determination to pursue your ideas—I want to argue that it is somewhat limited and falls short in explaining the complex processes of aesthetic experience. Yes, when people are overwhelmed by the power of art, they understandably and justifiably use phrases like "being lost in" or "mesmerized" or "completely taken" by art. Artists also use similar phrases to describe the unwavering attention they paid to their creative work. These expressions of dissolution are real, but they are only the starting point or an intermediary step in the development of aesthetic consciousness. Where there is surrender, there is only genuflection, not aesthetics. It is the world of art that dominates and all other parties are subordinated to its power. In a situation like this, we are dealing with a religious and not an aesthetic experience; as Bakhtin says, "when the other consciousness is the encompassing consciousness of God, a *religious* event takes place (prayer, worship, ritual)" (1990, p. 22).

Let us consider an actor trying to play a role. Initially he has to get under the skin of the character he sets out to play and immerse himself in all the attributes of that character and merge with that character. This is the first step and is absolutely crucial for the actor in his evolving role. Having fully felt the character he is playing, he must come out of the character to play the character. If he remains in the character, there is no acting and consequently no art. But if he had never entered the "body and soul" of the character, then the artistic activity had never begun. Only when you are in the ambiguous zone of "being in the character" and "being out of the character" with dialogic movements between the two, are you dealing with aesthetics.

To give another scenario, let us say a singer has to render a melancholic song and if she managed to make her listeners sad through that rendition, then she has succeeded as an artist. But if she herself felt sad on the stage, it would be a failure of art. If your audience cries and it thinks you are crying, then it is art. But if the artist cries, it is no longer art. Perhaps it would be a laughable moment. The singer cannot be emoting the emotions she is trying to convey. But how does she develop the capacity to make her listeners feel the melancholy? During the process of learning and perfecting the art form, she feels the emotion, and yes, she feels it with a great deal of intensity and even cries. In other words, she is moved by the emotion and has fully experienced the emotion. Once she comes out of the experience, she is able to transform the experience into an art form. Had she been "lost" in the experience as Dewey and Csikszentmihalyi claim, then she would never be able to deliver the emotion in the right proportion. She must vacillate between "feeling" and "not feeling" the emotion so that it is delivered in the right measure. To bring the artistic effect the emotion can neither spill over nor be inadequate, and she must be mindful of various other factors—the musical notes, rhythm, lyrics, musical accompaniments, and other considerations of stage. Because these multiple factors have to be carefully woven to bring the desired effect, she must be undistracted and thus appears to be "lost" in her art.

Aesthetic philosophies that guide performance traditions in India explain with a great deal of clarity how the artist must churn the emotion to enhance its effect and transform it into an aesthetic sentiment. According to *Natya Sastra*—a treatise on the aesthetics of dramaturgy—the artist must use the basic emotions of the human heart, such as love, courage, sadness, anger, fear, and so forth, and present them through a story, dance, music, or whatever the art form is, such that the spectator experiences an aesthetic sentiment. Sage Bharata, the author of *Natya Sastra*, describes the sublime emotion as *Rasa*—literally meaning "juice," "taste," or "flavor." This gastronomic metaphor is ideal for explaining the dynamics of aesthetic experience. Like a chef who takes the basic ingredient and cooks it with spices and condiments to make the dish tasty and flavorful, the artist takes the basic emotions and seasons them with the right measure of gestures, bodily movements, and other devices for the spectator's delight. In art one receives a gourmet version of an ordinary emotion. Abhinavagupta, an aesthetic philosopher who wrote extensive commentary on *Natya Sastra*, explains that the artist's task is not only to express an emotion but also to offer an exposition of an emotion (Unni, 1998). As the spectator absorbs the essence of the emotion, he or she cultivates finer taste and slowly develops into a connoisseur of art. The artist squeezes the *Rasa* and combines it with the body of poetry, music, dance, and so forth to both mimic life and create newer possibilities for life. Art becomes at once mimetic and poetic for the creator and the receiver, setting the stage for art and life to answer each other.

Between the Creator and the Creation

If the world of art and the world of life must connect in the "unity of answerability" as Bakhtin claims, how, then, is it achieved, and what are the indications that this necessary process is taking place for the aesthetic vision to emerge? First of all, answerability is not a given entity; it is achieved through a long and an arduous task. It is not something that can be readily identified in a dialogue at a given moment; rather it is something that is realized over a period of time. Furthermore, for Bakhtin, aesthetics is not defined by a set of properties or conditions, thus making the concept elusive. Unlike Kant, Bakhtin had very little interest in fixed categories and operational definitions. In the Kantian world of transcendental aesthetics, concepts gain validity as long as they pass through fixed categories and synthetic judgments that are a priori, providing grounds for making sense of all experiences. In Kant's highly abstract philosophy, there can be no traces of concrete life experiences; they have to be far removed from the specifics, the local, and the real time, for these are considered contaminants of the pure, transcendental aesthetic. Bakhtin, on the other hand, had very little patience with anything so far removed from the specifics of life. He practically shunned *phantom* philosophies—be they on aesthetics, ethics, or epistemology. In his early work on the Philosophy of the Act, Bakhtin asserts:

> There is no aesthetic ought, scientific ought, and—beside them—an ethical ought; there is only that which is aesthetically, theoretically, socially valid, and these validities may be joined by the ought, for which all of them are instrumental. These positings gain their validity with an aesthetic, a

scientific or a sociological unity; the ought gains its validity within the unity of my once-occurant answerable life.

(1993, p. 5)

For Bakhtin, when the prescriptive "ought" dominates the theorizing activity, it simply loses its veridicality. Once an action or thought has achieved its validity in the "now-ness" of life, in all its fullness and contradictions, then we may very well be able to detect the "ought." But, when the "ought" dominates, we are looking at a hierarchical organization that does not entertain differences, and without differences there is no dialogue. Bakhtin asks us to place our faith in the ethically acting subject to understand ethics rather than using ethical norms that do not have validity in their own right to judge a subject. Ethics must meet its obligation to life and to human sensitivity.

In his early works, Bakhtin approached aesthetics with all its complex dimensions from a philosophical perspective. His long essay *Author and Hero in Aesthetic Activity* often is repetitious, elaborate in the explanation, and the tone is covertly theological. It is an open question whether Bakhtin was trying to redeem aesthetics in theological terms or address theological concerns in aesthetic terms. Bakhtin, like his favorite author, Dostoevsky, had a very complex relationship with God. One of the members of the Bakhtin Circle, Sergey Bocharov (1994), recorded some revealing conversations with Bakhtin in the early '70s, and during those conversations Bakhtin reflected on many topics that occupied him for his entire life. About the interconnections between aesthetics and religion, Bocharov opines that "The religious aspect of Bakhtin's aesthetics is deep but concealed, an unspoken, implicit theme, evidently because of the external conditions of writing in the Soviet period and as if he sought to prevent us from judging it too decisively" (1994, p. 1019). Like any intellect living under oppressive conditions, Bakhtin had to write in riddles, hint at something more profound, while writing something seemingly acceptable in the political climate. During his conversation with Bocharov, Bakhtin confesses that he made compromises in his writings. "Everything that was created in this graceless soil, beneath this unfree sky, all of it is to some degree morally flawed" (p. 1012). When pressed about the "moral flaws" in his work on Dostoevsky, Bakhtin said that he would have written it differently and addressed the "main question," which he says he never addressed. When Bocharov sought clarification, Bakhtin said:

Philosophical questions, what Dostoevsky agonized about all his life—the existence of God. In the book I was constantly forced to prevaricate, to dodge backward and forward. I had to hold back constantly. The moment a thought got going, I had to break it off. Backward and forward. I even misrepresented the church.

(p. 1012)

In his mind, Bakhtin considered his works on Dostoevsky merely literary criticism, without any scope of leading the ideas to "other worlds." In Bakhtin's self-assessment about the discovery of the "new word" in Dostoevsky's works, those words that capture the non-merger of voices, in his view, "won't be examined in the highest council. *Up there* it won't be read" (p. 1013), because in his judgment he did not and/or could not sketch an image of a world that he shared with Dostoevsky in which one sees "the church as a communion of unmerged souls" (p. 1012).

I draw attention to these personal reflections of Bakhtin because they enable us to understand why he so strongly proposed the kind of relationship between the author (the creator) and the hero (the created), in which every voice retains its originality and integrity even while engaging in a dialogue. Bakhtin did not approach religion as an abstract code of conduct—he was not interested in the "do's and the don'ts," but in a feeling for your creator, who embodies the "synthesis of ethical solipsism" with "ethical-aesthetic kindness toward the other" (AHAA, p. 56). Bakhtin consistently displayed an amazing predilection for un-appropriating relationships not only between fellow human beings, but also between the creator and his or her creation. It was not the abstract or institutional religion that interested him, but it was faith, a living faith or a feeling for faith, that energized him. Bakhtin says Dostoevsky was drawn toward, "Not faith (in a sense of a specific faith, in orthodoxy, in progress, in man, in revolution, etc.), but a *sense of faith*, that is, an integral attitude (by means of a whole person) toward a higher and ultimate value" (TDP, p. 294). Bakhtin, in short, celebrated Dostoevsky's artistic vision because as an author he created characters that were philosophers in their own right; they were not mouthpieces for the author's worldview. The author may unequivocally disapprove of his characters' worldview, but their voices were never silenced. In Bakhtin's view, Dostoevsky was endowed with special radar to pick up multiple voices, with all their intermittent pauses, to hear dialogicality in our social life.

Bakhtin's approach to the relationship between the creator and his creation is similar to Nietzsche's, whose Zarathustra firmly asserts, "The creator seeks companions, not corpses or herds or believers. The creator seeks fellow-creators, those who inscribe new values on new tables" (1961, Zarathustra's Prologue, No. 9). The creator cannot and must not have the final say on his or her creation. That is why Zarathustra famously proclaimed, "I should believe only in a God who understood how to dance" (1961, Of Reading and Writing). While Nietzsche sought dance, Bakhtin sought a dialogue with the creator. The crux of aesthetics lies in this evolving dialogue between the artist, the art, and the audience.

Aesthetics is not a given, but achieved, and even this achievement cannot be identified at specific nodal points in a dialogue or a conversation. It is a certain way of relating to others and other abstract entities. The mere existence of multiple voices in a fragmented form in a conversation does not constitute an aesthetic relationship. One has to consider extralinguistic features and the positionality of various parties and entities and their shifting relationship with ample loopholes, leaving them open-ended. The unfinalizability that is essential for aesthetics does not mean that it is devoid of any anchoring points or periodic closures. Bakhtin sets the free flow of experience and dialogue to what he calls the "rhythm," which provides some systematization and channels the flow. Morson and Emerson explain, "rhythm expresses closure in the present moment, as the loophole expresses openness" (1990, p. 193). In many ways, it is a meta-experience, which makes the distant past, the immediate present, and the potential future ubiquitous. Bakhtin explains:

> Rhythm is the axiological ordering of what is inwardly given or present-on-hand. Rhythm is not expressive in the strict sense of the term; that is it does not express a lived experience, is not founded from within that experience; it is not an emotional-volitional reaction to an object and to meaning, but a reaction *to* that reaction.
> (AHAA, p. 117)

For the activity to become creative, one cannot get too complacent enjoying the cadences of the experience "present-on-hand"—the rhythm must transition into the "extrarhythmic" mode—the necessary dissonance must occur so that "what-is-given" mutates into "what-ought-to-be" (AHAA, p. 118). In Indian aesthetics, rhythm is considered the science and melody the art of music; thus aesthetics integrates rules, laws, structure, and the free-flowing, open-ended melody taking music to great heights, keeping the potential for creativity intact and ever alive. By insisting on the rhythm and the loophole in activities and relationships, Bakhtin makes sure that laws are not compromised in the free and open world. He is also making sure that there is unity in the diverse elements necessary for aesthetic vision to emerge. There is wholesomeness to aesthetics even as it leaves the "window open" for the birth of new ideas.

How does the relationship between the artist and the art develop? What does it look like in the nascent stage, when the head must create what the heart has conceived? We are dealing with the groping consciousness of the creator struggling with a nebulous idea, and even after achieving some clarity, the craftsman must search for suitable materials for the craft—an author for words and utterances, a painter for colors, and so forth. At this stage we are certainly dealing with only one consciousness, for there can't be any face-to-face meeting with the creation. The hero's stable image is yet to be formed, and achieving this image, according to Bakhtin, is to a considerable extent the author's struggle with himself. The author at this stage does enjoy the benefit of "surplus of *meaning*" (PDP, p. 73); after all, he is the creator and the hero is not yet voiced. During this phase, the author is at liberty to play with the hero's "grimaces, masks, actions, gestures, responses" (AHAA, p. 6), and so forth at his whims to shape the countenance of the hero. This process of building the image of a hero cannot be traced back accurately, and the attempt itself, according to Bakhtin, is flawed. One can only arrive at some plausible explanations because we have to deal with "meaning-related laws" (AHAA, p. 6) governing this process. To assume that the steps can be traced back implies that the process is systematic and sequential. Furthermore, once the image of the hero gains some stability, the very way we look at the formative moment changes; in other words, its "history on the plane of meanings" (AHAA, p. 6) changes, and furthermore, in Bakhtin's view, a microscopic examination of the temporal causes and sequence of this process is not relevant to our concerns about aesthetics. This point is highly instructive for psychologists, developmental psychologists in particular, who are more than eager to draw a flow chart of the creative processes. They design fancy experiments with some literal and figurative "magnifying lenses" and "precise timers" to accurately record the sequence of artistic activity. What concerns Bakhtin with respect to aesthetics is the nature of the relationship between the author and the hero where neither party is in possession of the other. The "surplus of meaning" that the author naturally possesses is slowly relinquished to allow the hero to find meanings in culture and history. Aesthetics emerges at the meeting point of these multiple voices.

Aesthetic contemplation then involves a certain way of relating to objects, individuals, and, for that matter, to our own creation as equals in a dialogue. Furthermore, it is a certain way of positioning the other on a horizontal plane and a certain way of relating *to* meaning to ensure that there is no finality or exclusive ownership. Also, it entails a certain manner of questioning to invite the other into a dialogue so that the response generates another question. In this kind of give and take, human sensibilities are heightened and human sensitivities are strengthened, subtleties and nuances are grasped and responsible choices are made possible and ethical freedom is guaranteed.

Bakhtin found the realization of such an aesthetic vision in Dostoevsky's polyphonic novels and in Goethe's works. Both were able to give life to their creations—to the characters, to the world around them, natural and cultural—and both were skillful in temporalizing all aspects of reality. While Goethe possessed the *"art of eye"* (Bakhtin, 1986, p. 27), Dostoevsky, we could very well say, was endowed with the "art of ear," and both were capable of going beyond what their senses perceived. The aesthetic eye and ear sees and hears what others fail to see and hear. The *seeing eye* of Goethe was just as capable as the *hearing ear* of Dostoevsky to grasp the complex configurations in society and the historical forces that reconfigure the cultural landscape.

The sharp visual and auditory perceptiveness that contribute to the aesthetic vision of Goethe and Dostoevsky is not necessarily restricted to literary and other forms of fine art. Similar features can be found in creative works in the field of hardcore science, and exemplary scientists also have an unusual type of relationship to the topic of their study. Noted philosopher of science Evelyn

Fox Keller, who studied the life and work of Barbara McClintock, a geneticist who won the Nobel Prize, observes that this extraordinary scientist had a rare ability to "feel for the organism" and "hear what the organism" has to say and see the "organization and behavior of DNA" (1983, p. 200), and this ability not only set her apart from other scientists, but also enabled her to study movements and pattern formation of biological cells. This creative approach contributed to the amazing discoveries she made in the field of biological science. When Fox Keller asked McClintock how she was able to uncover the mysteries of genetics, McClintock's responses were, "hear what the material has to say," and have a great deal of patience to wait for the organisms to "come to you," and, above all, McClintock insists, one must have "a feeling for the organism" (p. 198). McClintock goes on to explain, "No two plants are exactly alike. They're all different, and as a consequence, you have to know the difference" (p. 198). Note how she relates to a plant over a period of time. "I start with the seedling and I don't want to leave it. I don't really feel I really know the story if I don't watch the plant all the way along. So I know every plant in the field. I know them intimately, and I find it a great pleasure to know them" (p. 198).

These brief snippets carry all the features of aesthetic activity that Bakhtin emphasized. First and foremost, the biological organisms are not some dead cellular structures for McClintock, but living entities with eccentric behaviors, interesting forms, and distinctive voices having their peculiar interaction with the surrounding environment; above all, they have their exclusiveness in undergoing change. Like Goethe, who was able to see changing shades in the cultural landscape, McClintock was able to recognize differences between plants and variations in the corncob. Just as Dostoevsky renounces his "surplus" vision to allow his created hero to speak with him, McClintock allows the biological cells to speak and reveal themselves to her. The same approach that enabled Dostoevsky to uncover the dialogic sphere of human consciousness facilitated McClintock's discovery of the dialogic sphere of the natural world.

Bakhtin explains how and why an aesthetic activity is distinct from cognitive processes and performed actions. In a basic cognitive act, there can be a division between the knower and the known, for the latter is simply available for comprehension. Aesthetic activity is not an opposite of cognitive activity, but rather it "enriches and completes" what has been understood through cognition. This completion and ornamentation is achieved by a whole new way of relating to the object in hand and in turn with this new relationship, further discovery of new laws governing the scientific or cultural phenomena are possible. Aesthetic activity is marked by its receptivity to the aesthetic object, and in this process the subject and the object of the activity may momentarily merge or temporarily switch places. The difference between the art and the artist is not so visible, or, in Bakhtin's words, "*it creates the concrete intuitive unity of these two worlds. It places man in nature, understood as his aesthetic environment, it humanizes nature and* naturalizes man" (CMFVA, p. 279). It is precisely this humanizing of nature and naturalization of an individual's relationship with the natural world that we see in McClintock's approach to science.

Creative Composition of Self and Life

Creativity need not be restricted to works of art alone. The processes that apply to creating a work of art may very well apply to the ways we compose our lives and the manner in which we relate to others, understand our past, and learn from other cultures to find solutions to our sticky problems. We are fundamentally social animals. It is a given, and hence we cannot afford to be too aloof. We cannot be lost in the crowd either. Types of relationships are as varied as human beings themselves. Just as there are no ideal marriages, there are no ideal relationships. If we take this as a given, how then do we ensure that a relationship is not exploitative or manipulative? When is an individual's action charmingly innocent, and when is it foolishly naïve? When does the individual's inability or unwillingness to abide by the written and unwritten rules of culture become a sign of mental disorder? When is it an admirable act of nonconformity? After all, adapting to an inherently sick society is no sign of sound mental health.

We are not only cultural subjects but also bearers of history, even the past that was created long before we were born. History may facilitate and/or burden human interactions. How, when, and why do we invoke history selectively to our advantage? How, when, and why should we unburden ourselves with the baggage of history? Globalism has pushed human relations into a new phase. Nothing is far away and exotic. New patterns are continually forming—some break free from provincialism, while others create local tribes in the global village. Globalism has brought cultures very close; in big cosmopolitan cities, interracial, interethnic, and intercultural marriages are all too common. The same globalism has reopened old wounds and cultural heterogeneity has produced anxiety among many, and hence we also see a "return to the roots" phenomenon giving birth to the most virulent form of cultural chauvinism. Whether these ever-changing patterns in culture lead to what pundits have called "The End of History" (Fukuyama, 1989) or "The Clash of Civilizations" (Huntington, 1993) or both is an open question. Bakhtin did not live to see this new global reality. He died in 1975, and naturally he didn't have much to say about it. But when we examine Bakhtin's works from this new reality, we discover that we have much to learn that might be apropos to our times.

Bakhtin constructs human relations based on a triadic equation—I-for-myself, I-for-others, and Others-for-me. These are the parameters within which Bakhtin says we can pose questions about self and other operating in the world. None of these categories are static for Bakhtin; individuals are always developing in an ever-changing world. Bakhtin had no patience for a mechanical "interactionist" approach. The essential categories are to be understood as a unit; they are interdependent and cannot be separated. Bakhtin does not necessarily view the interdependence between self and other as a virtue or as a sign of tolerance or as a way to build a harmonious society, rather he points out that it is inevitable because we cannot transcend our solipsism. At a fundamental level, we are invisible to ourselves—I cannot see my own face—I need the other as a mirror. Our view of the world is partial; hence I need the other to fill in. The other's filling in may not be complete, but at the least, it shows clearly that my view is limited.

The necessity of the other, Bakhtin asserts, can be recognized by addressing the fundamental manner in which we experience our "outward appearance," the "outward boundaries of the body," and the "outward physical action, both in relation to oneself (in one's self-consciousness) and in relation to another being" (AHAA, p. 47). The face is the index of our outward appearance and this elementary indicator is not available to our vision. Hence we need a mirror and the expression we see in our reflection, according to Bakhtin, is made up of several other expressions. They include the actual emotion or attitude of the moment; let us say we react to a wrinkle or a pigmentation or grey hair and so on that automatically produces a response. Additionally, on another plane we also see in our reflection the evaluation of our expression by possible others—it could be someone specific or a phantom character—and the next plane is our response to the evaluation of our expression by the other. Bakhtin is careful to point out that looking at our reflection in the mirror is precisely that—a reflection and not ourselves—we are in front of the mirror, not in it. This act is neither pure perception nor is it, psychologically speaking, a solitary activity. Simultaneously, we "see" our exterior and we "see" what we think others see and we "see" our response to what others see. This composite view of the outward appearance does not translate into the whole self; it only becomes important material for self-consciousness. The outer vision is important—contributing to the development of inner vision—but taken in isolation it becomes deficient. The pivotal point for Bakhtin is that we are never alone when we look at ourselves in the mirror even in the privacy of our home. The "eye" of the other is always there. Even the simple act of seeing our reflection in the mirror encompasses the triadic relationship that Bakhtin stressed—the I-for-myself (how I see myself), I-for-others (how others see me), and Others-for-me (how I see others). The perception, the cognition, the evaluation, and the response are one, inseparable unit.

Bakhtin takes the limitations of self at a perceptual level to build his case for the necessity of the other at an aesthetic level. The need, the respect, and the love are not a prescription Bakhtin offered for promoting harmony and peace in society; he was not interested in building utopias; he says the categories for seeing ourselves operating in the world are simply unavailable. We are equipped with the capacity to see the contours of the external body against the backdrop of the surrounding world of others, but the same view of ourselves is impossible. The panoramic view is available only to see others, not ourselves. This perceptual limitation is compensated by the cognitive awareness that the others are equally limited in their view. The same principle would apply for our actions. Bakhtin asks us to consider how absurd it would be if we focus on our actions while we are acting; we must concentrate on the thing we are acting on, but not on the action itself. We can't be actors and observers at the same time. Bakhtin says it would be fatal to watch the movements of our feet while we are running, jumping, or driving. In sum, we simply do not have the analytical categories to "see" our outward appearance, our actions, or be able to draw our silhouette with the world as our background. Furthermore, the outer boundaries of the body are stretchable and unlimited. It is like entering into a hall of mirrors and every turn of the head offers only a partial view of the body. The bottom line is, we never get the complete picture of ourselves.

How does this perceptual limitedness set the stage for how we relate to each other? For Bakhtin, first and foremost is love—a revised version of Christian love—love the other not as you would love yourself, but love the other because they are the other. Loving the other as the other does not entail any self-sacrifice or self-denial. The self in no way is diminished because the self and other occupy a unique position in time and place, which cannot be transcended. To affirm self, one need not negate the other. Negation of the other only leads to false consciousness, for true consciousness needs the input of the other without being dictated by the other. Bakhtin reiterates again and again that "Pure, solitary self-accounting is impossible" (AHAA, p. 144) because there is simply no vantage point for that kind of reflection. Besides, even a solitary self-accounting, in a literal sense, implies a presence of a fictitious other or others who serve as interlocutors. "In an absolute axiological void, no utterance is possible, nor is consciousness itself possible" (p. 144). Recognizing the necessity of the "other" does not mean that one must feel besieged by the cacophonous voices of the others. Nor is Bakhtin suggesting naïvely that social organization is fair and equal. To live mindfully, one must understand the cultural atmosphere to actively embrace and reject cultural codes; as Bakhtin asserts, "The life which has no knowledge of the air it breathes is a naïve life" (p. 144).

In Bakhtin's worldview, love is neither absolute nor undifferentiated; he calls for that kind of love that honors outsideness, boundaries, and non-merger. In his later works, he recommends flexible boundaries between self and other and suggests, "The more demarcation the better, but benevolent demarcation, without border disputes. Cooperation" (FNM 70–71, p. 137). The borders, for Bakhtin, must be open and shifting in order to play a meaningful role in the lives of each other and to enhance a deeper understanding of self and other. Above all, the porous border allows one to exercise ethical freedom amidst the historical necessities and material forces of the world.

Disregarding the borders would be counterproductive in human relationships. Let us say, a fellow human being is suffering and you are cognitively aware of the circumstances that cause the suffering; but the knowledge alone cannot heal the person—the counsel you want to offer will not be effective—because at this point there is no contact between the two consciousnesses. The first step, Bakhtin says, is to project yourself into the other person and experience his life as he experiences it. The empathy or the co-experiencing is only the first step. But a meaningful counsel can be given only when the individual returns to his position, his life, and his self and sees it as an "outsider," and having seen it as an "insider" earlier can now see and feel the inner and outer dimensions of the problem. Bakhtin makes a clear distinction between empathy and sympathetic co-experience. Empathy involves complete merger, and as a result a creative solution cannot be found. Besides, it lacks all the vantage points. The sympathetic co-experience operating on the border of two consciousnesses acquires the capacity to be creative and the sensitivities become soothing and effective. Bakhtin explains this transformative process:

> From the very outset, sympathetic co-experiencing introduces values into the co-experienced life that are transgredient to this life; it transposes this life from the very outset into a new value-meaning context and can from the very outset rhythmicize this life temporally and give it form spatially.
> (AHAA, p. 83)

The self–other relationship is not a simple mechanical interaction or a mechanical balancing act between two individuals. It raises a host of questions on the disjunction between experiences and the narrating of those experiences, and the value- and history-laden context that gives meaning to those experiences, and the degree to which the self or the other exerts authority over the range of meanings. The crucial factor for creative living and aestheticized consciousness is to selectively collect meanings scattered in the world of the present and the past to construct and reconstruct the self and to explore new vantage points from which to view the human world. In an attempt to construct a desirable selfhood, individuals often strive to be "good" and do "noble acts" and "help others" and so forth. While Bakhtin insists on *love* as the foundation for human relations, he also warns against becoming too overbearing or mistaking ingratiating behavior for love. As detailed as Bakhtin is in explaining the distinctive features of aesthetic consciousness, he is equally detailed in explaining those modes of consciousness that may be mistaken for the former.

Bakhtin identifies two types of biographical consciousness—one the "adventurous-heroic type" and the other the "social-quotidian type." The individual in the adventurous-heroic type is driven by the "will to be a hero" in the lives of others. He strives to "win fame and glory" and wants "to grow in and for others, and not in and for oneself" (AHAA, p. 156). This individual selects heroes of the past and present, builds a shrine for them, and seeks to "become a participant in such a pantheon" (AHAA, p. 156). The individual here loves only to quench his "thirst to be loved," to achieve significance in the lives of others. In this mode of consciousness, the I-for-others dominates at the expense of

I-for-myself and Others-for-me. This individual thrives only in the state of being possessed by the other's love. Bakhtin argues that this mode, while being infused with warmth and perhaps to some degree even sincere feelings, is still immature. He calls this "naïve individualism"—a belief that one has all the necessary traits and sincere intent to perform the noble deeds. Bakhtin emphatically says that you are never your own hero, nor can you feel entitled to be another person's hero by performing the deeds that you think are worthy of merit. Heroism is bestowed upon you as a gift by the other because what the self cannot see, the other sees and offers it back as a libation. Bakhtin had a strong distaste for self-aggrandizement. In his view, this search for glory boils down to "unmediated parasitism" (AHAA, p. 156) because "everything inward and everything outward strives here to coincide in the other's axiological consciousness" (AHAA, p. 160). More important, the individual perceives the world around him as static, as if it is established and the heroes of the present and the past he wants to emulate possess a set of given traits. Bakhtin cautions that once this individual feels thrown out of this imaginary world or slighted by the other, the individual wilts and his heroism collapses and desperation sets in. An amorphous identity is not a mark of maturity and development.

The second type of biographical consciousness is the "social-quotidian type," which, in contrast to the adventurous-heroic type, lives in a humanity that is socially given. In other words, it only deals with values that are given at the present living conditions and does not draw inspiration from the heroes of the past who are dead and long gone. The social-quotidian type strives to be *with* the world—abiding by familial and social values—but not *in* the world. While the adventurous-heroic type submits to the consciousness of the other to achieve the heroic status, the social-quotidian is a distant observer who is always outside, taking note of social expectations and sanctions, and lives accordingly.

Note that Bakhtin's characterization of the "adventurous-heroic" and "social-quotidian" must not be treated as equivalent to what psychology terms the "histrionic" and "conformist" types of personalities, respectively. They certainly share some resemblances, but the explanatory domains are different. Bakhtin certainly was not the first one to point out the limitations of an individual whose motto is "do good to feel good" or "play by the rules." Lawrence Kohlberg identified three levels of moral reasoning—the first pre-conventional level is that of a young child whose orientation to rules is to obey them to avoid punishment or to receive something in return, followed by the next conventional level in which the individual plays by the rules or is duty bound. For Kohlberg, these levels are developmental trajectories and all individuals follow this upward path to eventually reach the highest level of moral reasoning, where your actions are guided by universal principles of justice and morality. According to Kohlberg, only a few reach the highest level. Bakhtin entertained neither a sequence in the development of consciousness, nor an abstract universal value. Everything for Bakhtin was bound to the concrete specifics of life. He was also not interested in identifying traits purely as psychological constructs, as if they had independent existence.

Bakhtin's approach was not prescriptive either, and as such was not dealing with individual psychology in inane terms like "selfish," "selfless," "sacrifice," and so forth. His main concerns were with outsideness, shifting axiological points, uniqueness of the individual (because of the place we occupy at a given moment), and the unsystematizability of culture. What he finds problematic about individuals trying to fashion themselves as heroes or to simply play by the social rules is that they fail to recognize change in every realm. Striving to gain importance in the lives of the others entails a firm positioning of self and other in an equally immobile world. Whereas the fluid self freely moves in a changing world with the recognition that the genesis of self-awareness is in the other and yet can negotiate relationships without overpowering or being over-powered. Bakhtin shuns standard formulas and fixed timetables and his theory of aesthetics and, by extension, aesthetic love offers no prescriptives or particulars. What we understand from his account of author–hero relationships is that the healthy self welcomes and rejoices in the plenitude of differences in the world only to discover its image in the eyes of the other, leading to an ongoing dialogue with periodic closures.

In our lives, right from birth, everything about self—from appearances to primal self-awareness—comes from the external world through others. In fact, in the early years it is the other that dominates. Bakhtin says, "Just as the body is formed initially in the mother's womb (body), a person's consciousness awakens wrapped in another's consciousness" (FNM 70–71, p. 138). What is given does not automatically translate into self-consciousness. Like a painter who chooses from the infinite array of colors and mixes them in the desired measure to produce a work of art, the self must also select the images he or she sees in others to compose selfhood and life. It is the selective and transformative process that makes the self–other relationship into an art form.

There are only two points in life at which the self has no role or awareness and they are the terminal points—birth and death. Bakhtin argues that they do not belong in the realm of self-consciousness. For that matter, they are not even events in our lives that we are capable of experiencing. When a child is born, the parents and others celebrate—it is an event in their lives—the child is incapable of experiencing it. The same holds true for death. The one who is being born cannot have any awareness of his or her own birthing process. There is no outsideness. Similarly, there is no external vantage point to see one's own death. Those things belong only in the realm of imagination and curiosity, and the material for this activity can be supplied only by the other. Moreover, to imagine the significance of our entry into and exit from the world, we need to see it through the eyes of the other; as Bakhtin writes, "My birth, my axiological abiding in the world, and finally, my death are events that occur neither *in* me nor *for* me" (AHAA, p. 105).

What, then, is the ethical and aesthetic potential of this awareness that the beginning and the end of one's life are really events for others? What meaning does it have for the interval between life and death? Interestingly, Bakhtin sets up a dialogue between life and death, leaving it open-ended and unfinalized. Grappling with our death in life is not morbid for Bakhtin; it has neither finality nor any pathological overtones. It is the knowledge about the inevitability of death that allows one to compose one's life creatively and meaningfully as Bakhtin recommends, "The demand is: live in such a way that every given moment of your life would be both consummating, final moment and, at the same time, the initial moment of a new life" (AHAA, p. 122). It is precisely because I know that death is inevitable and that it has significance in the lives of others—the loved and the loving survivors—that I hold myself answerable to them. Answerability is not the same as the desire to be a hero for others; the former is a gift that is durable and the latter is a demand that could crumble in no time. How is it that death renews life on another plane? Caryl Emerson (1989) explains that, in Bakhtin's view, death itself is an "ultimate aesthetic act" in which all authority over your life has been relinquished and handed over to the other as a gift and the other begins the work of bringing wholesomeness to the life that has been received. Among many things that Bakhtin admired in Dostoevsky's artistic world is that death has no finality. Of course a person dies, but the "Personality does not die" (PDP, p. 300) because the departed person's words remain available for an open-ended dialogue. We must bear in mind, particularly from a psychological perspective, that we are not referring only to noble and heroic words. Bakhtin is not talking about martyrdom. He is insisting on the unfinalizability of life even after death, and the closure, the rhythm, and the organization of the plot structure is done by the other. Furthermore, Bakhtin is pointing to the longer life of words in comparison to the body. That awareness that words outlive us enables us to compose our lives creatively.

The outsideness that is crucial for our understanding of self and our lives applies even in the realm of culture. Bakhtin does not subscribe to the idea that "deep down people are pretty much the same" and that cultural practices are only surface manifestations. One side of this doctrine is utopian and the other side is imperialistic. To a great extent and for a very long time, psychology has been the most vociferous proponent of this doctrine. It operates on the assumption that psychology is the scientific study of human behavior or the human mind and with carefully designed experiments we should be able to uncover the laws governing every realm of human activity. By erasing differences we view the other through our lens without recognizing that the categories through which we interpret have grown out of specific cultural soil. Thus, unproblematically, the subjective assessment becomes an objective truth.

Another way of approaching culture is to assume that each one is so different and so unique that the only way to understand a foreign culture is to become a participant in that culture—mimic its mannerisms, follow its rules, consume its food, and don its costumes. Bakhtin warns that this is a "one-sided view." He does acknowledge that entry into the other's world is crucial, and, in fact, it is the first step. But to blindly put on the cultural garb would amount to participating in a fancy dress party. Forgetting "one's own culture" results in an imposter syndrome. Like the exterior body, particularly the face that we are incapable of seeing, the cultural codes that we imbibe during the course of our life are invisible to us. It is an unwritten script that we simply acquire and enact. These deep aspects of culture reveal themselves in encounters with a foreign culture. Bakhtin explains:

> *Creative understanding* does not renounce itself, its own place in time, its own culture; and it forgets nothing. In order to understand, it is immensely important for the person who understands to be *located outside* the object of his or her creative understanding—in time, in space, in culture.
> (RQNM, p. 7)

Thus, Bakhtin's argument is clear. Membership in a cultural group does not give one a special access to that culture's inner workings. You don't get the *inside scoop* because you are an insider. You may be privy to the specifics of events, but creative understanding requires outsideness. By the same token, one cannot be a distant observer either; remaining untouched by the other cannot provide any insight.

It is important to keep in mind how Bakhtin postulates creative understanding of cultures in our discussion of identity politics with respect to immigrants. On one side is the demand for complete assimilation—that the immigrants must suspend their cultural baggage to become Americans, as if cultural baggage is an external thing and the contents of that baggage (dress code, eating habits, mannerisms, ways of thinking, etc.) could be grouped together for disposal. The other extreme, which has become rather fashionable these days, is that each culture is different—so unique, so beautiful—and hence worthy of celebration, and so we have "Asian Heritage Month," "African Pride," and so forth to build a "multicultural" America. My objection is not with multiculturalism as such, but with the way it is conceived. When cultures are turned into products to be showcased, then we are essentially freezing them and converting them into empty signs for display, resulting in ugly chauvinism. It does not necessarily promote deeper understanding. Creative understanding entails an awareness of our cultured self that has hitherto been unavailable to us until we have had an encounter with another culture. With the new awareness of one's own culture and other foreign cultures, a deeper understanding of self and other emerges, and that would be a meaningful developmental achievement.

In sum, creativity is through and through dialogic—to hold us answerable through our lives to what has been learned in great works of art, and to answer our past with the present and the yet-to-be-achieved future. It means establishing a certain relationship even with our own creation—be it works of art or our children—in a way that facilitates the full play of each other's ideas and intermingling of voices to leave everything open-ended for future meanings to emerge. It also means being aware of our unique position vis-à-vis others so that we may mutually fill each other's insurmountable lacunae.

4

CARNIVALIZATION OF CONSCIOUSNESS

A Catalyst for Development

> My labor is in no way meant for those who are tainted even slightly by the symptoms of the disease, which is the conceit of sanctimoniousness. (3ab)
>
> Someone shamed by laughter will not persist in his wrongs. To help him, I myself have made this effort. (4)
>
> *Kshemendra,* Desopadesa *(Worldly Lessons)*[1]

The eleventh-century Sanskrit poet and satirist hailing from Kashmir was undisputedly one of the master philosophers of laughter, keen on exposing the folly of wisdom using the wisdom of folly as his device. On the surface level, his writings are blatantly vulgar and appear in poor taste. His defense was that he was only trying to release people trapped in the magic spell of sanctimoniousness. He was out to shame the mighty and powerful masquerading themselves as saviors of the world. As an upholder of the "higher level of truth," he resorted to crude tactics to jolt the complacent. In earthly life, sanctimoniousness is far more captivating than sanctity; often the difference between the two is difficult to recognize, and so the fake is mistaken for the real. Kshemendra described sanctimoniousness as "a paralysis induced by delusion," leaving the individual in a state of "perpetual unawareness," and it triumphs by duping people into believing the unreal to be the real. Kshemendra calls sanctimoniousness the clever and effective tool of the powerful, and says it is "*a pillar of deceit erected to commemorate world-domination*" (The Grace of Guile: Sanctimoniousness. 1.45), and this strong pillar could be demolished only with derisive laughter and raunchy language. For a world plagued by the disease called conceit, Kshemendra offered boisterous laughter as a remedy.

What are the philosophical dimensions of laughter? How is it a response so spontaneous can also be so profound? What is the liberating potential of laughter?

Does it liberate you *from* the world or *in* the world? Is it mockery, rebellion, or revelation? How do we distinguish one from the other? From a psychological and social perspective, how do we distinguish between a rebel without a cause and one with a justified cause? How is it possible for an emotion so base to be so elevating? Is it a heuristic device to peel layers of hypocrisy? Is laughter a cheap amusement or serious business?

The world of carnival with its uninhibited laughter, coarse language, grotesque body images, and excessive indulgence in food and liquor, according to Bakhtin (1984a), brings wholesomeness to our cultural life. In this space and time, we see the world not through the rational dictates of the mind, but through the principles derived from the functions of the lower stratum of the body. The carnival space is a "certain way of being" in the world and a "unique way of seeing" the world. Only in this inverted world, one manages to break down the oppressive hierarchies, pull the veil off false claims, and peel various layers of hypocrisies. This special space in the cultural landscape has far-reaching significance for Bakhtin. Laughter is evergreen and triumphant in this field where opposites remain irreconcilable. Laughter does not patch the incompatible; it just shows that some entities remain incompatible forever. It is in the carnival space that people from all walks of life gather together to shed all their inhibitions to find relief from the tedious drone of cerebral activity. One need not adhere to any conventions of decency and décor or deliver the culturally scripted narrative. The carnival self sheds the excess of self-consciousness that has built up so much anxiety to affirm body matters hitherto deemed shameful. It is a loud proclamation of our corporeality. More important, the obsession with the uniqueness of self-identity that has created barriers between self and others in normal cultural life breaks down to affirm our undisputed commonality. The carnival space also is the open platform to freely mock all revered entities.

What is the developmental potential in periodic carnivalization of consciousness? I stress the word "periodic" because life is not a carnival, and one cannot and perhaps should not be in a carnival all the time. After all, what is so progressive about derisive laughter, profane utterances, and marketplace vernacular? In the current cultural climate, the glutton and the alcoholic are diagnosed as suffering from psychological disorders and are promptly sent for treatment. We certainly live in an age of "direct unmediated talk" and deviation from the cultural norm is quickly pathologized. Cultural norms are not enforced overtly as in closed cultures or tyrannical societies, but done covertly in this media-driven modern age, where words, emotions, and behaviors are judged in dualistic categories of normal and abnormal. In the era of sound bites and chat rooms, words are used and judged differently and the encouragement is for straight talk, clear words, and unfortunately literal interpretation and dangerous oversimplification of concepts. This trend is driven in part by the necessity of cross-cultural communication (use unambiguous words and concepts so that the non-native speaker can verify meanings in the dictionary) and in part by the tool (the computer) and the cultural setting that tool creates (anonymity of chat rooms and so forth). The point is, we cannot approach carnival as if it is ahistorical. The nature of carnival, the worldview *of* the carnival, and the worldview *about* the carnival have undergone enormous changes throughout history. In order to explore the carnival's developmental potential, perhaps we need to reclaim some of the worldviews of the past, so that laughter and philosophical anarchy may regain their rightful place in our individual and collective consciousness.

Bakhtin addresses the nature of laughter and its necessary counterpart heteroglossia in his essay entitled "From the Prehistory of Novelistic Discourse," in which he observes that during the earlier period, when there was no clear-cut break between tragedy and comedy, laughter was far more forceful, liberating, and revealing than its diluted modern-day version. He observes that every type of discourse, be it "artistic, rhetorical, philosophical, religious," or "ordinary everyday" language, had its own "parodying and travestying double, its own comic-ironic *contre-partie*" (PND, p. 53). Not only were the genres inseparable as "tragico-comical" or "serio-comic," the parodic doubles and mocking laughter were to a great extent accorded the same status as their lofty counterparts. What was idealized also had to be ridiculed. While seriousness sanctioned power to the revered entities, laughter as a corrective measure redistributed power. Comedy's role was to expose the inherent paradox in reality.

Parodying alone forces us to see the "other side," the "lowly side" of reality. Bakhtin writes, "Parodic-travestying literature introduces the permanent corrective of laughter, of a critique on the one-sided seriousness of the lofty direct word, the corrective of reality that is always richer, more fundamental and most importantly *too contradictory and heteroglot* to be fit into a high and straight forward genre" (PND, p. 55). The modern-day parody, in Bakhtin's view, is either cruel—mocking and belittling others—or it is a relief from reality, unlike the earlier period, during which it revealed reality. A worldview that treats comedy and tragedy as a unit enjoys freedom from "nihilistic denial" (PND, p. 55) because it is not the heroes who are mocked, but the process of "heroization," because elevating the hero to unrealistic heights could have tragic consequences for the hero. Why should degradation accompany idealization? In the classical traditions of India—be they performance or literary—satire was an integral part of the text. The satirist is an apotropaic priest who wards off evil eyes to protect the hero by resorting to ritual degradation through comedy. Everything is seriously comical and comically serious. The parodying of the "heroization" is the protective amulet. In ancient India or in the classical Western world that Bakhtin describes, these ritualized forms of parodying were considered neither superstitious nor literal. They were certainly wise enough to know that a ritualized "put-down" was not going to save the hero. Instead, laughter was used as a theatrical and literary device to restore ambivalences and indeterminacies back to reality. Bakhtin says, "The high genres are monotonic" (PND, p. 55), and hence laughter alone is capable of breaking this monotone to display its "profoundly productive and deathless" nature. Bakhtin deeply bemoaned the loss of this function of laughter in modern times because language—manner of speaking, writing—has become too "straight" and linear. Laughter thrives in a discourse full of twists and turns, zigzags and coils. While during the Middle Ages, parody "paved the way for a new literary and linguistic consciousness" (PND, p. 71), Bakhtin observes, "In modern times the functions of parody are narrow and unproductive" (p. 71). He adds, "Parody has grown sickly, its place in modern literature is insignificant" (p. 71). Parody does not and need not change reality—social inequities continue to exist and gross abuse of power goes on—but it gives the individual interpretive power to resist and retaliate in a comic revolt against the human condition. It opens up possibilities for defiance and even encourages one to consider defying acceptable and recognizable forms of defiance.

Laughter's Triumph: A Developmental Gain

Of all the human emotions, laughter is the most spontaneous and yet the least understood. The misunderstanding and misappropriation is inevitable as long as we see the world through the dualities of high and low, sacred and profane, and so forth. Laughter is one emotion that encompasses all the polarities. The clever trickster and the tricked fool together produce laughter. Sanskrit philosopher/aesthetician Abhinavagupta, who has written extensive commentaries on dramaturgy, also addressed the aesthetics of humor in the most comprehensive manner (Unni, 1998). He declared that all other *Rasas* (literally meaning juice or essence—an aesthetic exposition of emotion) are included in *Hasya* (laughter), thus establishing laughter's wholesome nature. According to Abhinavagupta, incongruities in the presentation of any emotion results in laughter. Comedy, in general, thrives on impropriety—when things are out of place, one responds with laughter. Wit is constructed on linguistic ambiguity. Straight talk does not produce laughter. Language must hint at something else. Abhinavagupta insists that the comedian must engage in "crooked" and "contemptible" speech to evoke laughter. Laughter also demands mental quickness, on the part of both the speaker and the listener. If explanation is sought, laughter loses its essence. Either you get it or you don't. It is a delight that occurs when suddenly everything appears transparent. In Hindu cosmology, the awareness that produces laughter is a significant moment of enlightenment and liberation because the phenomenal world is considered one grand cosmic trick, and seeing through the metaphysical flimflammery one is liberated *in* the world. Laughter simultaneously pulls you out of the world and into the world. It is heavenly and earthly, so to speak, and the recognition of these opposing movements results in laughter. Because it integrates ascending and descending modes of consciousness, laughter is considered a holistic emblem of heightened awareness.

Bakhtin's interest in carnivalistic laughter also stemmed from its developmental potential—its ability to direct one toward some higher and interior form of truth. Bakhtin writes:

> Carnivalistic laughter likewise is directed toward something higher—toward a shift of authorities and truths, a shift of world orders. Laughter embraces both poles of change, it deals with the very process of change, with *crisis* itself. Combined in the act of carnival laughter are death and rebirth, negation (a smirk) and affirmation (rejoicing laughter). This is profoundly universal laughter, laughter that contains a whole outlook on the world. Such is the specific quality of ambivalent carnival laughter.
>
> *(PDP, p. 127)*

Carnival laughter alone can expose the impoverishment of the wealthy and the richness and freedom of the pauper, or the suffocating constraints of intellectual activity and the false feelings of superiority it creates. The recognition of this built-in paradox is crucial—laughter simultaneously reveals and responds to this truth. As a developmental model, carnival laughter has much to offer. When laughter is not situated on a developmental plane and its role as a catalyst for change is not recognized, it is then reduced to a level of cheap amusement. It becomes a vacuous concept. When it is stripped of its philosophical depth, it is deemed uncouth. Bakhtin was quite mindful of this danger. In fact, he begins his work on *Rabelais and His World* with this observation: "Of all the great writers of world literature, Rabelais is the least popular, the least understood and appreciated" (RAW, p. 1). Why is the Rabelaisian world detested? Because it is seen exclusively as demonic, countercultural, and anticivilization, although at a surface level all these characterizations are valid, but it also incorporates its opposite tendencies. When we want to identify the *products* of cultural development, then we look at cleaned up and polished institutions, norms, practices, and so forth, but if we need to understand the *processes* of cultural development, then we cannot disregard various aspects of carnival. Just as the birth process of an infant is accompanied by excreta, the birth process of a new idea, a new awareness, a new era happens through carnival laughter.

What are some of the features of carnival laughter that developmental psychologists must pay close attention to? What can carnival teach us about developmental processes? First of all, carnival laughter is not at the expense of someone else. It is certainly not an individual affair. It does not happen in isolation. Like Vygotsky's claim that the genesis of all higher mental functions is in the social realm, the carnivalistic laughter that occurs in the collective realm is also the birth moment of a new awareness. It is a "festive laughter" (RAW, p. 11), says Bakhtin, an hour of celebration. Second, it is universal—directed at everyone—the performers and the participants. Everybody laughs, at themselves and at others. It is primordial. It is not an hour for analysis or contemplation. It is pure experience. Third—which, in Bakhtin's view, is the most important—laughter's ambivalent nature "is gay, triumphant, and at the same time mocking and deriding. It asserts and desires, it buries and revives. Such is the laughter of carnival" (RAW, p. 12).

The universal and festive nature of carnival laughter breaks down all the constraining hierarchies of the world and mind. It is a ritualized mockery of all things sacred and serious. Excessive and unreflective deference to the mighty and powerful creates confusing emotions, eventually resulting in painful servility, with no scope for growth and renewal. Carnival laughter in its wholesomeness affirms all that is earthly and corporeal. Moreover, it erases all that is "cultic"—it jolts the individual from blind adherence to ideologies and worldviews—killing all that is stale and irrelevant to give birth to a fresh perspective. Carnival laughter does not create utopias; in other words, it does not take you to a permanent paradise. For that matter, it does not change anything in the world, but it retains the "utopian element" to direct our attention "toward the highest spheres" (RAW, p. 12). Laughter frees the individual from oppressive and gloomy categories like "eternal," "immovable," "absolute," and "unchangeable" to expose one to the "gay and free laughing spirit of the world with its unfinished and open character" (RAW, p. 83). It shows endless possibilities in the world and activates unrealized potential in the individual. The mundane invades the sublime and the physical mocks the metaphysical; carnival laughter is anti-philosophical in spirit, but its function has profound philosophical implications for regeneration and renewal.

The psychologist who addressed the topic of laughter and humor was the indomitable Sigmund Freud (2003), and he dealt with this subject at great length in his classic work *The Joke and Its Relation to the Unconscious*. According to Freud, laughter, like a dream, expresses our unconscious motives and desires. Unlike Bakhtin, who suggests that we look into the collective realm of carnival space that is open and visible, Freud insists that we take a journey into the mysterious zone of the unconscious, which is closed and carefully guarded to pick fragments of unacceptable psychological traits to make sense of laughter. For Freud, the individual forever is driven by a wild and primitive libidinal energy called the *id* that seeks instant gratification, which in turn faces constant censure from the *super ego*—the morality principle emanating from the social realm. The internal psychological pleasure principle is always at odds with the prohibitions and sanctions that society imposes. Thus, forbidden and sinful desires, which, in Freud's view, are inherent to the individual, must be pushed into the hinterland of the psychic world. While the buried emotions and feelings have the need to erupt, escape, and express themselves, the psychological apparatus called censorship maintains strict vigilance. In order to cross the check-post, a few fragments from the unconscious backyard adopt disguises—a labor that Freud labeled "dreamwork"—and these disguised forms are jokes, puns, and riddles. Unlike dreams that are raw and unedited, which occur in deep sleep over which the individual has no control, but are meant for exclusive viewing for the individual, the joke is a disguised form of the unconscious world, meant for social consumption; as Freud states, "The dream is always a wish, however unrecognizable this has been made; the joke is developed play" (2003, p. 173). According to Freud, they even serve different purposes; dreams spare us from "unpleasure" while jokes are meant to "gain pleasure."

Freud maintains that humor is a way of being economical with our "psychical apparatus"—a way of regaining energy spent on inhibitions, imagination, and feelings. He cites several examples of gallows humor and absurd decisions made by individuals wielding power or conceptual errors made by children in their naïveté to explain that laughter, as a form of parsimony, helps the individual to save the energy that would otherwise be spent on brooding and analyzing. In his introductory remarks to Freud's work, John Carey (2003) observes that "Freud's theory of jokes itself is a kind of joke" (p. xxvii) that merits analysis through different analytical categories. One cannot help but notice the inordinate number of anti-Jewish jokes he cites to build his theory. Most of these are mean-spirited and directed at someone else. This form of laughter cannot be all-inclusive. It is one-sided. Furthermore, this kind of laughter has no developmental potential. The gallows humor, the type that Freud refers to, could serve only as a cover or a lid to save energy from being spent on something so morbid. Freud's view does not have the multidimensionality that Bakhtin bestows on laughter. In fact, we may say that they hold diametrically opposing views. While laughter veils undesirable truths for Freud, it bares the truth in all its naked form for Bakhtin.

The Renaissance period captured laughter in all its profoundness, says Bakhtin. In his view, "Certain essential aspects of the world are accessible only to laughter" (RAW, p. 66), and that is why it carried deep philosophical meaning. The view that laughter provided was not trivial or lighthearted. If anything, it was serious and thus carried enormous epistemological significance. Many hidden and dormant truths are revealed and activated only through the boisterous laughter in the carnival space. The eleventh-century philosopher Abhinavagupta explains this dimension of laughter more succinctly. Commenting on Bharata's *Natya Sastra*—a treatise on dramaturgy—Abhinavagupta explains the comic sentiment as *Kuhaka*, meaning tickling of *Kaksa*, armpits, or literally meaning "hidden place" (Siegel, 1987). Tickling is a form of cute aggression; you never know whether it is aggression-as-affection or affection-as-aggression, and, whatever the case might be, one realizes the sensitivity and vulnerability of various zones in the body. Abhinavagupta saw laughter as a tactile equivalent of intellectual and aesthetic processes in which the hidden and "untouched" zones of meaning-making spheres are brought to life. Bakhtin would concur with Abhinavagupta that laughter is not simply a fun way of knowing but the only way of knowing some serious truths. Laughter is the tickling of the mind—leaving it squirming and squealing to lose a sense of balance and composure and to drop all false pretensions and seriousness of cerebral activity to witness the exposure of bare truth. The act of tickling always retains its ambiguity—you want to be tickled as much as you want to escape it. We all know that children attempt to run away or dodge when you chase them to tickle, and yet they get disappointed when you stop the chase. It is simply mock aggression. It is real and yet not real. Surrendering to the power of the tickler is an acknowledgment of the pleasure of aggression. In laughter, the contradictory forces converge, not necessarily to synthesize but to coexist while asserting their unique power. The aggression and the cuteness of tickling leave both the tickler and the tickled feeling triumphant. Bakhtin explains that Rabelais built his theory of laughter on the "Hippocratic novel," in which Democritus' laughter was based on "a certain spiritual premise of the awakened man who has attained virility" (RAW, p. 67). Laughter is the mind's equivalent of bodily virility, enabling it to act and produce new forms of knowledge. Herein lies the significance of laughter to human development.

The second philosophical dimension of laughter in the Rabelaisian world, according to Bakhtin, was the recognition of its exclusivity to human beings. Like speech that leads to thought, which is hidden and private, public carnival laughter leads one to hidden truths and both speech and laughter are uniquely human. That's what separates us from other species. Do other species have their unique language and communication systems? Yes, of course. But human language and meaning-making systems allow for ambiguities and contradictions. An utterance that is complimentary in one situation could be derogatory in another situation. Seen from a cosmic plane, laughter is God's gift to humanity—to make earthly life bearable and to be able to mock the heavens. It is defiance, a revolt against authority. Even if you cannot eliminate power, you can at least laugh at it to affirm your being.

The third philosophical dimension was laughter's relation "to the underworld and to death, to the freedom of the spirit and to the freedom of speech" (RAW, p. 70). Laughter not only mocks the heavens, but also death. Laughter does not eliminate death, but brings new life from death. Bakhtin stresses over and over that laughter's real power lies in its regenerative capability.

The freedom of carnival laughter is not at the expense of responsibility, even while marked by ruthlessness and radicalism. During the Middle Ages, it was licensed to operate outside the official sphere—in the marketplace and on feasting and festive days. It was in this time and space that "material and bodily principle" found its unfettered expression. In this topsy-turvy world, the fools feasted and the rogues were crowned and the gluttons and drunkards reveled in the festive atmosphere. This inverted world did not take people away from truth, but, in Bakhtin's view, brought them closer to the "unofficial truth" (RAW, p. 90), and hence the aspects of culture that were berated in officialdom gained veridicality in carnival laughter.

What, then, is the value of recognizing the unofficial truth for human development? To answer this question, we need to examine how cultural systems operate. Cultural systems are driven by centripetal and centrifugal forces, and generally organize themselves hierarchically, privileging some practices and prohibiting others (Lotman and Uspenski, 1985). The sanctioned practices in the course of time have a tendency to lose their original intent or they become anachronistic. When this occurs, the practices or values become hypocritical, rigid, and even oppressive. Therefore, carnival laughter is a search for truth—at a social level it seeks justice, and at an individual level its goal is to regain honesty. When cultures turn tyrannical, the individual consciousness takes on false seriousness and individuals become fearful and weak. Bakhtin explains that "Laughter is essentially not an external but an interior form of truth" (RAW, p. 94).

The lesson one learns in the carnival is that nothing is as it appears to be. The fool in the carnival knows fully well that he is a fool and with this meta-awareness ceases to be a fool, whereas in non-carnival space and time, the fool thinks he is wise and thus continues to be a fool. Once you know that you don't know, you will make an attempt to know. This awareness brought about by carnival laughter then becomes a catalyst for acquiring higher and truer forms of knowledge, whereas if one is too incompetent to recognize one's own incompetence, one is doomed in false consciousness. Carnival laughter is both the cure for and prevention of this malady. Bakhtin asserts:

> Laughter showed the world anew in its gayest and most sober aspects. Its external privileges are intimately linked with interior forces; they are a recognition of the rights of those forces. That is why laughter could never become an instrument to oppress and blind the people. It always remained a free weapon in their hands.
>
> *(RAW, p. 94)*

Laughter reveals hidden truths and catalyzes new truths. It is not antiestablishment at a deeper level, but it pulls you away from the establishment that has become stagnant and putrid. It cautions you against consuming stale and rotten ideas, which were actually desirable when they were fresh. Laughter is the antidote for ideas and ideals that have turned dogmatic. Like great emperors who wanted to build open and free societies were bold enough to have court jesters to speak the truth to them, "true open seriousness" (RAW, p. 122) never fears parody and laughter. Bakhtin explains that it comes from the awareness of our incompleteness. A good emperor knows that he is surrounded by panegyrists, who intentionally or unintentionally hide the truth from him. Praise has a built-in paradox of fabrication. That is why he needs the jester to deliver hard truths. The jester is forever on a "fact-finding" and "fact-delivering" mission. He is devoted to the king and the kingdom. Laughter that is needed for good governance is needed as well for the thinking mind. The jester is not meant for the lowly amusement of the emperor. His acts are cheap and he uses street vernacular and appears completely ridiculous, but his role is a serious business. It makes the bitter truth palatable. It easily pushes the bitter pill down for it to do its curative job. It pulls you from the stagnant cultural waters that have become foul and filthy to lead you to the fresh stream. Laughter transports the individual from inertia into the realm of possibilities. Bakhtin writes:

> True ambivalent and universal laughter does not deny seriousness but purifies and completes it. Laughter purifies from dogmatism, from the intolerant and the petrified; it liberates from fanaticism and pedantry, from fear and intimidation, from didacticism, naïveté and illusion, from the single meaning, the single level, from sentimentality. Laughter does not permit seriousness to atrophy and to be torn away from the one being, forever incomplete. It restores this ambivalent wholeness.
>
> *(RAW, p. 123)*

When unholy acts are committed in the name of holiness, laughter is needed to expose them. When you become a prisoner of your own liberation theology, it is a laughable moment. When you are stuck in unproductive and routine formulas, you need laughter to change your habits. When you think you are indispensable to the world and assume false seriousness, laughter exposes your insignificance. It tells you not to take yourself so seriously and points out your limitations and the strength of the others. Laughter does not favor any self-appointed saviors. When unbridled power is exerted, primordial laughter is the defiant response. When the hierarchically organized world sees itself as the norm, laughter shows an inverted world to suggest other possibilities. When morals and ideas are frozen in time and space, laughter melts them to let them flow in the cultural landscape to pick up other dimensions. The fallen and the downtrodden get their due respect in carnival laughter. Laughter loots precious values that are hidden. When officialdom suffocates, laughter releases the individual. These functions are of paramount importance for a sound mind and a healthy society, and hence psychologists—developmental, clinical, and other branches—cannot afford to ignore the power and value of carnival laughter.

The Virtue of Street Talk: Bawdy Voices and Body Images

What happens to ideas of development when we bring in images of the body with all its orifices and anatomical parts, and the coarse language of the street with its bawdy voices, profanities, and curses? We begin to see consciousness in the act of becoming. Body becomes a metaphor for understanding developmental processes. Like the birthing body that is accompanied by bodily fluids and excreta, the developing consciousness is precipitated by factors that society does not necessarily sanction. Bakhtin's observations about the culture of the marketplace with its raunchy language and raucous ribaldry must *not* be viewed as a prescription for development, but as an ineluctable part of the birthing process. The birthing process is never clean and sanitized, and a construction site is never without its necessary scaffolding. Every usage of profanity and every act of defecation is not a birthing moment, but birthing is invariably accompanied by other bodily discharge and the tongue responds with some salty language to the pain that comes in the act of birthing. After the birth the newborn is cleaned up, and after the construction the scaffolding is dismantled, but during the process the ugliness is inevitable. Carnival is not a permanent state, but it is a transitional state from one mode to another mode of viewing the world. It blows away the veil separating body and mind, folklore and high culture, to reveal the transition from one state to another. Ever since Rene Descartes proclaimed *Cogito Ergo Sum*—"I think, therefore I am"—the body has been ferreted out of the philosophical system and has become private, shameful, and inferior. For Bakhtin, the Rabelaisian preoccupation with anatomical fantasy and imagination restores philosophy back to the body.

How did Bakhtin read Rabelais' language that others considered filthy depravation or plain impertinence? Bakhtin saw the topography of the body as a powerful and effective epistemological tool that emerged from collective gaiety. This is the way our ancients understood the workings of the cosmos. According to Bakhtin, it is the genre of "festive gaiety that was gradually formed during many centuries" (RAW, p. 146). Understanding the self and the world entailed drawing parallels between heavenly bodies and parts of the human body, which resulted in some laws of homomorphism. Thus, the functions of the human body became a microcosm of the universe. Furthermore, the lower stratum of the body, with its contradictory functions, retained its essential ambivalence. It is a source of disgust and relief. It is the zone of elimination and fertilization, thus linking death with renewal and birth. Bakhtin saw the indispensability of the body and its functions in understanding the interconnectedness of life, death, and birth. That is why the images of the body in all their grotesqueness retained their philosophical force and were not considered vulgar.

The atmosphere at the marketplace is filled with debasing gestures and mud-slinging. The colloquial language of the street is full of images of sex and scatology. It is through references to "shit," "spit," or "sneeze" that one hurls insults and curses. Bakhtin appreciated Rabelais for his detailed observation of the unofficial world. Knowledge about the unofficial world is crucial to our understanding of the forces of history that bring about cultural change. To understand the human world, one must not only examine cultural institutions, high literature, and official language, but also the marginalized practices, folklore, and coarse vernacular of the street. Popular fairs and festivities draw all aspects of the unofficial world—herbalists sell aphrodisiacs, vendors promise cures from magic potions, quacks give their diagnoses, acrobats display their skills, and buffoons ridicule the mighty. It is a grand display of absurdity showing the flip side of things considered sensible and desirable. Like the juggler tossing objects, the joker produces wit by playing language games. He breaks words, twists concepts, juggles meanings, amplifies sounds, and in doing so always maintains ambiguity and multiplicity of meanings to amuse the passers-by at the fair. The joker is not unintelligent; if anything, he displays the plasticity of language, at both the sonic and semantic levels. His speech is filled with palindromes, tongue twisters, mind teasers, anagrams, and riddles to beckon the market-goers. The acrobatic language is charged with sexual and scatological images, simultaneously causing disgust and delight. In this carnival space, one rediscovers the body. Routine bodily functions and natural urges of the body assume a whole new dimension. Everything seems new and fresh, and everything that is forbidden and shameful is granted license for collective expression.

The carnivalized consciousness is a counterpoint to the rational mind. The former is an experiential mode meant for display and release, while the latter is the thinking mode meant for analysis and contemplation. The individual dissolves in the cultural universe during the carnival time; there are no differences between performers and spectators. It is a collective affirmation of our corporeality. After all, that is what we share in common. Carnival provides an avenue for the body to revolt against order and discipline. The body challenges any pretensions of polish and perfection; it defecates, farts, perspires, belches, sneezes, and emits foul odor. In short, it has a temperament of its own and routinely disobeys the rational dictates of the mind. The carnival world is not a fractured one, but it is the space for confrontation between the lower and upper strata of the body. Carnival has no room for false modesty and strict codes of conduct; it is meant to show us the folly and vice that we otherwise fail to see. The loud chorus of the carnival awakens the masses who have become inured and blind to the foolish dictates of the powerful. The inverted world is not so mechanistic; it is not a simple role reversal. It does not simply announce that the body is better than the mind, but shows how the glorification of the mind all along has been at the expense of the body. The excessive display of food and liquor is not a direct call for gluttony and dipsomania, but an acknowledgment of the primal gastronomic desire and the pull of intoxicating substances.

The carnival image is enlarged and the carnival voice is amplified to present a very detailed account of our social life. Food consumption is inherently a social activity, particularly the kind we relish and rejoice in. In almost all cultures, the kitchen is the hub of a family; relationships are built around the eating ritual. No celebration takes place without rich food. As Freud rightly pointed out, food is the first source of pleasure. Maternal love comes in the form of food. Family discussions take place across the dining table. Like the basic ingredient in a dish that blends with other ingredients and spices and condiments to produce a particular flavor, savoring and relishing the gourmet with others yields a collective fervor of joy and excitement. Fasting may be a private, individual affair, but feasting is social, joyous, and jubilant. Bakhtin observes that public feasting is a "banquet for all the world" and like the yeast added to the dough the banquet images "rise," "grow," and "swell" to "reach exaggerated dimensions" (RAW, p. 278). The larger-than-life image of ravenous individuals devouring food, according to Bakhtin, shows the individual's interaction with the world and the internalization of the world in its unfinished form. Even the ones with the strongest appetite cannot consume the variety of food at these popular feasts. For Bakhtin, these images have immense philosophical and psychological significance. Like the huge array of dishes presented at the banquet, the world presents an innumerable menu of choices for the individual to selectively internalize and triumph over the world. The image of collective feasting is universal and interestingly egalitarian, as Bakhtin observes about the banquet:

> Here man tastes the world, introduces it into his body, makes it part of himself. Man's awakening consciousness could not but concentrate on this moment, could not help borrowing from it a number of substantial images determining the interrelation with the world. Man's encounter with the world, in the act of eating is joyful, triumphant; he triumphs over the world, devours it without being devoured himself. The limits between man and the world are erased, to man's advantage.
>
> *(RAW, p. 281)*

One may raise questions about social inequalities and people's access to food. We must bear in mind that carnival is open to all—the rich and the poor, the powerful and the powerless—everybody feasts. Bakhtin points out that "They feast heroically, but they are not heroes" (RAW, p. 291). The open festivities also create opportunities for the disadvantaged to ambiguously poke fun at corrupt individuals. The image of the fat belly becomes an emblem of a greedy official who plunders public wealth. It is instructive to recognize the double-voicedness of "excess"—in the case of the deprived, consumption is a sign of prosperity—a reward for having toiled day and night, and in the case of the privileged, it signifies the "paunch of the insatiable" (p. 292). The expression "he eats a lot" is a subtext for "he takes a lot of bribes." Even as it affirms the universal spirit of food as a reward for labor, it also makes a dig at private feasts with "hungry beggars at the door" (p. 302). Carnival is a defiant call for social justice and collective rights. If the image of eating and drinking is assigned to private life, it would then lose its universal symbolism, and in such a case we are talking about pathos of obesity and alcoholism. The important thing is that the images and words retain their ambiguity in the true spirit of carnival.

The primary element in the carnival, Bakhtin maintains, is free laughter and unrestricted curses filled with unabashed display of bodily functions. Carnival language thus becomes a way of translating the individual-biological into social and vice versa (Ivanov, 1991). The skin does not seal the body. If anything, layers of social fabric cover the skin and carnival language facilitates the dialogue between the biological and the cultural. Bakhtin takes the cultural realm even further and says the "grotesque body is cosmic and universal" and "can merge with various natural phenomena, with mountains, rivers, seas, islands and continents. It can fill the entire universe" (RAW, p. 318). Bakhtin observes that the legends and literary works from the "Indian Wonders" were a source of "direct and indirect influence" in Rabelais' works. In the Hindu cosmos, all the scriptures describe the original creation as a form of bodily dismemberment. Brahma, the androgynous primeval being, is said to have dismembered his body to create various cosmic and earthly bodies. These tales are filled with images of sucking, devouring, swallowing, and tearing. In short, the cosmic topography is synonymous with bodily topography. As in the Rabelaisian period that Bakhtin describes, descriptions of the body with all its orifices, anatomical parts, and internal physiology have deep philosophical meanings in Hindu philosophy. Anatomical fiction and fantasy elevated body to an aesthetic level. In the carnival language, the concrete physical body becomes an idea, a concept, and a metaphor and vice versa.

In the Hindu cosmos, the goddess Kali with her grotesque body image represents the aesthetics of horror and revulsion. She is the dark side of the idealized mother. She wears a garland of skulls, leaves her hair unbraided, chews on flesh, sticks out a blood-drenched tongue, and dances wildly on cremation grounds with terrifying necrophilic laughter. One of the epithets of Kali is *Vikarala*, which in Sanskrit means ugliness, and it also refers to a "transitional state" and the "changing of the form" (Monier-Williams, 1899). The inference to be drawn from this heteroglot word is that a changing phenomenon is grotesque, odd, and ugly, and Kali represents such a process. Kali's monstrous body and her activities in the cremation grounds are considered neither tragic nor terrifying, but a necessary link between death and birth. Kali's mouth is seen as the fertile soil in which death in the form of the bones and flesh that she swallows is sown as seeds for the generative growth of collective life. Bakhtin observes that "Generative time is a pregnant time, a fruit bearing time, a birthing time and a time that conceives again" (RAW, p. 207), and Kali represents such a time. That is why the image of her gaping mouth represents the fertile earth ready to conceive and her permanently bloated belly represents the ever-pregnant earth ready to give birth to new life.

Folklore and literature have always used ghastly images of the body to drive home a point, to pose a metaphysical question, or to show the absurdity of artificial dilemmas. The main purpose of grotesque body image is educational. The image and the language of body, particularly the lower stratum, is a powerful genre with a very long history. Bakhtin argues that the carnival genre, having passed through various cultural terrains in different historical periods, "became a *powerful means* for comprehending life" (PDP, p. 157), and more important, because body structure is what we share in common, the genre has an "extraordinary capacity for *symbolic generalization*" (p. 157). While the upper stratum of the body is equipped with the ability to discriminate, differentiate, and theorize, the lower stratum is capable of "*generalization in depth*" (p. 157). Bakhtin insists that the multifacetedness and multilayeredness of certain aspects of life can be identified, understood, and conveyed only through this metaphor.

Because Bakhtin describes the ancient tales from India as the mother lode of the world's stories that rely on graphic body images, I shall take a short tale from *Kathāsaritsāgara*—literally meaning "Ocean of the Seas of Story"—which Acharya Somadeva (1994) compiled sometime in the eleventh century to show the carnival genre's versatility. These short and simple tales narrated by various ministers were meant to educate the king and the queen. In this anthology of stories, nothing is conclusive, and, like the ghosts that often pose the question, the dilemmas haunt the listener, who must rework the plot over and over to consider every dimension. Here is the story of *The Heads That Got Switched*, narrated by *Vetala*—the ghost to the king who must arrive at some provisional conclusion. It is about a young woman traveling with her husband and her brother; they stop at a local temple where the principal deity is Goddess Kali. The husband goes inside the temple while the young woman and her brother stay outside. The husband is moved by the fierce image of the goddess and feels guilty for having entered the temple without any offering. At the spur of the moment, he decides to offer himself and so pulls the sword from the idol's hands and beheads himself. The young woman, concerned by the delay, sends her brother, who in horror also cuts off his head. The young woman then enters the temple to find the decapitated bodies of her husband and her brother. When she is about to end her life, the goddess appears and instructs her to attach the heads to the respective bodies. The young woman in her haste attaches the wrong head to the wrong body and so faces a potentially incestuous situation no matter which body she chooses as her husband. When the ghost asks the king to resolve the dilemma, the king decides that the one with her husband's head should be the woman's choice. In the king's mind, the head rules, but whether the woman considers this solution is an open question. Besides, the king, swept by the waves in the "ocean of tales," is bound to confront in another tale a challenge to the resolution he arrived in an earlier tale, keeping the system open-ended forever. In his retelling of this tale in *The Transposed Heads*, German writer and thinker Thomas Mann used it as an occasion to challenge the split between mind and body, biological and psychological. Based on Mann's challenge to this ancient tale, Indian playwright Girish Karnad (1994) wrote a play entitled *Hayavadana*—literally meaning "Horse Man"—to explore the reality of sundered identities in a world of tangled relationships. The world proposes completeness and the reality shows incompleteness.

The peculiarities of head transplants and animal heads with human bodies push the boundaries of what we take for granted. Changes in the body bring about changes in psychological phenomena and sociological categories. Take for instance the ethical problems that advances in reproductive technology and genetic engineering have presented us with. One may ask the question, who is the mother? Is it the conventional mother who gave birth (genetic, biological birth and socially recognized), or the adoptive mother (socially recognized), or the egg donor (genetic and biological), or the surrogate (genetic, biological, and birth), or the womb-renting mother (she does not contribute her egg, but the fertilized egg of another woman is transplanted into her womb)? The dismemberment at a very cellular level poses questions at an ethical and political level. The advances in technology may put an end to the stigma of infertility, but it is also the beginning of another dilemma of surrogacy.

Carnival forms are meant to show incompleteness or, more precisely, to show that the end of one thing is also the beginning of another. While its role as a catalyst for change is a shared feature across literary and cultural traditions, the mechanisms or the processes of carnivalization vary from culture to culture and from writer to writer. The commonalities and specific differences between writers like Boccaccio, Rabelais, Cervantes, or Dostoevsky are not relevant to our study. But as cultural psychologists concerned with sociohistorical epistemology, we must consider the specifics of the cultural atmosphere in which the individual is operating to understand the developmental changes at a greater depth. Time and again Bakhtin cautions against oversimplified application of carnival. The carnival image is certainly bold and provocative, and carnival language is boorish and indecorous, but carnival itself is neither vulgar nor bohemian. It is meant to show a glimpse of life otherwise hidden in the normal course of life. Every theatrical pageant is not a carnival, and being a passive spectator of a carnival procession does not constitute carnivalization of consciousness. Simply witnessing a Halloween or Mardi Gras parade, or, for that matter, even mechanically participating in it, does not automatically translate into carnivalization of consciousness. But a new revelation of collective significance that registers at that moment or a new idea that emerges during the contemplation of the carnival hour does constitute carnivalization of consciousness.

To appreciate the ambivalent and paradoxical nature of the body, it would be instructive to consider the role of the body or rather the absence of a very vital part of the body in Bakhtin's life. From a very young age, Bakhtin suffered from osteomyelitis, an infectious bone disease that can be difficult to detect at early stages. As the disease progresses, which was the case with Bakhtin, abscesses form on adjacent soft tissue and emit foul odor. Bakhtin was born in 1895, and by 1921, which means by the time he was just twenty-five years old, the disease had spread to his thigh and hip joint and he became permanently handicapped. Bakhtin, a bold theorist of the body, had to constantly wage a bold battle against his body, and often his diseased body could not be subdued; he had to learn to live with his fleshy imperfections (Clark and Holquist, 1984). By 1938, his right leg had to be amputated, and for the rest of his life he was dependent on his wife, who tended to his every need, and he relied on crutches for mobility. Clark and Holquist note that Bakhtin never spoke about his body directly, but we certainly see inscriptions of his grotesque and uncompromising body in his theory. His imperfect body was a constant reminder of the perfect revolt that the body is capable of. He could not hide it, either. Clark and Holquist wrote that sometimes "The pain was so great that he conducted his classes while lying on a couch" (1984, p. 51).

To add a political dimension to disease and handicap, in January 1929, at the height of the Soviet Union's effort to silence intellectuals who even remotely disagreed with the official line, Bakhtin was sent to jail. Within six months, by June 1929, Bakhtin's disease shifted him to a hospital bed. The body was both his curse and his savior. The carnival body is essentially ambivalent, says Bakhtin, because glory and humiliation coexist. Bakhtin says rather definitively, "It is impossible to trace a sharp line of distinction between the praise and abuse," and you never know "where one ends and the other begins" (RAW, p. 418). That is why Bakhtin wouldn't consider laughter at physical imperfections offensive; instead, he would consider it a moment of supreme awareness of the power that an imperfect body could exercise. In his own life, his imperfect body became a perfect excuse for transporting him from a prison to a hospital. Without the glaring visibility of contradictory forces, the body wouldn't lend itself to laughter. Had Bakhtin just perished in his illness, it wouldn't be a laughing moment. When he was suffering from unbearable pain, that was not a moment for laughter. Laughter triumphs when you arrive at a moment when you don't know whether to laugh or cry. When contradictory forces converge to reveal the paradox of body, then laughter is an appropriate response. The carnivalized consciousness celebrates this revealing moment with unabashed laughter.

Carnivalized Consciousness: Iconoclastic Wisdom

The great Moghul emperor Akbar once asked his court jester and minister, Birbal, "What is the basic difference between an intelligent person and a fool?" Birbal replied, "Your Majesty, the first one knows his limitation and other's freedom, while the second one knows only his freedom and others' limitation."[2] Like the great emperors who were bold and secure enough to have excellent jesters to bring them closer to truth, consciousness itself must be strong enough to be periodically carnivalized, so that we may recognize that we are one among the many, because each of us is limited and therefore must join the chorus to loudly affirm our collective freedom. The boorish carnival voice is not a selfish call for individual freedom; it is not selfless, either; instead, it is collective. It is a joyous and free merger into the masses. Carnival space is not a platform for every disgruntled voice to express itself. It is not a place to seek validation for subjective feelings and thoughts or, for that matter, a personal truth. The carnival language gives expression to the hidden and tacitly forbidden truths, the kind made hush-hush because of prevailing cultural norms and ideologies. Bakhtin observes that the loud voice of the carnival captured the "marketplace frankness that concerned everyone" (RAW, p. 271). The individual drops all pretensions of uniqueness and superiority to operate on a leveled field. The carnival way of looking at the world, first and foremost, breaks down the barriers between self and other to sense and feel the world as "one great communal performance" (PDP, p. 160). The colorful masks worn at carnival festivities only externalize the layers of psychological masking that we so routinely apply to ourselves. The carnival vision expresses everything with a guffaw to expose the charlatan in every individual. It is a carnivalesque way of neutralizing differences.

Bakhtin observes that all aspects of carnival—behavior, action, and expression—are characterized by exaggeration, hyperbole, and superfluity. These fundamental attributes do some service to the changing consciousness. Like a modern-day laser surgeon who needs an image of an eye enlarged on a computer screen to correctly identify the problem, the consciousness needs enlarged images, amplified voices, and excess display to correctly recognize the contradictory forces in reality. Every image and every utterance alludes to something else without forsaking its literal meaning. The human body is a microcosm of the universe. Physical disfigurations are metaphors for spiritual and ethical deformities. Hyperbole and excess are used to show emphasis of a reality, but they also show vehemence against that reality. The absence of division between spectators and performers draws attention to artificial and/or rigid barriers between inside and outside, pure and impure, truth and pretense. Carnivalized consciousness wants nothing to do with absolutes and claims of purity. Laughing at lustful mendicants or bishops is a way of recognizing that the garb of holy men is only to cover their unholy acts, and the one who looks like a scoundrel may very well show amazing piety. It is not a wholesale rebuke of holy men, but it most certainly is a caution against wholesale valorization of holy men. Carnivalized consciousness pushes one to look for truth and humanity in the most unusual of places and people. Such a realization is a plus point for the evolving consciousness.

It must be reiterated that the concerns of carnivalized consciousness are about raw truth. The crowd in the marketplace is an emblem of the collective truth it seeks. Like the mighty elephant that is capable of lifting huge stacks of timber is just as capable of picking up a small needle with its trunk, the carnival genre is capable of visualizing the universal and even cosmic truths, and yet it shows incredible capacity to reveal concrete truths bound by local conditions. Bakhtin was impressed by the Rabelaisian images that combined "an extreme breadth and a cosmic character with an exceptionally concrete feeling, with individuality and a journalistic response to the events of the day" (RAW, p. 436). The carnival "way of looking" captures the panoramic view and the close-up shot of reality with all the details. If these carnivalized lenses are so efficient in capturing the contours and the specific details of reality, the cognizing subject then must acquire them. After all, they seem to possess immense epistemological value. As significant as they are to the "mind's eye," Bakhtin cautions against treating them as readymade mechanical devices. He explains this point succinctly:

> Carnivalization is not an external and immobile schema which is imposed upon ready-made content; it is, rather, an exceptionally flexible form of artistic visualization, a peculiar sort of heuristic principle making possible the discovery of new and as yet unseen things.

(PDP, p. 166)

Because the carnival "way of looking" at the world is faithful to both the universal and the local, the genre is essentially an evolving one. Although carnival is marked by boisterous laughter and corrosive language with extensive references to sex and scatology, we cannot and must not treat every laughing moment or curse as an indication of carnivalization. The tirades of the marketplace indicate a firm refusal to conform to strict demands of etiquette, civility, and respectability in the interest of freedom and frankness—freedom for all people and frankness that concerns the public. Despite its celebration of chaos, the carnival genre is neither illogical nor alogical. Bakhtin points out that "*the logic of genre is not an abstract logic*" either, but it "possesses its own organic logic" (PDP, p. 157), specific to the time and place. The important lesson here is to refrain from making mechanical application of carnival concepts.

Take, for example, the expression "bullshit," a commonly used generic term of abuse with a direct scatological reference. The modern-day usage is markedly different from the way Rabelais or Dostoevsky used profanities. Bakhtin observes that when the carnival genre was woven with other literary genres, it allowed these creative writers to express first and foremost the ambivalent nature of reality, leaving everything in an open-ended and unfinished form, and hence "love is combined with hatred, avarice with selflessness, ambition with self-abasement, and so forth" (PDP, p. 159). Carnival as a literary and analytical device brought one in close contact with truth in a disguised form or a truth that is not so apparent. In the modern day, when we refer to something as "bullshit," we are referring to speech that takes you far away from truth. Frankfurt (2005) argues that "bullshit" does not represent either willful misrepresentation or deliberate lying because both require a sound knowledge of truth. The modern-day "spin doctor" routinely hired by political campaigns knows the truth and gives it a quick spin so that it forces the listener to consider different interpretations of the politician's talk. It is a clever deception. Frankfurt argues that the liar also must know the truth to invent a persuasive lie. Frankfurt makes the following distinction between the truth-teller, the liar, and the bullshitter:

> It is impossible for someone to lie unless he thinks he knows the truth. Producing bullshit requires no such conviction. A person who lies is thereby responding to the truth, and he is to that extent respectful of it. When an honest man speaks, he says only what he believes to be true; and for the liar, it is correspondingly indispensable that he considers his statements to be false. For the bullshitter, however, all these bets are off: he is neither on the side of the true nor on the side of [the] false. His eye is not on the facts at all, as the eyes of the honest man and of the liar are, except insofar as they may be pertinent to his interest in getting away with what he says. He does not care whether the things he says describe reality correctly. He just picks them out, or makes them up, to suit his purpose.
>
> *(2005, pp. 55, 56)*

A mindless construction of reality with no relevance to social life cannot be interpreted as a carnivalized act. Frankfurt's characterization of what constitutes contemporary "bullshit" appears an idle exercise, a monologue that the "bullshitter" carries out with blatant indifference to and disregard for the other. The act is neither iconoclastic nor triumphant. On the other hand, consider some late-night comedy shows in American culture: they certainly engage in bawdy language and boisterous laughter, but they consistently maintain ambivalence. For instance, *The Daily Show* by Jon Stewart and *The Colbert Report* by Stephen Colbert on the Comedy Central cable channel are classic examples of carnivalization of current events. These shows are incredibly popular, and many viewers receive "real news" from these "fake news" shows. While the "real news" frustrates and misleads individuals with layers and layers of needless commentaries, creating "false seriousness," the "fake news" shows break the dogma and hypocrisy to present a carnivalized view of current events. The "bullshitter" who runs away from truth and the "satirist" who takes you closer to truth both use profanities, but their philosophical meaning and their impact are worlds apart. Furthermore, the carnival space is not meant to be a safe haven for those who seek refuge from harsh realities; if anything, it is the site for insurgency.

Carnivalize to Develop and Develop to Carnivalize

I want to suggest that a carnivalized consciousness is both an *indicator of* developmental progress and a *mediator for* developmental progression. The benefits of the carnival "way of looking" at self and others in the world are clear in every domain of development.

In the domain of cognition, hidden truths are clearly exposed. Untouched dormant zones in the semiotic field are activated. While the "authoritarian word" in a monologic discourse restricts the range of meanings, the carnival language expands to present a multilayered and multidimensional account of reality. It is just as local as it is universal. In Bakhtin's view, the novel is an emblem of life and its hero personifies the emerging consciousness. In short, the hero is the developing individual. By introducing carnival motifs in literary works, writers like Rabelais and Dostoevsky showed developmental changes in the hero and in the world around him. Bakhtin insists that in the carnival world, death is always followed by birth—the transition from the demise of one worldview to the birth of a new one leads to a very crucial "realization that established authority and truth are relative" (RAW, p. 256). The carnival space and time are the junction where one mode of thinking reaches its termination and a new thought process begins its journey, so that life events may find their denouement.

The carnivalized consciousness is faithful to the "interior truth" and it validates "unofficial truth." Lev Vygotsky (1987) tells us that the genesis of thought is in social speech. The early forms of a child's speech are external and there is no distinction whatsoever between thought and speech. The fluid social speech slowly becomes private speech (children talk to themselves as loudly as they would talk to others), and slowly the private speech goes deeper and deeper to become semi-fluid inner speech, to finally condense into solid thought. If the transformation of social speech into private thought is one kind of developmental process governed by its own laws, the transformation of thought into social speech or written words is yet another kind of developmental achievement. As the thought travels from the mind to the tip of the tongue (for speech) or the tip of the finger (for written work), the self must intervene. Only in a child we can accept thought in an unedited form. The law that "thought equals speech" holds good only in early childhood, and with or without this knowledge the world accepts that trait in young children. As one develops, the individual must become a skillful craftsman to carefully choose words to make them suitable for public reception. The disjunction between thinking and speaking is a developmental law, a reality (one struggles to express thoughts), and a social demand (think before you speak). It is not a mark of maturity to say what you think in an unedited form, and not being able to express your thoughts clearly is not desirable either. In other words, one must develop the skill to speak/write in a manner that is faithful to the thought and yet convey it with some tact to the listener/reader. Thought must be carefully cast in suitable words; otherwise the words would amount to unofficial language. Ivanov (1991) made a very interesting observation at his talk at the Fifth International Bakhtin Conference at Manchester, England, in this regard. He said that "words, intonations and intra-verbal gestures" normally are cleansed and polished to make them presentable to the evaluating social audience, whereas the carnival language is a way of "connecting the lower levels of inner speech with [the] broader social sphere." I want to extend Ivanov's argument to suggest that the public carnival language being so close to the private inner speech, particularly speech held back because of fear of public censure, erases the boundaries between the inner and the outer. The deep condensed thought gains validation in a public realm. Besides, you realize that others think like you and gain some relief. The walls separating self and others are also demolished. Ivanov points out that the "I-experience" in its extreme form moves toward annihilation—it loses its verbal form. In order to recharge and rejuvenate, the "I-experience" must blend into the "We-experience," or, as Vygotsky would say, thought must become speech so that it can achieve greater clarity and strength. Taking these arguments as my foundation, I suggest that consciousness must periodically dip into carnival mode to achieve clarity in the way we view our position, our role, and our responsibility in the fields of culture and history.

The carnival genre has had a very long history, or better put, the genre changed its form in the course of history; therefore one must be careful not to adopt and deploy the genre taken from history's reservoir in a mechanical and uncritical manner. Nietzsche, in his usual vitriolic manner, cautions against this danger in his work *Beyond Good and Evil*, and he says there is nothing virtuous about claims of hybrid identity if all one does is treat "history as a storage room for costumes" (1989, p. 223) for a fancy dress party. Despite the high risk of banality in this activity, Nietzsche finds a glimmer of hope and argues that when moralities, gods, customs, and "articles of faith" are assembled in the form of "costumes" for "a carnival in grand style," the individuals donning the garb may or may not be aware of its significance, but, according to Nietzsche, the "historical spirit" still works its way through to show the creative potential:

> Perhaps this is where we shall still discover the realm of our *invention*, that realm in which we, too, can still be original, say, as parodists of world history and God's buffoons—perhaps, even if nothing else today has any future, our *laughter* may yet have a future.
> (1989, Beyond God and Evil, #223)

The carnival laughter, by its sheer collective force, can never lose its potential to show innumerable possibilities and herein is the significance for human development. The loud chorus and collective feasting is a bold show of defiance against the vanities and hypocrisies of the world. In the domain of social development, the carnivalized consciousness freely tears down the barriers between self and others to participate in collective struggles. The spirit is always democratic, and the lesson is to laugh for the sake of laughter, for the sake of collective freedom, and for the sake of liberation from the constraints of righteousness and seriousness. For the individual, separation and individuation are crucial for identity development, but just as crucial is the awareness that you are one among many—to merge and dissolve in the crowd and shed the false sense of superiority is critical to function as a social entity. The collective revolt seen in the carnival does not mean that it is a permanent enemy of authority; the carnival world is only revolting against authority that has become hollow and duplicitous. While the critics of Rabelais found him a "foe of royal power" (RAW, p. 119), Bakhtin understood the progressive meaning in Rabelaisian language and tactics. The revolt is meant to restore sincerity to power.

The carnivalized consciousness has a significant impact on our emotional development, helping us overcome fear, despair, and stagnation. It is also an effective cleanser of negative emotions. Bakhtin says, "Laughter purifies the consciousness of men from false seriousness, from dogmatism, from all confusing emotions" (RAW, p. 141). The carnival mind rejects "false seriousness," *not* "seriousness" as such, if anything, as Bakhtin points out, "True ambivalent and universal laughter does not deny seriousness but purifies and completes it" (RAW, p. 123). Carnivalized consciousness is driven by folk sensibilities, which know no repression. Folk culture is more faithful to frankness in the public square than to emotions held in the private realm. With its free use of profanities and curses, it is an antidote to the toxicity of passive aggression. Carnival language prefers blunt talk to restraining, polite conversation that goes in an endless loop, leaving all the parties even more confused. Carnival attacks political, social, and psychological repression. Carnivalized consciousness is earth bound and unabashedly carnal. Its language and behavior confirm the reality of flesh, show how triumphant the physical is over the metaphysical, and demonstrate the power of instincts over abstract ethics. Finally, the collective subsumes the individual and humans overshadow the gods. This realization leads to emotional empowerment.

In the realm of morality and ethics, the carnivalized consciousness rejects phantom ideals. Real dialogue is not possible unless the interlocutors are prepared to recognize that their traditions, religious practices, ideals, and even modes of thinking are subjected to spatiotemporal upheavals. Lev Vygotsky (1987) demonstrated convincingly that the content of our thought and, more important, our ways of thinking—the cognitive apparatus—undergo change along with the advances and changes in cultural tools. Changes in every realm of psychology follow technological change. Bakhtin asserts, "every entry into the sphere of meanings is accomplished only through the gates of chronotope" (FTCN, p. 258). We must bear in mind that the word "chronotope," literally meaning "time space," is referring not to abstract categories, but to historical time and cultural space. A consciousness that is not periodically carnivalized risks losing the critical angle in assessing various aspects of cultural life. A living faith that grows with life and responds to change turns into terrifying ideology—an instrument for exploitation. Carnivalizing the faith becomes a corrective measure against this danger. The main function of carnival is to renew, refresh, and transform, and retain its core value. Bakhtin maintains that one cannot understand culture in all its wholesomeness, if we ignore the folk humor and marketplace language. I would extend this postulate to suggest that the emergence of consciousness cannot be comprehended in all its multifacetedness if we ignore the mischievous, the defiant, and the irrepressible nature in us—the carnivalized self that precipitates change and development.

I repeat, there are real dangers of misapplication of carnival, particularly in the current cultural climate. Mass media, having its greatest influence in our collective life, frames issues in a dangerously oversimplified manner—demanding not nuanced explanations but neat categories of affirmation and repudiation. The carnival genre with its inevitable propensity to detect ambivalences and open-endedness may be easily dismissed and rendered undesirable. Or, there is the opposite danger as well; undifferentiated laughter (making no distinctions between laughter at others and the all-inclusive laughter of the carnival) and indiscriminate foul language (usage of curse words due to weakness in vocabulary) may very well be erroneously identified as carnival. Bakhtin was quite mindful of this danger, as noted in his concluding remarks on Rabelais, and he reiterated, "every act of world history was accompanied by a laughing chorus. But not every period of history had Rabelais for coryphaeus" (RAW, p. 474). It would be a shame if psychologists fear studying and promoting carnival because of the risks involved. After all, carnival is a cure for irrational fear and not its symptom, and it would be the height of irony to fear the remedy. Whether the healers and the theorists of the mind are bold enough to lead the laughing chorus is an open question.

Note

1. Cited by Somadeva Vasudeva (2005) in his Introduction (p. 19–20) to Vasudeva, Somadeva. (Editor & Translator) 2005. *THREE SATIRES by Bhallata, Kshemendra & Nila-Kantha*. Clay Sanskrit Library. New York: New York University Press.
2. Transmitted orally and recorded in *Akbar Birbal's Jokes*. Diamond Series. New Delhi: Diamond Pocket Books Pvt. Ltd., p. 32.

5

AUTHORING THE SELF—ANSWERING THE OTHER

Epistemological Necessities and Ethical Obligations

> Man as a knower, is not fully himself—his mere information does not reveal him. But as a person he is the organic man, who has the inherent power to select things from his surroundings in order to make them his own.
>
> Personality, *Rabindranath Tagore*, 2002c, p. 12

During this era of "selfies" when the self is both the photographer and the photographed, a commodity and a marketer of the commodity, it would take more than a shout to signal the necessity of the "other"—the other not as a passive spectator or a cheerleader for the self, but the "other" as a recipient of the *soul* of the self as a gift. It would demand a deep sense of urgency and impatience with our current digitally mediated constructions of self, for as fashionable as they are, they reduce the self to a display object and the other to a passive onlooker. Perhaps the same degree of urgency and impatience is needed to critically examine our long tradition of Western individualism that has celebrated autonomy, self-sufficiency, and privacy. The mechanics of the digital world and the intellectual tradition's absolute faith in the power of the individual undermines the significance of the other. The ego-centered individualism fails to engage with others on relational basis. For Bakhtin, the world of mutual dependency is more than a celebration and certainly not a prescription either; instead, it is a necessity for we cannot transcend our solipsism, and this ontological reality creates the need for the other to fill in what the self is incapable of perceiving. Furthermore, the interdependent world demands ethical answerability and responsibility to sustain a community and to avert identity from becoming amorphous. The main concern for cultural-developmental psychologists would then be how to maintain that delicate balance—a dance between authoring the self and being coauthored by the other. More importantly, how do we draw that very crucial line between coauthorship and defining, dominating, and appropriating the voice of the other? After all, social relations are rarely worked out on a level playing field.

Something incredible happens when humans congregate; they talk, argue, gesture, and grimace. One intends to say one thing and says something else, and what one meant in saying what one said is interpreted and understood differently by the other, so much so the scene becomes a performance where the focus is not on just the act *of* saying something, but how the performance is produced by all the acts involved *in* saying something. Purpose, energy, intent, anticipation, and affect play a role in making sense of this performance. Perhaps that is why Vygotsky rightly equated the entire enterprise of psychology with drama, because, to him, man is "*an aggregate of social relations*" (1989, p. 66). Meanings are bargained and contested in human conversations, and this clash is inevitable; that is why Vygotsky asserts, "A drama cannot be otherwise, i.e., it is *a clash of systems.*" The clash is intrinsic even to our understanding of self, as he observes, "I am a social relation of *me* to myself" (p. 67). In this social drama, roles are never set and the script never prewritten, and therefore roles shift and the script evolves. In human conversations, words are not necessarily tossed into the air like a badminton ball awaiting response from the other in a neat sequential back-and-forth exchange; instead, even as words are being tossed out, the act of interpreting, twisting, responding, and rejecting begins in a simultaneous manner. Thus it seems that even as the self begins to present itself—author itself—it invariably has to answer the other. In his landmark essay on Bakhtin's trans-linguistics, Michael Holquist treats "answering" itself as "authoring" and argues that just as the body responds to its physical environment by sensing and adjusting, the mind "responds to social stimuli by authoring its own experiences" (1983, p. 317). Therefore, if authoring is a distinct feature of consciousness, then embedded in it is the act of answering.

Self: Ideas, Concepts, and Imageries in Psychology

Perhaps, William James (1900), a proponent of functionalism, pragmatism, and radical empiricism, must be credited for putting forward a rich account of self in his most influential work—*The Principles of Psychology*—written in 1890. James conceived of self as the sum total of all the things an individual can make claims to, from his body, psyche, lineage, friends, and family, to material possessions. He identifies two aspects of self: "I"—the self as subject—and "Me"—the self as object. James goes on to identify three aspects of "Me"—the material self, the social self, and the spiritual self. Because consciousness operates in a *stream of thought*, according to James, the multiple selves are always evolving and occasionally enter into a conflict with each other, and when that happens the "I" as the knower chooses one from the many possible selves to suit the occasion (Barresi, 2002). Thus, James set the stage for the multiple and dynamic nature of self in psychology.

Another classic work in the field of the self is George Herbert Mead's *Mind, Self and Society* (1934), which comes from a social behaviorist standpoint and which set the stage for symbolic interactionism. For Mead, the genesis of self is a developmental process, and he identifies two stages—the play stage and the game stage. During the play stage, children take on the attitudes of particular and significant others like parents, teachers, and peers toward them, and this play becomes the simplest form of roleplaying. In this sense, Mead shares with Bakhtin the idea that the "other" dominates during early stages of self-awareness, and Bakhtin addresses this issue from the vantage point of verbal exchanges. "I realize myself initially through others: from them I receive words, forms, and tonalities for the formation of my initial idea of myself" (FNM 70–71, p. 138).

The play stage is the first step in the developmental processes of the self, where the child internalizes how significant others see him, but still lacks a sense of self independent of others. A fuller sense of self where there is negotiation between self and others happens during the game stage. Play can be a solitary activity with partially imagined others, whereas in a game there is competition that involves strategy, anticipation, and negotiation with real others, and hence only during the game stage does a fuller sense of self/other develop. In his discussion of the game stage, Mead (1934) introduces one of his perhaps most widely known and contested concepts—*the generalized other*—referring to how the self perceives the attitude of an organized community or social group. The question that comes with this concept is whether the generalized other is singular and undifferentiated or a diverse body of differentiated particulars. It is precisely this question that leads us to Bakhtin, but before getting there, it is important to engage with an offshoot of Bakhtin's theory that has gained a lot of traction in the study of the self.

Influenced by James's distinction of "I" and "Me," informed by Mead's developmental trajectory of self-awareness from the play stage to the game stage, and inspired by Bakhtin's ideas on shifting positions of multiple voices in a polyphonic novel, a whole new trend proposed by Hubert Hermans and his colleagues called the "dialogical self" has emerged in psychology (Hermans and Kempen, 1993).

The dialogical self is modeled after Bakhtin's thesis on the polyphonic novel that characterizes Dostoevsky's works, and the prominent feature of this type of novel is the "plurality of consciousness"—meaning independent, unique, and mutually opposing voices engage in open-ended and unfinalized dialogic relations. As in polyphony, the self in this school of thought has the potential to move between multiple "I positions" and engage in a dialogue with these multiple selves. What, then, is the impetus for multiple selves to engage in a dialogue? Hermans and Kempen (1993) identify four developmental prerequisites for the dialogical self—act, memory, imagination, and language—and because these prerequisites are an integral part of life, the authors argue, the self inevitably becomes dialogical. The authors contend that every act of a child is bound to be interpreted and responded to by others, and hence actions and gestures have dialogic potential. Second, in the act of remembering, multiple memories from different moments in time converge to enter into a dialogue. The authors explain that in the third prerequisite the individual pushes some elements from real and perceived events into the imaginative horizon to transform reality into something novel, and this act would require dialogic interpenetration between the real and the imagined. About the last prerequisite, the authors explain that "language is indispensable" for exchanging actions, memories, and imaginations, told from divergent positions. Hermans and Kempen highlight the multiplicity of I positions and asymmetrical relations and the power struggle between these multiple selves as the main defining features of the dialogical self and argue that the self is a "highly contextual phenomenon" that is "bound to cultural and institutional constraints" (1993, p. 78).

Although the proponents of dialogical self theory make very strong claims of Bakhtinian influence, the imprint of many of Bakhtin's key concepts or close approximations of them like answerability, spirit, soul, rhythm, and loophole are barely visible. The movement of multiple selves certainly provides the foundation for Bakhtin to develop other sophisticated concepts to address larger issues like the ontological realities of self–other relations, the epistemological necessities of the other for the self, and the ethical obligations that we need to fulfill toward each other, and in the absence of these concepts, the dialogical self comes across as somewhat interactional. Numerous critics have pointed out many shortcomings like integrity and unity of self within its diverse manifestations (Sullivan, 2007), the "otherness" that already exists within the self (Burkitt, 2010), and the self as a social entity even in its embodied experience rather than being social only in intersubjective exchange (Cresswell and Baerveldt, 2011).

The proponents of the dialogical self conceive the notion of dialogue in a far more narrow sense than what Bakhtin had in mind. In his collected works, Bakhtin developed the idea of dialogue in at least three distinct senses, and, as Morson and Emerson observe, considerable misunderstanding has occurred due to our failure to tease out these multiple senses of dialogue. On one level, they observe that it is a global concept—"dialogue as a view of truth and the world" (1990, p. 131). In order to participate in the world dialogically, one must first and foremost see the world itself as dialogically structured, and that is the very foundation of Dostoevsky's artistic vision; as Bakhtin observes, Dostoevsky went beyond the "monologic model of the world" (PDP, p. 292) to uncover the "dialogic nature of societal life" (p. 298) and the "life of a human being" (ibid.). While Hermans and his colleagues identify the prerequisites that are primarily individualistic and psychological in nature for the emergence of the dialogical self, Bakhtin takes it to a very wide macro level to link the dialogic view of the world with dialogic consciousness. The next sense in which Bakhtin discusses dialogue is grounded in the problem of language, and language in action, by its very nature, is dialogic, and much of the school of the "dialogical self" is premised on this sense. In the third sense of dialogue, Bakhtin recognizes that several factors—the predisposition of an individual or the person he or she is conversing with or the conditions under which exchanges occur—may allow some utterances to be dialogic and the rest to be non-dialogic or monologic. If anything, Bakhtin recognizes that in human thinking (intra-psychic conversation) and in human interactions (interpersonal conversations), monologic impulses are unfortunately rather strong and it takes a great deal of maturity and courage to engage in intra-psychic dialogue of competing ideas and interpersonal dialogue with others who hold different views. The idea that very often dialogue ceases to exist is not a part of the theory of the dialogical self, and therefore it would appear as if it is a state and that it is automatic. In fact, I would argue that evolving to dialogic consciousness is a major developmental achievement, and even if an individual moves in that direction, the expression and manifestation of dialogue is not always possible because of the refusal of the other to participate or the cultural conditions being unfavorable. Surely, an individual must be willing to engage in a dialogue by accommodating the other on a horizontal plane, and even if one regards the utterances of the other in a dialogic spirit, the other might shut down the dialogue with his or her monologic impulses. A similar trend could occur between readers and texts, and in both cases cultural conditions may facilitate (as in open societies) or restrict (as in closed societies) dialogue. How cultural conditions enable or disable dialogue is not accounted for in the school of the dialogical self. Furthermore, as Cresswell and Baerveldt point out, Bakhtin's account "sheds light on the embodied ambivalences inherent in dialogicality" (2011, p. 275) to go beyond "a conception of dialogue that only involves inter-subjective exchange" (p. 275).

Authoring Self: Concerns in Psychology, Literature, and Philosophy

Authoring a self—is it a compilation of individual psychological traits, predisposition, temperament, and experienced events; or is it a creative work of writing narratives on lived life; or is it a deeply philosophical endeavor that examines our duties and ethical obligations toward self/other and society? Perhaps the activity of authoring and answering in and of itself is at the very intersection of these three disciplines. Note that Bakhtin did not have a special interest in self as a topic per se, and yet he presented a very sophisticated account of the self while exploring polyphony, chronotope, and genres in novelistic discourse and, more important, while addressing the relationship between art and life and the philosophy of the act. Therefore, literary and philosophical concerns were at the forefront in discussing various "images of the man" and man in relation to the surrounding world and historical forces, and in this process he provides incredible insights for psychology. It would be instructive to hear what Bakhtin says about the issue of the "soul"—a term that rarely appears in psychological theories—and if we substitute "soul" with "self," Bakhtin's argument would still hold true. In addressing the "Problem of the Inner Man," Bakhtin says:

> The problem of the soul, from a methodological standpoint, is a problem in aesthetics. It cannot be a problem in psychology—a science that is nonvaluational and causal, for even though the soul evolves and becomes

in time, it is a whole that is individual, valuational, and free. Nor can the soul be a problem in ethics, for the ethical *subiectum* is present to itself as a task—the task of actualizing itself as a value, and it is in principle incapable of being given, of being present-on-hand, of being contemplated: it is *I-for-myself.*

(AHAA, p. 100)

The takeaway from this rather esoteric passage for our current discussion is that psychological science operating on the principle of causality and assuming self bound, is bound to pluck the individual out of the cultural soil and study it as a sterile entity and to subsequently treat self–other relations as interactive and not necessarily as inter-penetrative, where the other always is an integral part of the self. As is typical of Bakhtin, he addresses any topic—be it readers, texts, authors, or cultures—at the intersection of philosophy, literature, and anthropology. Relationship is everything for Bakhtin. Therefore, the most insightful accounts of the self–other relationship emerge in his discussion on "authoring," "ethical, aesthetic and scientific validity," "responsibility," emotional and moral significance of "outsideness," and "*non-alibi in Being*" (TPA, p. 40), and these philosophical ideas are substantiated and validated in his discussions of typologies of novels, where Bakhtin clearly delineates various images of a man.

Another point becomes very clear in Bakhtin's discussion of the soul when he says that the soul cannot be a problem for ethics either. If I may replace "soul" with "self," we can still say that Bakhtin never entertained the idea of the self as exclusively autonomous, although autonomy is certainly an aspect of the self. Similarly, Bakhtin never entertained phantom ethics or "ethical ought," and therefore the idea of an "ethical subject" defined by certain features was unacceptable to him. Instead, what he sought was an "ethical validity" that is achieved in the unity of the "once-occurrent answerable life" (TPA, p. 5). Bakhtin argues that the answerable act is not necessarily subjective and psychological, but "a truth that unites both the subjective and the psychological moments, just as it unites the moment of what is universal (universally valid) and the moment of what is individual (actual)" (TPA, p. 29). Therefore, abstract universal principles converge with concrete acts that honor a truth at a given time in a given space, and this meeting point between the abstract/universal with the concrete/particular is the answerable act. In such a Bakhtinian formulation, neither the integrity of the acting individual, nor the universal ethical principles, nor the significance of time and space where the act occurs are compromised. No entity is subordinated to the other, and not any one of them could be understood without the other.

The necessity of the other for authoring the self is fundamentally a philosophical and an ontological issue for Bakhtin. In sharp contrast to Kant's transcendental subject, who overcomes his solipsism, Bakhtin argues that individuals always occupy a unique position in time and space that cannot be transcended, but only mediated, and it is precisely this uniqueness of one's axiological position that gives birth to the necessity for the other. For Bakhtin, we simply do not have fixed, a priori categories to know the world or the self in their fullness, and therefore we need the other to fill in what we are incapable of perceiving. In his early philosophical works, Bakhtin expresses immense frustration with Kant's abstract theoreticism. He is unconvinced by Kant's claim "that a hundred real thalers are not equal to a hundred thinkable thalers" (TPA, p. 8), and argues that the world of theoretical science has no room for real people performing actual deeds and answerable acts. Due consideration for actual, lived life, according to Bakhtin, does not in any way "deny the autonomy of truth," nor does it descend to relativism. On the contrary, Bakhtin avers, the answerability factor preserves the "autonomy of truth, its purity and self-determination" (p. 10) because purity itself is premised on the fact that "truth can participate answerably in Being-as-event" (ibid.) and truth divorced from life is vacuous.

Self as the lone seeker of knowledge is possible only in theory, but in real life it is impossible both at a sensory perceptual level and at a cognitive conceptual level. Bakhtin asks us to consider the problem of seeing ourselves at a very perceptual level. It is impossible to get a complete picture of the self against the backdrop of the surrounding world. I cannot see my contours, my face, the top of my head, my back, and much more, and even if I turn my head in all possible directions, I must concur with Bakhtin's observations: "I can succeed in seeing all of myself from all sides of the surrounding space in the center of which I am situated, but I shall never be able to see myself as actually surrounded by this space" (AHAA, p. 37).

If my eyes cannot see my own exterior, would my photograph make that possible? Bakhtin says that in a photograph, we see only "our own reflection without an author" (AHAA, p. 34), and it is nothing more than "material for collation" (ibid.). Note that Bakhtin was not writing this in the age of selfies, and even had he lived in such an age, he would have still said that it is a piece without an author because to him verbal or photographic compositions created by the self are still incomplete, fortuitous, and artificial, as they do not capture the self as an ongoing event. However, a portrait by an artist has greater legitimacy because the self sees itself through the eyes of the other and in the world of the other.

Acknowledging the Need for the Other and Resisting the Oppressive Other

By making an impassioned case for the indispensability of the other in authoring the self, has Bakhtin overlooked the lived reality of innumerable people in every culture who occupy a position so marginal and whose voices are so fragmented, muted, and discredited by dominant groups that they are forever silenced and cannot define themselves and must only accept the definitions of the oppressive other? Rendered as objects by dominant others, how do such individuals begin to retaliate and reclaim selfhood when they were never even given a chance to be proper subjects? Colonized nations, racial groups, women, members of certain castes, classes, or communities have faced the scourge of dominance and tyranny, and it takes several generations for them to come to their own. Systemic oppression feeds poison to annihilate the oppressed groups. One cannot expect the dominated mortal beings to be like the Hindu god—Lord Shiva—to consume poison and still sustain and even make it part of their identity, and if and when the slightest awareness of being poisoned by the other dawns on them, they may resist consuming the toxic substance, but must still figure out a way to find some nectar to revive and nourish the self. In her very provocative and influential essay "Can the Subaltern Speak?" (1994), Gayatri Spivak, referring to postcolonial subjects and other marginalized groups as "subaltern," answers her own question with an emphatic no—"the subaltern cannot speak"—because their languages and ways of being are not sanctioned and whatever they say is bound to be interpreted only in terms of sanctioned language. Imperialism has robbed them of their histories and practices and pulled their diverse languages into the unitary monologic language of the colonizer.

The history of slavery, as bell hooks (1990) observes, not only snatched away the dignity, humanness, and identity of blacks, but also left no "home place" where there is a possibility of recovery. In Bakhtin's parlance, no chronotope seems secure and validating, and even if one looks into the chronotopes of the past, they do not seem promising either. The image of a person is chronotopic, says Bakhtin, and, if that is the case, how, then, do we deal with images of the self violently distorted by the other? Was Bakhtin unmindful of such social pathos or can we find some explanatory capability for this dilemma in dialogic theory if we plough through his works?

At the very outset, we can categorically say that Bakhtin had very little to say about social inequities and institutionalized injustice and did not necessarily embark on a journey to rid the world of exploitation. Although he was finetuned to hear the cultural chatter, Bakhtin evinced no particular interest in the shrill voices of political slogans. Addressing concerns about what Bakhtin had to say about "Keeping the Self Intact during the Cultural Wars," Caryl Emerson observes:

> In his philosophical orientation Bakhtin was a personalist, an intentionalist, something of a Stoic. He had little sympathy for depersonalizing grids and predetermined trajectories of the Hegelian or Marxist-Leninist historical models endemic in his homeland. And on a personal plane, he was uninterested in those psychological prime movers so popular in Western theorizing about personality: resentment, envy, guilt, self-doubt, self-rejection. About such powerful motivators of human behavior, Bakhtin has almost nothing to say. He insists on love.
>
> *(1996, p. 109)*

Bakhtin discovered the potential for liberation, self-discovery, and dignity not in the mass social movements (not that he said anything against them), but in an *I am not like you but I like you* approach to tender human interactions. By choice, circumstance, and temperament, Bakhtin's philosophy and his own lived life have the quality of human beings interacting in a cozy chamber space—one-on-one or heart-to-heart kinds of personal interactions (Emerson, 1997). When an individual performs a deed for a political cause or as a religious ritual, he or she does that "in the capacity of a representative" (TPA, p. 52), and that means the collective force has already accorded the individual the status and the power, and under these circumstances the individual acts with pride and not in humility, and, so Bakhtin insists, "One has to develop humility to the point of participating in person and being answerable in person" (ibid.). Jumping onto the bandwagon of social movements and shouting political slogans is the easy part, but to cede your territory and make room for the different other as an equal partner in a dialogue requires humility, patience, and respect, and this was Bakhtin's main concern.

Bakhtin himself was no stranger to marginalization and exile, and his physical body was both his curse (crippled because of bone disease) and his savior (illness released him from prison); these factors restricted his movement, and therefore solitude was perhaps the only option, which might explain Bakhtin's preference for everyday one-on-one human relations (Emerson, 1996). For psychologists, the benefits from Bakhtin's works come from his intense focus on differentiated particulars and the uniqueness of the individual in our interconnected world.

Bakhtin addresses the issue of composing a self in the realm of architectonics: How does one group gather together and connect select heterogeneous parts of lived life and eventually achieve a consummated whole, with ample loopholes to aestheticize the self? For Bakhtin, the very moment of consummation is also a moment for a new beginning when the other must enter the picture, not as an alibi but as a coauthor bringing new dimensions, as he suggests:

> live in such a way that every moment of your life would be both the consummating, final moment and, at the same time, the initial moment of a new life. As such, this demand is in principle incapable of being fulfilled by me, for it includes an aesthetic category (a relationship *to the other*) which although attenuated, is still alive in it.
>
> *(AHAA, p. 122)*

In every moment of consummation, the *I-for-myself*, the image and feel of the self to its own consciousness, includes the otherness and outsideness; the *I-for-others*, how self appears in the eyes of the others; and the converse, *Others-for-me*, how others appear to the self; and the components of this triadic equation, by their very nature, are bound to be different. One party could see the other through a biased or bigoted lens, and working out these equations never occurs in a just world or under ideal conditions, but it is precisely in this process that there is room for answerability and responsibility toward others and to self. I have to be true, answerable, and responsible to myself, even as I extend the same courtesy to others. (Emerson [1996] points out that, in Russian, the same word—*otvetstvennost*—denotes answerability and responsibility.)

The disjunction between *I-for-myself*, *I-for-others*, and *Others-for-me* perhaps creates the space for the self to affix its personal signature to performed deeds and lived experiences. Furthermore, the disjunction makes room for selection, rejection, reflection, and correction from the available surplus of meanings. For Bakhtin, ethical conduct is not immanent in the constitution of selfhood; rather it is a position, a point of view, and an attitude toward the other in a dialogic relationship. Bakhtin's (1993) emphasis on "ethical validity" rather than "ethics" per se clearly points out that he developed not a formulaic notion, but a processual notion of ethics predicated on non-coincidence of the subject with itself and a radical openness to the other. This reciprocal formulation makes room to affirm agency and to recognize the necessity of the other and still resist the violence of the oppressive other, and this position, as Daphna Erdinast-Vulcan observes, is "both all-too-human and thoroughly humane" (2013, p. 105).

Because the subtitle of this book is "A Bakhtinian World," I want to push the argument that in Bakhtin's world, words, concepts, and determinations assume different meanings in different spheres of reality—be they about tyranny and oppression or any other form of social disharmony—and none of these can be defined by some standard features; instead, the surrounding context determines their validity. Take, for example, the multiple meanings that silence could generate—it could be a sign of ignorance or enlightenment, a form of tyranny (refusal to hear the other) or a type of resistance (refusal to internalize others' insulting words), it could be consent or disapproval—ground realities alone can determine the meaning. Bakhtin (2001) puts it nicely in one of his early lectures on "Grounded Peace": "Tranquility or peace of mind can be either the tranquility of self-complacency or that of trust"; and he goes on to say that the silence of inertia must be disrupted by disquietude and through repentance—that is, holding yourself answerable to a *super addressee*, be it God, society, or conscience—and in doing so the passive form of silence develops into an active form of trust. Answerability and personal participation hold the key to the transitional process.

Appealing to an agreed-upon super addressee in a discourse diminishes the "danger of relativism" because the participants recognize the super addressee in a judicial capacity (Erdinast-Vulcan, 2013), and hence answering each other without compromising the integrity of self is made possible.

In freely recognizing the need for the other, consciousness is risking itself, for the self could be taken advantage of, silenced, or stepped over, and this anxiety would seem normal, understandable, and even justifiable. This is akin to open societies with porous borders that risk infiltration and abuse of that openness, but the answer to this problem is not sealing the border, but negotiating border crossing. For the individual, there is great danger in thinking that the "other" is not needed; consciousness certainly is an attribute of an individual, but the formation of consciousness is located not in the individual, but between individuals. It is that in-between space that gives us joy and sorrow, and it is in this space that we can bargain, plead, reject, and retaliate. But rejecting the necessity of the other is tantamount to giving up oneself. When consciousness falsely imagines itself to be absolutely free, it disconnects itself from the interconnected world and ceases to feel that it is part of nature, culture, and history. When this happens, the self can shirk responsibility and rid itself of conscience, and this distorted self-image loses the ability to sustain criticism—because of either self-aggrandizement to the point of imagining playing the role of a demiurge, or self-effacement to the point that the self no longer holds itself accountable for anything. Strangely, both are two sides of the same coin.

Emotional Responsiveness: Empathy, Sympathy, Pain, and Healing

Among the most remarkable aspects of Bakhtin's works, particularly his early philosophical works on author–hero and self–other relationships, is the sophistication he displays in articulating emotional responsiveness. Ethical concerns are embedded in his exposition of emotions. Incredibly insightful for understanding the psychology of emotions, these sections in "Author and Hero in Aesthetic Activity" have direct relevance in many branches of psychology, in particular clinical and developmental branches. But sadly, these works have hardly caught the attention of psychologists, and the reasons could be many. Bakhtin's imprint on psychology in general is still indistinct, and references to his early works rarely appear even in journals open to interdisciplinary approach. Furthermore, his insights on emotions are couched in dense theological language with emphasis on confession, repentance, feeling for faith, and so on, and secular-minded psychologists may be less inclined to sift through the material. But I want to make the case that this exercise is worthwhile and there is much to gain.

Discussions on empathy and sympathy appear in Bakhtin's examination of "Expressive" and "Impressive" aesthetics. When aesthetic activity is seen as an "outward expression of an inner state" (AHAA, p. 62), it is assumed that the outer is an exact replica of the inner and that there is no transition and transformation in the movement from the inner to the outer, and hence the aesthetic activity is akin to "empathizing"—complete identification with the inner life of the other. Empathizing is not restricted to aesthetic activity, says Bakhtin, for it occurs in "all dimensions of life"—"practical, ethical and psychological" (AHAA, p. 64), and in all these areas Bakhtin finds the absence of demarcation between the inner and outer and self and other problematic and asserts that it is "unsound at its very foundation" (ibid.).

What is so impoverishing about expressive aesthetics? Bakhtin asserts that it cannot "account for the *whole* of a work of art" (AHAA, p. 64). He asks us to consider viewing Leonardo da Vinci's *The Last Supper* and if empathizing is a precondition for aesthetic experience, then one would have to identify with Christ and each and every one of the apostles—a task that would virtually be impossible because they are all different, and even if we consider the possibility of partial identification with each one of them, the aesthetic response to the work of art cannot be the sum total of identifications with the characters in the painting. Setting aside the work of art and identifying with the author, Bakhtin says, would still be erroneous because the author is placed "on par with his heroes" (p. 65), falsely assuming that the author and his heroes share the same "emotional-volitional position" (ibid.).

How do we extend this line of reasoning to psychological empathizing? I turn to the incredibly insightful work of Peter Good (2002), who brings Bakhtin to the "landscape of psychiatry"—a terrain defined by monological language that attempts to pull the diverse languages of tormented individuals into its orbit and subsequently certify them as "cured" and "normal." Peter Good challenges this practice to propose a new "language for those who have nothing," and does so by invoking Bakhtin's versatile concept—polyphony—that recognizes the shifting positions and uniqueness of each and every party in the healing process and gives a fair hearing to every voice—official and unofficial or supposedly normal and abnormal.

The field of mainstream psychiatry or clinical psychology is built on sameness and identification. If the long litany of woes the patient gives matches the long list of diagnostic criteria in the manual, a label of illness is attached to the patient, and the healing process is to eliminate all indications of those woes. Therefore the narratives in the mainstream "care chronotope," according to Good, are built on "what is and what ought to be" (2002, p. 24), and as such are designed to "heal the inadequacies of the past" only to justify "all the anomalies of the present" (ibid.).

It would be instructive to draw parallels between expressive aesthetics and mainstream psychiatry. In the former, to perceive something aesthetically is to "co-experience its inner states (both physical and psychological) through the medium of their outward expressedness" (AHAA, p. 63)—thereby bringing the private feelings and public expression of the contemplated subject/object in alignment with the contemplator. In psychiatry, the healer (the contemplator) also perceives the physical symptoms (tremors, weeping, and so on) and the patient's (the contemplated) reported inner state of turmoil to align them with the list of symptoms in the diagnostic manual and assume with certitude that they have accessed the inner life of the patient. Bakhtin's impatience with "expressive aesthetics" is echoed in Peter Good's frustrations with the mainstream psychiatric landscape, and he proposes a new way of wandering as he reflects:

> To travel polyphonically is to learn to read a landscape in the company of some improbable voices. My own dialogue with Bakhtin has fundamentally altered the way I see mental illness and means by which it is managed. I am increasingly aware that the way psychiatry continues to manage

psychopathology is one driven by a need to become more and more exact. This very determination means that the background voices on the landscape are made to become more muted, more insignificant. I believe that it is a paradox the more and more *correct* observations we accumulate the less and less we seem to know what it is that is worth living for and what it is that makes us all unique.

(2002, p. 18)

The second shortcoming of expressive aesthetics, according to Bakhtin, is its inability to "provide a valid foundation of *form*" (AHAA, p. 67). In expressive understanding, form is viewed as revealing the inner life, whereas Bakhtin argues that form is bestowed upon the work of art in our relationship to it. In other words, form consummates content while introducing something new from outside. Bakhtin asks us to consider the story of Oedipus—quite apropos to psychology—as this has direct relevance to how we understand and treat pain and suffering. Oedipus' actions have a certain value and meaning in the context of his own life, and his confession and penitence hint at his inner emotional state, but within himself "he is not *tragic*" (AHAA, p. 70), says Bakhtin, because "a lived life is incapable of expressing and shaping itself as tragedy from within itself" (ibid.). Therefore, empathizing with Oedipus—not situating yourself outside this character—does not permit the contemplator to feel and understand tragedy. It would be highly tragic to "nullify tragedy" because of a total merger with the contemplated Oedipus. Helping to heal is not possible in empathy, and for that to happen one needs the outsideness of "sympathetic co-experiencing." Peter Good puts it nicely: when healers and the healed walk into the landscape of psychiatry as polyphonic wanderers with clear benevolent demarcation between them, one appreciates how "other voices give meaning to suffering" (2002, p. 139), and healers begin to recognize that their "unitary language is only one voice among many that offers wisdom and commentary on abnormal mental activities" (ibid.). This appreciation does not in any way deny the debilitating nature of depression or anxiety; if anything, according to Good, when the healer, assuming an outside position, is attentive to the voice of the patient and can restrain himself from imposing a predetermined healing method and discover ways of healing that might be unique and custom made for the patient, "Even in the darkest inner voice of depressive dialogue there is a faint glimmer of some other, more positive, connection" (p. 139). The bottom line is, the outsideness of sympathy has incredible dialogic and healing potential.

Soul: Spirit's Gift to the Other—Melodic Flow and Rhythms of Life

It would seem incredibly farfetched for most humans to think that we have no proprietorship over our souls, and it would be unsettling to feel that our innermost entity must proceed to the category of other to be shaped, validated, and consummated. That the contours of our exterior body are invisible and inaccessible to self and one needs the other to get a bigger picture seems intuitively persuasive, but to consider that our innermost, well-guarded soul does not exist for me and cannot be engendered by me would seem counterintuitive to the habitual mind. Interestingly, the very nucleus of Bakhtin's dialogical world is the idea that the soul can be saved and preserved not through the efforts of self, but only by the grace of the other. Bakhtin makes a strong case for the necessity of other by pointing out the concerns of the soul, which is the problem of immortality; therefore, long after the demise of the mortal body, it is the other—survivors, future generations, history, the people you impacted—that takes up the job of keeping the soul alive. Both during and after one's lifetime, the soul relies on the other to gain form because giving form is not possible from within and it must come from outside—the other and another consciousness—to give rhythmic closure. About the nature and purpose of soul, Bakhtin says:

> The soul is the self-coincident, self-equivalent, and self-contained whole of inner life that postulates another's loving activity from outside its own bounds. The soul is a gift that my spirit bestows upon the *other*.
> (AHAA, p. 132)

The key words that one must attend to are *gift, grace*, and *gratitude*. In order for gift as an idea, a concept, and an act to gain validity, it must be given in grace—not expecting something equivalent in return—and the receiver accepts it with gratitude. If these sentiments are absent, the act then ceases to be a gift. In many ways, the "love" that Bakhtin insists on as the basis of human relations is itself a gift of life. Love can't be demanded, for that would amount to invading the other's interior. Desperate need to be loved by the other or to be a hero in the world of others erases the distinction between self and other and robs each of them of their uniqueness.

I often repeat in my classroom like a mantra—*Love Is a Gift of Life*—and I do this being acutely mindful of the fact that many students, particularly female students, enter into abusive relationships in search of that wonderful thing called "love," and they often mistake being "possessed" by the other as "love," and once that turns into stalking and abuse, considerable damage has been done to their exterior body and interior soul, and sadly their spirits no longer soar. Students often tell me that initially it was difficult for them to accept my mantra, but eventually it allowed them to pull themselves out of an oppressive relationship. Love as a gift you give and receive is not disempowering; if anything, the realization of this allows one to overcome childish neediness and desperation and seek healthy relationships on equal footing. Perhaps, it is a developmental achievement and a mark of maturity to reach this level.

The thirst to love and be loved is certainly human and vital for our development; as Bakhtin would like us to believe, it "constitutes growth in the atmosphere of another's loving consciousness" (AHAA, p. 157) because it "impels and organizes" (ibid.) life in many of its dimensions. In a loving atmosphere where one doesn't dominate the other, but joins hands with the other, life's "fabular" possibilities can be pursued in full strength and vigor, whereas possession of one by the other constitutes "naïve, unmediated parasitism" (p. 156) for Bakhtin.

Bakhtin describes spirit as the *I-for-myself*—how I sense my own experiences from within—and because it is within, it has no firm points of consummation. In search of consummation the spirit wanders, as it always looks for loopholes to take the flight, and as a consequence of encounters with others—the *I-for-others*—the soul is consummated. Does this mean that every encounter in our daily life is a moment of consummation for the soul? Do we and should we absorb every definition by the other, however erroneous and biased they might be? What Bakhtin says about Dostoevsky's underground man could come to our rescue:

> The hero from the underground eavesdrops on every word someone else says about him, he looks at himself, as it were, in all the mirrors of other people's consciousnesses, he knows all the possible refractions of his image in these mirrors.
>
> *(PDP, p. 53)*

The underground man gathers all possible *I-for-others* images, and in addition to them he has "his own self consciousness"—the *I-for-myself* image—and despite being in possession of all these "definitions, prejudiced as well as objective" (p. 53), Bakhtin points out that the underground man still cannot "finalize them precisely because he himself perceives them" (ibid.); however, the wandering spirit, always in search of loopholes for escape, "can go beyond their limits [the definitions of the others] and can thus make them inadequate" (p. 53). So the self is not beholden to the definitions of each and every other person. The open and reasoning mind has the power to render biased opinions inadequate.

The spirit by its very nature, like the melodic flow of music, just flows, retaining its unfinalized, unclosed, and indeterminate character. But every self and every story needs momentary closure, and that is provided by the rhythm that consummates the soul. Without the momentary closure of rhythm that comes from outside, the free wandering of the spirit could be risky. The self could be lost in the cultural flux; as Morson and Emerson (1990) point out, "Successful imposition of rhythm overcomes the open and risk-laden future," and so it is the other that gives momentary shelter—the protective tug—to the potentially reckless wandering of the spirit. So in authoring the self, it is the other that brings a chapter to its provisional conclusion, so that the next chapter may begin.

Encountering Different Others for Creative Understanding: A Global Truth

In order to understand my self and my culture, encounters with different others and foreign cultures are needed to bring to the surface the aspects that are invisible and dormant. Individuals are also bearers and enactors of cultural codes. We deliver the cultural script almost automatically and only when our culture comes face to face with another culture; deeply entrenched aspects become visible and even questionable. Such encounters with other cultures open up the possibilities for creative understanding, as Bakhtin observes:

> A meaning only reveals its depths once it has encountered and come in contact with another, foreign meaning: they engage in a kind of dialogue, which surmounts the closedness and one-sidedness of these particular meanings, these cultures. We raise new questions for a foreign culture, one that did not raise itself; we seek answers to our own questions in it; and the foreign culture responds to us by revealing to us its new aspects and new semantic depths.
>
> *(RQNM, p. 7)*

Do individuals always respond to this creative potential opened up by encounters with other cultures? I must emphasize the word "potential" because encounters with different others only open up possibilities for creative understanding, but it is not so automatic. If anything, how we respond to the revelations in the encounter with other cultures could indicate whether the interpretations or responses to the questions raised have been refreshingly new and creative or whether one becomes rigid and defensive in the interpretation. The very nature of our responses could be an indicator of developmental achievement or lack thereof.

In my earlier work on how immigrants with varying degrees of enculturation into the American culture understand self/culture (Bandlamudi, 1994), I found that very few engage in creative and dialogic understanding that entails seeing culture and self as an open-ended process and report gaining new insights into self and cultural practices. The vast majority fell into various modes of monologic understanding: (a) Non-relational subjectivism/objectivism, in which culture is seen as something that the self dons, focusing mainly on superficial aspects of appearance, dress code, and so forth; (b) Relational-unilateral, in which the self is the perceiver of multiple cultures focusing on distinctions, contrasts, and peculiarities; (c) Relational-bilateral, a view of cultural determinism in which culture is seen as rule-governed and fixed, such that the self simply abides by them; and last, (d) Multilayered/multifaceted, in which there is a more complex understanding of self in cultural systems, but it is not transformative—a trend found in dialogic understanding. All the subjects report that encounters with other cultures expose something about themselves and their cultures—things that they never thought about—but the variation is in how they respond to this unsettling feeling. Many respond by stubbornly clinging to what they perceive as demands of their ethnic culture, as if culture stages them in a certain way, and reject and harshly criticize broader American culture, or they want to shed their ethnic culture and pass harsh judgments on it to embrace unquestioningly the broader American identity. In dialogic understanding, the encounters with others have an "aha" moment of having discovered something new, so that they can now be selective about what aspects of any culture they want to hold on to and why they want to do so, and recognize the aspects of cultural practices that have outrun their time or have been so unjustifiable that they deserve to be tossed out. I found a similar trend in another work (Bandlamudi, 2010), in which I studied how Indian immigrants interpreted segments from a cultural epic text—The Mahabharata—and here too many, in response to anxieties about the immigrant experience, were eager to construct "imaginary homelands" and wholesale "romantic pasts" or "dreadful pasts"—as Bakhtin (1984b—PDP) would say in a monologic world, one only affirms or repudiates. Different others, different cultures, and different time periods do not coexist to enter into a dialogue; instead, one must negate the other to affirm self or vice versa.

I have made references to my earlier works to drive home the point that dialogue is both an indicator of development and a mediator for development—dialogue is both the product of development and the basis for processes of development—and that is why in the very title of the introductory chapter in this book, I have equated dialogue with development. Encounters with different others and foreign cultures only open up possibilities for creative understanding, but the individual must respond dialogically for that to happen. A simple assemblage of divergent viewpoints and diverse cultures does not translate into dialogicality, for each could remain untouched by the other or identities could become amorphous and cultures fragmented. There must be serious engagement.

Bakhtin's discussion of the relationship between the spirit and soul—the free, wandering spirit always in search of loopholes and the stable soul that sets the rhythm for momentary closure—is basically a journey of growth, learning, and the unfolding of personal and collective experience. It is the journey of life itself: journeys in self-exploration and self-realization. Learning to feel at home in the world of other people is eventually to find comfort in your own skin, and to find truth and beauty in the surrounding world. The movement between the spirit and the soul allows one to find humanity in the most unusual places and have the courage to defy recognizable forms of defiance; in other words, nothing about life is standardized or formulaic. It is all about finding and giving meaning to experiences and observations, as Bakhtin writes eloquently that the purpose of entering the world of another is "to be able to go on from confession—to objective aesthetic contemplation, from questions about meaning and searching for meaning—to the world as a beautiful given" (AHAA, p. 111). Poet Rabindranath

Tagore (1971) puts it nicely in his famous work "Gitanjali" ("Song Offerings"): *"The traveller has to knock at every alien door to come to his own, and one has to wander through all the worlds to reach the innermost shrine at the end"* (Stanza 12). The bottom line is, as one travels in the wide-open world, one goes deeper into the self.

It would be erroneous to think that frequent encounters with foreign others is a new reality of our globalized world, and hence assume that the world is getting more dialogic. It would be akin to saying that human communication—in the true sense of its meaning—has improved because of advances in communication technology. If anything, we see the opposite trend. Therefore, it is not unique to the modern world, because traditional societies had their own ways of recognizing the need for the other as a global truth, or accepted variation in creation as the workings of a higher or an unknown power, and hence were far more accommodating to differences. Ashis Nandy observes that in traditional and pluralistic India, "heaven and hell, sanity and insanity, the self and the other, more often than not spill into each other" (2001, p. 8). Traditional societies like India rarely tried to demarcate between these dualities and therefore were far more accommodating of eccentric and peculiar individuals and their seemingly inexplicable practices or spiritual pursuits. The modern world, on the other hand, is more likely to attach a label of pathology to eccentric or atypical behavior. Globalization also has led to dangerous levels of homogenization, and, sadly, the consequence of this is the loss of creative potential in understanding human relations.

Authoring the self is not the sole activity of self and, interestingly, according to Bakhtin, the activity of authoring does not end with death. If the soul is given to the other as a gift for the sake of consummation, Bakhtin says, death itself is a complete gift to the other, so that the other might continue with the activity of authoring. Entry into the world and exit from the world do not hold any significance to the self because they are events in the lives of others:

> My birth, my axiological abiding in the world, and finally, my death are events that occur neither *in me* nor *for* me. The emotional weight of my own life *taken as a whole* does not exist for me myself.
>
> (AHAA, p. 105)

Bakhtin's idea of death as a gift to the other reminds me of verses of various mystic poets from India, who have communicated in various languages in a variety of ways a fundamental philosophy of life—*you enter the world crying, while others are rejoicing, but live in such a way that you leave the world rejoicing with a smile on your face, while others are crying and it is in their bereavement that the soul continues to live and grow*—one must live in such a way that your death becomes a worthy gift for the other.

Death does not finalize anything. The other continues with the activity of authoring . . .

6

DIALOGIC METHOD FOR HUMAN SCIENCES

Between the Message Giver—Message—
Messenger—and Message Receiver

> So you see it as if you knew *that* about it.
> And if this seems a foolish way of putting it,
> Then it must be kept in mind that the *concept* of seeing it is modified by it.
> Ludwig Wittgenstein, Remarks on the Philosophy of
> Psychology, *Vol. II, #386, 1980, p. 71e*

Equipped with grand theories, the message seeker confidently begins the research project, almost assuming that he knew something or many things about *that*, which he sets out to investigate. But that *that* doesn't always fit the frame that the researcher has in mind, and so what, then, are the available options? Change the methodology assuming that the experimental apparatus has been inadequate or inappropriate for the study? Or change the framework for presenting the findings by carefully highlighting the desired results? Or question the paradigm? Or recognize the inherent paradox that can be neither ignored nor accounted for and perhaps this would be most difficult because academic writing wants certainties and not ambiguities, even if the former is false and the latter is the very nature of inquiry in human sciences. The monologic impulse and demands are so forceful at every step of the research process, and recognition of that impulse is perhaps the first step in a move toward dialogic methodology. Between the extremity of "utter skepticism," which is nihilistic and crippling to the researcher, and "dogmatism," which results in unjustifiable interpretations and unreal claims, there is a middle course of "partial skepticism" that allows you to venture out to research with confidence and yet find room for reflection at every phase (Pepper, 1942).

Vincent Crapanzano likens the researcher to the mythical figure Hermes—an inventive genius and a prankster—a messenger of gods who escorts dead souls to the underworld. The researcher, like Hermes, is a trickster in search of a message, and to get it, he must trick the message givers into believing that he will deliver their message, despite the fact that the message givers never sought him out in the first place. The messenger is also eager to convince the message receivers, and therefore must resort to alternating between mystifying (in order to beckon the message receivers) and demystifying (in order to display his competence in analysis) the message. About the desire and predicaments of a researcher, Crapanzano observes:

> He lives in a world charged with value, with loyalties, and with animosities. He cannot simply repeat the message he has heard. (Even direct quotation requires reframing.) He has to understand the message, to interpret it, translate, contextualize, and elaborate it, and he has to justify all these procedures. He has responsibility!
>
> *(1992, p. 3)*

In the spirit of dialogism, I want to extend Crapanzano's "He has responsibility" to "we have responsibility" to recognize and acknowledge that in the movement from gathering message to representing and interpreting it and drawing theoretical conclusions there tends to be inevitable gentle transitions and transformations and occasionally even dramatic shifts. But often our academic compulsions force us to mask or deny the activity that occurs during the transitional phase. Acknowledging this cannot be the sole responsibility of the researcher. The research community—the philosophy of science—needs to acknowledge the dialogic movement between the message giver–message–messenger and message receiver.

Investigative Practices and Their Resistance to Dialogicality in Psychology

Methodology was the very basis for the birth of psychology as a discipline. Psychology established itself as a scientific discipline at the time of its birth, and, having borrowed the principles of investigation from hardcore sciences, it embraced logical-technical features and celebrated rational virtues. Therefore a variety of psychometrics like ratings on Likert type scales, test scores, and distribution of responses, among others, are treated as admissible evidence. Methodological orthodoxy that claims to present "definitive" results, even if they are questionable, is favored over theoretical sophistication that points out ambiguities, open-endedness, and context dependency. Kurt Danziger aptly points out that our preoccupations with the "purity of method frequently deteriorate to a kind of method fetishism or 'methodolatry'" (1990, p. 5).

When psychology established itself as an independent discipline in the late 1800s, it tried to break free from its roots in philosophy to align itself with physiology and physics, thus making legitimate claims for a scientific status. Therefore, all traces of social thought had to be erased.

Is it because of psychology's unwavering commitment to scientific method—borrowed from hardcore sciences—that it shows stiff resistance to dialogicality? Well, that would imply that dialogic method is contrary to science. Or is it the case that dialogism's notion of what constitutes science is very different from the positivist definition? Bakhtin's "methodological introduction" to the study of the science of art in his early lectures and comments of 1924–1925 clarifies his position on the differences between what constitutes "science" in the natural sciences and in the human sciences:

> The tendency of *Kunstwissenschaft* [is] to establish a distinct scientific discipline that deals with art and is independent from general philosophical aesthetics. Meanwhile, the scientific character of a branch of knowledge is defined in terms of two exact (constitutive) characteristics: its relation to the empirical and its relation to mathematics; such is the scientific character of natural sciences. Another type of scientific (of the two solely existing types) is the scientific character of the human sciences, defined by their relation to empirical reality and their relation to meaning and purpose. The type of experience in the human sciences is quite different; what is important here is its intensiveness. The fact that one kind of experience is fully formed while the other is still in [the] process of formation leads to the attempts to transpose the methods of positive science upon artistic creation.
>
> (2001, p. 206)

A few points deserve our concentrated attention in engaging with Bakhtin's cautionary account of the dangers of mechanically extending the principles and methods of natural sciences to human sciences. First of all, he asserts that the very nature of the subject matter is different because the science of the natural world is established by "its relation to the empirical" and subsequently the relation of the observable to logic and mathematics, whereas the science of the human world is characterized by its relation to the empirical reality—meaning the vantage point of relating to the observable—and, more important, the connection between the point of view and meaning and purpose. Furthermore, unlike the natural world that is somewhat "fully formed" and voiceless—meaning it is incapable of directly challenging the observer's interpretation—the social world is forever in the "process of formation" and is fully "voiced" to challenge your interpretation. Bakhtin argues that to transpose a product-oriented approach that lends itself to logical and mathematical scrutiny on to a process-oriented phenomenon that resists principles of mathematics would be problematic and erroneous. Moreover, consistent transposition of the methods of positive sciences on human science would be impossible, says Bakhtin, and the inconsistency leads to rash scientific claims and "pretended judgments that are numerous and yet completely disconnected from each other" (2001, p. 207). Therefore, in a very Bakhtinian sense, copying the methods of the physical sciences for studying the human world amounts to being not anti-science, but being unscientific. Hence, this would mean that dialogicality is at the very heart of human sciences, and in fact dialogicality alone establishes the scientific integrity of studying the human world. In his later works on methodology, Bakhtin further reiterates the indispensability of dialogicality for studying and understanding the human world:

> The exact sciences constitute a monologic form of knowledge: the intellect contemplates a *thing* and expounds upon it. There is only one subject here—cognizing (contemplating) and speaking (expounding). In opposition to the subject there is only a *voiceless thing*. Any object of knowledge (including man) can be perceived and cognized as a thing. But a subject as such cannot be perceived and studied as a thing, for as a subject it cannot, while remaining a subject, become voiceless, and consequently, cognition of it can only be *dialogic*.
>
> (TMHS, p. 161)

One might very well want to question Bakhtin's clear demarcation between exact sciences and human sciences and the knowledge of the former being monologic and the latter being dialogic, and such a discussion, although worthwhile, is beyond the scope of this book. However, we can acknowledge that Bakhtin's argument on the dialogic nature of the human world is persuasive enough to lead us toward the dialogic method.

It is imperative to recognize the multiple senses of Bakhtin's argument on dialogicality. First, because the various elements in the world are interconnected dialogically, our worldview must be built on the principles of dialogism. Second, dialogism is more than a worldview; it is a method. Interestingly, the dialogic method does not necessarily dispense with concepts and phrases like precision, accuracy, and depth that are endemic to the natural sciences; instead, Bakhtin distinguishes what these concepts mean in each of these sciences:

> The limit of precision in natural science is identity ($a = a$). In human sciences precision is surmounting the otherness of the other without transforming him into purely one's own (any kind of substitution, modernization, nonrecognition of the other, and so forth).
>
> (TMHS, p. 169)

The equation "$a = a$" would be valid in the exact sciences, but in the human sciences it would be invalid because doing so would silence the very subject you are trying to study. Therefore, imposing depersonalizing grids and predetermined trajectories would be antithetical to the dialogic method.

Framing the Issues and Raising the Questions

Theoretical assumptions are embedded in the very way we frame the issue, and the manner in which questions are articulated determines the range of possible answers. Ambiguity, multidimensionality, and open-endedness, I believe, are integral to human experiences and processes of thinking, speaking, and emoting, whereas the vast majority of psychological research is based on a cause and effect, stimulus-response model that tends to break consciousness down into its constituent elements and establish mechanical links between them. Interestingly, almost 100 years back, William James cautioned about the dangers of arresting the flow of consciousness:

> Consciousness, then, does not appear to itself chopped up in bits. Such words as "chain" or "train" do not describe it fitly as it presents itself in the first instance. It is nothing jointed; it flows. A "river" or a "stream" are the metaphors by which it is most naturally described.
>
> *(1920, p. 159)*

If consciousness is a free-flowing stream, then it can be studied only in relation to the surrounding conditions, as a live entity and not as a thing composed of parts. In an attempt to mimic hardcore sciences, psychological research has been primarily preoccupied with the "what" question—what is consciousness made of?—as if by identifying the constituent elements and adding them up, we arrive at the wholesome picture. William James points out the dangers of arresting the flow. "The traditional psychology talks like one who should say a river consists of nothing but a pailsful, spoonful, quartpotsful, barrelsful and other moulded forms of water" (1920, p. 165). Whereas, how the free water continues to flow—whether as a calm stream or a rapidly flowing stream—is dependent on the nature of the landscape it is flowing in, and hence a scoop of water from a flowing stream cannot in any way offer explanation about its nature. That being so, if scooping water from the stream to study it gives an erroneous and/or inadequate account of the stream, then perhaps one needs to go with the flow to understand how and why it takes several directions and when it tends to be calm and when it becomes forceful. Interestingly, almost 100 years after William James announced the stream of consciousness, John Shotter (2011) proposed a "Withness-Thinking" as a way of studying the flowing stream instead of a "whatness-thinking" that is so prevalent in psychological research, and makes a persuasive case for the dialogic method as an appropriate way to pursue withness-thinking.

Because human activity entails the presence and participation of the other, the "withness-thinking" not only considers the phenomenon under study as a joint activity with multiple participants, but also sees the very nature of research as a joint activity. In this model, one breaks free from "aboutness" thinking that accords undue power and authority to the researcher to give his supposedly neutral and roving perspective on the topic he is studying, while the "witness-thinking" situates both the researcher and the researched—the messenger and the message giver—on a horizontal plane in a dialogic relationship.

What, then, is the difference between the dialogical "witness" thinking and the monological "aboutness" thinking in terms of the information they yield? Shotter opines that the difference is not so much in the information as in our attitude and ways of relating to the queried phenomenon: "withness-talk and writing can move us toward new ways of being *with* and *relating to* the others and otherness around us as we talk or write, whereas aboutness-talk and writing leaves us 'unmoved,' leaves us resolutely adopting the same standpoint during our talk to the one we adopted prior to it" (2011, p. 180). Fixed, stable, and neutral position in relating to the investigated phenomenon demands that one remains unmoved and unchanged, lest it should contaminate the presumed scientific purity. Human nature and lived life are marked by incertitude, and hence trying to force tumultuous and contradictory reality into the straightjacket of an objective and absolute truth ironically takes one far away from reality, subsequently making it unscientific.

The "aboutness" method is fundamentally Cartesian—that is, when something is approached with a set of given rules and obeyed exactly as stipulated, then the knowledge of that something is made possible and others who obey the very same rules are sure to arrive at the same conclusion. Thus, verification validates both the phenomenon and the systematic rules.

The challenge to the Cartesian method came long ago, almost 300 years back, when Italian thinker Giambattista Vico (1990) gave his most comprehensive and compelling criticism in his early work—*On the Study Methods of Our Time*—fundamentally opposing the encroachment of the mathematical method not only in the humanities, but also in other fields of science like medicine, cosmology, and physics. Vico's differences with Descartes are not only on methodological issues, but also at a much deeper level as they have different conceptions of man. For Vico, more than rationality and intellect marks man; he is driven in addition by fantasy, passion, and emotion and, more important, linked to history and culture (Gianturco, 1990). In such an integral approach, the individual is seen not as an isolated and independent entity, but in relational terms—in relation to the surrounding system, to the world that lies beyond its borders and the dynamic interplay between them. Gianturco explains that Vico approached the study of man with the mind-set of a "jurist" in a "spirit of erudition," while Descartes approached it with the mind-set of a mathematician, guided by the principles of "exact sciences" (1990, p. xxviii). Vico insists that studies in the human sciences must be guided by the spirit of erudition because it not only captures "what is" but also "what could be," and such possibilities are made visible only in a humanistic education and method. In his introduction to Vico's work, Gianturco observes that "Vico is the true forerunner of educational, and especially child-educational, psychology" (1990, xli). Although Rousseau is often recognized as the father of developmental psychology, Gianturco believes that Vico is the "authentic precursor of Rousseau" (ibid.). In sum, Vico insists on humanistic education that resists compartmentalization of knowledge and pursues a historical method to make sense of the human world. Historical method does not mean taking snapshots at different points in history to show before and after or past and present contrast, rather, to study historically means to study something as it is undergoing change and transformation, or something that resists change despite the passage of time.

For Vico, the spirit of inquiry is based on and determined by our conceptions of knowledge and learning, and he finds value in the art of using language—eloquence—as the ancients did to frame issues and posit questions. He says that the methodology of the sciences may provide valuable data on what is measurable, but the method of eloquence reaches areas of human consciousness that go way beyond the reach of the measuring instruments of the exact sciences. Wisdom and changing structures of consciousness are not easily measurable, but detectable and definable, and moreover they are not quantifiable, but nevertheless cognizable, and, therefore, to access them, one must repossess the ancient art of eloquence because, as Vico eloquently puts it, "wisdom, which is mind and language, is the perfecter of man in his properly being man" (1990, p. 90). In sum, methodology in the human sciences must be skillful in the art of language—to frame questions that make room for numerous possibilities, and to detect in the answers the various meanderings of the flow of consciousness.

What, then, is the nature of the relationship between question and answer in this history-sensitive dialogic method? If the method is concerned with macro- and micro-historical processes, then temporalities become central, and question and answer cannot be seen as a transfer of information in space—to and fro between the questioner and the answerer—instead they generate each other, as Bakhtin observes:

> *Question* and *answer* are not logical relations (categories); they cannot be placed in one consciousness (unified and closed in itself); any response gives rise to a new question. Question and answer presuppose mutual outsideness. If an answer does not give rise to a new question from itself, it falls out of the dialogue and enters systemic cognition, which is essentially impersonal.
>
> (*TMHS*, p. 168)

In the witness-thinking of the dialogical method, posing fixed questions would be problematic because it would then recognize only one subject—the subject of the research—and the voice of the researching subject that plays a significant role is masked or downplayed in the name of neutrality and objectivity. Bakhtin argues that when question and answer fall out of dialogue, the responses of the answerer are mechanically turned into abstract concepts, but the reality, in his view, is that "the subject can never become a concept (he himself speaks and responds)" (TMHS, p. 169). Because the uniqueness of the chronotopes occupied by the questioner and answerer is disregarded in the "neutral" world, the "question and answer are inevitably depersonified" (p. 168). Bakhtin asserts that only contextual meanings that emerge in interrelationships between the *other and I* have the scope of becoming personalistic. In other words, only in a true dialogue where there is a question, an address, and an anticipation of a response would a tacit recognition of one or more "super addressees" carry greater authenticity. Does this mean that objectivity is compromised? Bakhtin clarifies that "personalization is never subjectivization" (TMHS, p. 167) because only in interrelationships with other personalities can the uniqueness of each voice be heard. Context-dependent personalized voices, in Bakhtin's view, are open-ended and unfinalized, always striving toward the limit of reification and personification, but never reach it. Herein lies the developmental potential of dialogicality.

Dialogue is both an indicator and a mediator of development, and hence the process-oriented dialogic method can trace developmental pathways and also lead one to developmental milestones along the way, and this was a central concern for Lev Vygotsky when he addressed methodological issues in studying higher mental functions:

> The search for method becomes one of the most important problems of the entire enterprise of understanding the uniquely human forms of psychological activity. In this case, the method is simultaneously prerequisite and product, the tool and the result of the study.
>
> *(1978, p. 65)*

In sum, the methodology that Vico, Vygotsky, and Bakhtin, among many others, propose is the one that simultaneously uncovers the directions that forms of life take and sets up other directions that one could take, so that there is a creation of novelty, new developmental moments. Such a methodology clearly identifies the factors that enhance or inhibit growth and change.

Play of Language and Modes of Communication in the Dialogic Method

The central focus in the dialogic method is on the play of language—what happens when two or more individuals come into living, responsive contact with each other—so much so that there is a continuous creation of new realities. The unit is more than an amalgam of mechanically connected parts; they constitute an indivisible whole. To understand and appreciate meanings that emerge in the communicative activity, one must be sensitive to use of language and cultural context. As a wholesome unit, how is language used in conversation? Is it inflexible or pliant or is one party using words in ways that are rigorous and unbending, while the other party is more relaxed in its usage? The researchers, I would argue, have greater responsibility to make language more supple and adjustable to human habits and customs. In other words, create conditions that are conducive to open-ended dialogue.

What, then, is the relationship between language as a system and individual consciousness? Volosinov offers some cogent explanations in this regard, as he challenges the position of abstract objectivism that views the system of language as independent of individual consciousness. He observes that "representatives of abstract objectivism are inclined to assert *the unmediated reality, the unmediated objectivity of language as a system of normatively identical forms*" (1986, p. 67). If language as a system is disconnected from its users, then it would be reduced to mechanical signs—an "inert system of self-identical norms"—but in reality what we witness is "ceaseless generation of language norms" (p. 66). Volosinov argues that the speaker only picks up words, phrases, and utterances from normatively identical forms, and for the sake of argument, assuming they exist in the cultural atmosphere according to prevailing conventions, and applies them to a specific context, thereby investing utterances with unique meanings that are changeable and adaptable.

The issues that concern us in formulating research design and questions are about sensitivity to the subjective nature of word meanings and also about setting up communicative patterns that allow for change and reflection. Take, for instance, studies that generate an adjective checklist on what men and women are like, and, if men are described as strong and competitive and women as emotional and cooperative, one must be mindful of the fact that what the respondents meant in stating the adjective could be very different. It is more than dictionary meaning. Words can have positive or negative connotations and be charged with sarcasm or uttered with a sideward glance. Associating women with emotions could have many meanings—that they are essentially emotional, or considered emotional, or their actions are indiscriminately interpreted as emotional because of assumptions of patriarchy in societies, or it can have a positive ring, meaning women express emotions freely, or it could be said in a pejorative sense, translated into "they nag"—and hence context and tone matter in endowing words with meanings. Thus, generating an adjective checklist without proper explanations could lead to an erroneous or a limited interpretation of what was meant.

On setting up conducive communicative patterns in research interviewing, it would be instructive to review Lotman's discussion on two communication systems; he identifies "I-s/he" as the most typical form of communication, in which the message or information is transmitted from one party to another—a mechanical transfer in space—whereas another kind is the "I-I" system, where the information/message generated by the self is re-transmitted to the self, and in this process, the content and the code of information undergoes transformation. In the "I-I" model, there is a dynamic change in the content and code, and information is transferred in time. Lotman explains that in the "I-s/he" system, the movement of the message is from addresser to addressee, and so the bearer of information changes but the message and its code remain as constants. In the "I-I" system, the bearer of the information remains the same, but the "message is reformulated and acquires new meaning during the communicative process" (1990, p. 22). This qualitative transformation of message in the "I-I" system, Lotman (1990) explains, "leads to a restructuring of the actual 'I' itself." A genuine research on development must then be ultra-sensitive to set up an "I-I" system to detect shifts that occur in thought processes. Lev Vygotsky also argues that any study of development demands a method that "reconstructs all the points in the development of a given structure" (1978, p. 65), and that would imply studying something historically, meaning to study it in the process of change, and Lotman's "I-I" system would enable it. The "I-s/he" system, according to Lotman, can generate and transmit quantity of information, whereas the "I-I" system shows qualitative shifts that occur, capturing the micro-genesis of developmental events that concerned Vygotsky.

In an earlier work on narrating life stories and interpreting an ancient epic text, The Mahabharata, I structured my research method along the "I-I" communication model to give ample opportunities for my subjects to reflect on their life events and restructure the "I," and I found that despite the beckoning call of the model for reassessment of their earlier account, many resisted the call and a few entered the dialogic space to reflect and reconstruct. Here is my description of the method and the nature of the narratives generated:

> My questions were open-ended and the respondents constructed their own plots. I did not approach my subjects with a standard set of questions, but had some themes, such as chapters in their life stories, turning points and twists and turns in their stories, significance of geographical locations and/or the relationships that were important in their lives. I tried to explore and elaborate on whatever themes the respondents focused on. I was an attentive and an active listener and periodically would relay their own recollections to facilitate extra semantic layering and/or shift in semantic codes. My pull was towards temporality in the narratives, to which some responded while others simply resisted and spatialized time. In the former there was the fullness of temporality in the narratives, and during the joint construction of the narratives, we not only communicated with each other, but also with ourselves trying to grope for common points of reference. This process of autocommunication created layers of meaning both for the self and for the cultural process, leading to a sharper image of the self in a broad episteme. Whereas in the narratives dominated by spatial categories, the communication model was unilateral, the respondents narrated their account of events in their lives and resisted revisiting them to explore other possible meanings.
>
> (Bandlamudi, 2010, p. 41)

A few observations about the trends in my earlier research: despite the deployment of the dialogic method, not all subjects responded to the dialogic potential. This trend is indicative of something very crucial about dialogue itself; many factors play a role in generating dialogue; that is, willingness on the part of the subject, favorable conditions—meaning research methodology that enables it—and probing questions and attentive inter-listening on the part of the researcher and the intersection of these factors play a critical role. Furthermore, as I have been suggesting all along in this book, dialogue is an indicator and a mediator of development, and despite the availability of mediators, not all subjects avail them; instead, they stick stubbornly to their monologic habits. But if the methodology does not create possibilities for dialogue, we would not be able to understand and appreciate the intersection of multiple factors that enable or inhibit dialogue. In an effort to advance the dialogic method, Paul Sullivan and John McCarthy observe that the Menippean genre of dialogue makes room for imagination and ethics, in contrast to Socratic and Magistral dialogues that lean toward monologue. The authors observe that the "Menippean dialogue points us in the direction of inquiry as a personal and creative act that places voices (including the authorial voice) in contact with each other with the capacity to enrich and change each other" (2005, p. 621). In a related article, Sullivan and McCarthy (2009) point out that the dialogic method has the unique capability to capture the perception and production of art as a lived experience, thus showcasing the centrality of selfhood in artistic processes. In sum, the message giver, the message, and the messenger have the potential to evolve in the dialogic method.

Making Sense: Analytical Tools of the Dialogic Method

Having generated rich narratives through the dialogic "I-I" model, the equally important next step is to deploy sharp analytical tools that can point out stasis and movement in the narratives. Questions that concern us in approaching the narratives are about ontological positioning, worldview or worldviews presented by the individual, shifts that might occur during the narrative production, and so on. What is the image of the person sketched out in the narrative? Where is the positioning of the subject in the cultural matrices and what is the nature of the relationship with the surrounding culture and historical forces? And, for analytical purposes, how then do we draw connections between "what was said" and individual consciousness?

Because all areas of human life involve using language in one form or another, we need to be attentive to the nature of the forms of its use. Bakhtin tells us that "Language is realized in the form of individual concrete utterances" (PSG, p. 60) and "thematic content, style and compositional structure" (ibid.) constitute utterances. Because language in action cannot be separated from cultural conditions, "each sphere in which language is used develops its own *relatively stable types* of utterances" (ibid.), and these context specific utterances, according to Bakhtin, are called *"speech genres"* (ibid.). While individuals make utterances, the range of meanings they acquire is dependent on cultural conventions, thus establishing interconnections between the individual and cultural conditions. Furthermore, genres are not mechanical linguistic devices, and in order to use and understand them, we need to move beyond linguistics to metalinguistics. Because various spheres of cultural life have their own stable form of genres, Bakhtin observes that the individual needs more than a mastery of vocabulary to effectively communicate in each sphere; one needs the ability to "command a repertoire of genres of social conversation" (PSG, p. 80). That is why one could be a great conversationalist in one sphere of cultural life and embarrassingly inept in other spheres.

For the researcher, the first step in analyzing narratives is to recognize and understand the sphere from which the message giver is generating the narrative because the sphere would say a lot about the genre used. For instance, in my earlier work on interpreting segments from a television production of The Mahabharata, my respondents were entering different spheres. Some of them, particularly the older generation, saw themselves as participating in the "epic culture," and it so happened that the medium was television, whereas other subjects saw themselves as engaging in "television culture" and the program happened to be the epic text (Bandlamudi, 2010). The differences in spheres clearly contributed to differences in lexicon and phraseology. In short, the mind's eye was seeing things differently, while the physical eyes saw the same thing.

The mind's eye is the genre that perceives and conceptualizes reality, and seeing and understanding is inseparable from the process embodying it in a specific genre. As Bakhtin and Medvedev explain, "the reality of the genre and the reality accessible to the genre are organically interrelated" (1985, p. 135). Therefore, it would be erroneous to think that one perceives and understands reality and then uses genre as a device to give form and express it. It is the organic relationship between them that links the produced narrative with human consciousness:

> We think and conceptualize in utterances, complexes complete in themselves. As we know, the utterance cannot be understood as a linguistic whole, and its forms are not syntactic forms. These integral, materially expressed inner acts of man's orientation in reality and the forms of these acts are very important. One might say that human consciousness possesses a series of inner genres for seeing and conceptualizing reality.
>
> *(p. 134)*

While there is an organic connection between consciousness and genre, Bakhtin and Medvedev stress that neither does the consciousness finalize the functions of genres and nor do genres finalize consciousness. The task is conceptualization and not finalization. Similarly, the relationship between genre and reality is also a complex one; as Bakhtin and Medvedev say succinctly, "Genre appraises reality and reality clarifies genre" (p. 136).

A genre is also incredibly selective in picking only a few aspects of reality, and by this token it sheds light on some aspect and is equally blind to other aspects of reality; it also decides on the range it wants to cover and how deep it wants to go, and that is "why people and cultures need continually to learn new genres as the compass of experience expands" (Morson and Emerson, 1990, p. 276). A dialogic consciousness, ever interested in expanding its horizon, would then be in perennial search for new genres, and hence the narratives could have an interesting mix of genres, unlike the fixed genres of monologic consciousness.

How do we make generic distinctions between various types of genres? Bakhtin offers another tool—the chronotope—spatial and temporal relationships that are intrinsic to genres. Bakhtin demonstrates that various types of novels could be classified effectively using this analytical tool. Using chronotopic analysis, I have classified various theoretical models on development in "The Novel and the Hero" chapter in this book, so I shall keep the discussion on this topic somewhat brief. But it is worth reiterating the key functions of the chronotope— that the "image of man is always chronotopic" (FTCN, p. 85) and that "every entry into the sphere of meanings is accomplished only through the gates of [the] chronotope" (p. 256).

In a dialogic approach, we are interested in the image of a person in relation to the cultural space and historical time. Rich narratives display intricately interwoven chronotopes that may coexist, or replace each other or render the other chronotope somewhat insignificant, or they may clash with one another. These complexities mark dialogicality.

Does this mean that quantitative data are anathema to dialogic method? With so much focus on analyzing qualitative narratives, it would appear to be the case. Interestingly, Bakhtin does not dismiss quantitative statistical data, but points out important differences between them. Toward the end of his long essay on the forms of time and the chronotope, Bakhtin addresses chronotopic analyses in numerical and narrative data:

> In conclusion we should touch upon one more important problem, that of the boundaries of chronotopic analysis. Science, art and literature also involve *semantic* elements that are not subject to temporal and spatial determinations, of such sort, for instance, are all mathematical concepts: we make use of them for measuring spatial and temporal phenomena but they themselves have no intrinsic spatial and temporal determinations; they are [the] object of our abstract cognition. They are an abstract and conceptual figuration indispensable for the formalization and strict scientific study of many concrete phenomena.
>
> *(FTCN, p. 257)*

Interestingly, the dialogic method is not necessarily averse to numerical data; in fact, descriptive, correlational, and experimental studies do yield data to capture certain aspects of individual and cultural phenomena. But those phenomena must be endowed with meaning, and to do so we must bring them "not only into the sphere of spatial and temporal existence but also into the semantic sphere" (p. 257). Entry into the semantic sphere is not possible without passing through the "gates of chronotope." In short, numbers do speak for themselves and they also enter into dialogue when brought into the semantic sphere.

Does the dialogic method have a monopoly over qualitative data analysis? Apparently not, for there are many other models like grounded theory, discourse analysis, narrative analysis, and phenomenological analysis. How does the dialogic method stand in comparison to these existing models? To address this question, I turn to the comprehensive work done by Paul Sullivan (2012) in "Qualitative Data Analysis Using a Dialogical Approach," in which he draws clear distinctions between various qualitative methods. Borrowing the concepts of "bureaucracy" and "charisma" from Max Weber, Sullivan applies them to a few widely used qualitative methods to point out ways they establish authority in the interpretive process. He explains that the "Grounded Theory" engages in a "line-by-line" coding—in an almost reductionist manner—and every code is labeled and compiled to deliver the overall message. The "fine-grained discourse analysis" identifies the "interpretive repertoires" and turn-taking functions in the narrative, and goes great lengths to rhetorically protect the study from potential criticism, while the large-scale "discourse analysis" concentrates on power dynamics and linguistic features to substantiate the theoretical position. The "narrative analysis" concentrates on plot types, metaphors, and tropes to link narratives to lived experience, while the "phenomenological analysis" is keen on identifying themes and meaning units in an analytic style. Unlike these models that are strong on either bureaucratic or charismatic elements and are quite inflexible in establishing their authority, Sullivan argues, the dialogic method not only allows for greater flexibility between bureaucracy and charisma, but also makes room for the selective process in all phases of research.

> I am suggesting that a dialogic analysis can be used in a bureaucratic way—leaving an audit trail—but with charismatic elements nonetheless—e.g., choosing extracts that reflect personal interest; judging what transcription symbols to use; judging how the audience will react to particular directions in the analysis; judging how to present the argument and how the data fits in with this.
>
> *(2012, p. 80)*

In sum, from the time of conceptualizing an idea, a problem, to sketching a research design to framing questions to analyzing data to reporting the findings, there is an inevitable dialogic transition, and, according to Bakhtin, that would be the very nature of human sciences.

Delivering Messages and the Message Receivers Enter the Dialogic Platform

While preparing to write a book after conducting research, Vincent Crapanzano (1992) reports of a dream he had in which a voice said, "the I of the now is not the I of the now," and of seeing an equation "I≠I." The "I" that conducted the research and the "I" that is now eager to report the results are not identical. For Bakhtin, the apparent reason is that the former and the latter "I" occupy different chronotopes. The stakes are different and the concerns are different. The reporting "I" wants to challenge conventions, and yet knows full well that one must abide, at least partially, to conventions, just to be heard. There is a biographical dimension in conveying the message, says Crapanzano, and yet the writing conventions demand masking it and expect the researcher to assume a fixed vantage point:

> We write as though we had a single controlling voice, and expect to be read as such. We are distressed by changes of voice, changes in attitude, introductory stances, which announce the inconstancy of the self and the instability of our vantage point.
>
> *(1992, p. 9)*

To assume "singularity, coherence, and constancy" is an illusion for both the messenger and the message receiver, says Crapanzano, and it is tantamount to disregarding the very nature of exchange as a fundamentally social activity.

Because every phase in research is a social activity, how you *see* and *interpret* the phenomenon is a matter of negotiation. Therefore the process as a whole entails disruptions, revelations, and surprises. In one of my research works—from the starting point of "finding the actors" to "staging the drama"—I wrote about the inevitable and necessary challenges to my confidence and certitude I was assuming at each stage:

> Contemplating a research project seemed relatively secure only because it was [a] "behind the desk" activity—there was only one party, me—in many ways uncontested. There were no subjects, no potential "heroines and heroes" to challenge my assumptions and my methods. The security of the contemplation phase was also its limitation, because even though the configuration of various "grand theories" had some veridicality, it was not constructed out of sincere dialogue with living subjects.
>
> *(Bandlamudi, 2010, p. 28)*

If the message givers pose a challenge at the beginning of the research, the message receivers pose a challenge when the findings are reported. Therefore, the researcher's role is indeterminate at every stage.

The indeterminacy of the researcher does not mean losing command. Dialogism and the dialogic method are built on multiplicity—multiple voices, multiple meanings, multiple layers, and multiple dimensions—and this calls for skillful orchestration by the researcher. Surely, murkiness and chaos are aspects of the dialogic world, but there is a method to the madness and at every phase in research, demands are placed on the researcher to reflect and carefully interpret the findings. It is easy to get overzealous in celebrating multiplicity and overlook the nature of multiplicity. It must be kept in mind that a simple mechanical assemblage of divergent viewpoints does not constitute dialogicality; metamorphosis must be achieved. Similarly, sensitivity and tact must be shown in interpreting single-voiced monologic discourses. For instance, discourses of hegemony and dominance and discourses that resist them may very well show similar chronotopic features, but there is an ocean of differences between voices of brute force and voices of resistance. The former has no desire or intent for a dialogue, while the latter might want a dialogue, but their voice is silenced, leaving them with no option but to resist. Additionally, there are no multiple viewpoints on certain topics like sexual assault, slavery, genocide, and many more. There is only strong, plain condemnation on such topics. Therefore, even as we applaud dialogicality, monologism, under certain conditions, must be interpreted with care and sensitivity.

Dialogue as an ideal, where there is a genuine anticipation and hope that the other or others will give you a fair hearing, could very well be knocked down in practice in the real world. It could easily be hurtful and damaging when reality decimates an ideal. Bakhtin was not blind to such possible betrayals, as Emerson explains:

> Read Bakhtin carefully, and you will see that nowhere does he suggest that dialogue between real people necessarily brings truth, beauty, happiness or honesty. It brings only concretization (and even that is temporary), and the possibility of change, of some forward movement. Under optimal conditions, dialogue provides options. But there can still be deception, mountains of lies exchanged, pressing desires unanswered or unregistered, gratuitous cruelty administered on terrain to which only the intimate beloved has access. By having real other respond to me, I am spared one thing only: the worst cumulative effects of my own echo chamber of words.
>
> (1997, pp. 152–153)

The deployment of the dialogic method is done not in naïveté—in search of some absolute ideal—but with a hope that the "other" brings to the field what you have not considered or overlooked. It is pursued with the full knowledge that the potential may or may not be realized. It takes enormous maturity and confidence to prepare the self to be unsettled, challenged, and changed by others. The self-confident researcher must know when and what to accept and reject. Making this responsible choice is the strength of the dialogic method.

7

DIFFERENCES AS THE WILL TO POWER AND FREEDOM TO CHOOSE

> The world's deep contrasts are but figures spun
> Draping the unanimity of the One.
> Contrasts, Sri Aurobindo, 1999, p. 135

> No limit to the ways in which the world can be interpreted;
> every interpretation a symptom of growth or of decline.
> Inertia needs unity (monism); plurality of interpretations a sign of strength.
> Not to desire to deprive the world of its disturbing and enigmatic character!
> Nietzsche, The Will to Power #600, 1967

I purposely chose the phrase "will to power" to show what can be gained from navigating a world of contrasts, not so much in the Nietzschean sense as much as to give the Nietzschean force to the depth Bakhtin gives to a world packed with differences. Power, freedom, and choice are much sought-after ideals, and these very ideals are subject to varied interpretations. Also, they are much used and abused concepts—very often, individuals claim sole proprietorship over them, disregarding the other and disrespecting the differences. Difference is also a much dreaded idea, for it is mistakenly understood that even acknowledging a world of differences somehow denigrates or contaminates an ideal—an ideal of unity and an ideal of sameness—as if it is an affront to the fanciful idea that "deep down, we are the same"—which, perhaps, doesn't deserve to be idealized in the first place.

Power, freedom, and choice are much-celebrated concepts worked out in hyper-individualistic philosophies, and to bring them into the world of contrasting differences—the world that regards the necessity of the other—and to show their potency would require a dramatic shift in perspective. In the world of sameness, one seeks an alibi for being. In the world of differences, there is no alibi for being. Bakhtin asks what there is to learn when there is fusion between the self and the other. What is there to gain when the other becomes a narcissistic extension of the self? The very idea of choice loses its validity if there is no variety in the menu to choose from. Even the author/creator—be it God, writer, or artist—needs a surplus of meanings to choose from and to consummate them, and the created must generate an abundance of meanings to re-authorize the author. The very act of creativity rests on variety.

Ideas about freedom find expression in a few distinct themes in Western philosophy; one is the "freedom as autonomy" that John Stuart Mill advanced in *On Liberty* (1985); and the second is the "freedom as enlightenment" that Plato promoted in *The Republic* (1945). Jean Jacques Rousseau (1979) in *Emile* saw freedom accompanying the child at the time of his birth; nature made sure that man was "born-free," but culture usurps what nature gives to force humans to obey its laws and plans. For Rousseau, freedom was a necessary condition for growth and development, and cultural interference distorts the natural course. In the philosophies of Mill, Plato, and Rousseau, the focus is exclusively on the individual. For Mill, individual autonomy must be guarded at any cost unless the individual's actions have the potential to harm others. For Plato, the release from the dark cave of limited and illusory sensory knowledge and movement toward the mind seeking true knowledge is freedom. The lone seeker's ascent from ignorance to enlightenment is an affirmation of freedom, while those who fail to reach the pinnacle remain enslaved by falsehood. For Mill, the other is to be ignored unless the intent is to prevent harm. The other is virtually absent in Plato's rational world, while in Rousseau's romantic world, the self must be left alone for nature's plan to unfold and also because the other could intrude on the self's autonomy and freedom. The main feature in these philosophies, as Sharon Schuman (2014) observes, is not just disagreement with competing philosophies, but dismissiveness of other viewpoints. As an alternate, Schuman proposes "dialogic freedom" that participates in co-construction of meanings and views divergent viewpoints as essential to our own freedom.

In the dialogic world that Bakhtin envisages, freedom is sanctioned to all—one is not at the expense of the other—in fact, one could say that true freedom for one is guaranteed only when the other is also truly free. Think about the trappings of a prison guard; neither the guard nor the prisoner can move from their spaces. Recognizing and regarding the other is not at the expense of self (Cresswell, 2011). When the dialogic relationship with the other is realized at every moment in life, life is always on the threshold of new beginnings, new developmental possibilities emerge, and freedom, power, and choice remain uncompromised; as Bakhtin observes about the author–hero relationship, "Dostoevsky's polyphonic novel is a *fully realized and thoroughly consistent dialogic position,* one that affirms the independence, internal freedom, unfinalizability and indeterminacy of the hero"

(PDP, p. 63). The bottom line is the free author recognizes and respects the free hero, even when the hero happens to be his creation.

So, what then is the appeal of the world of sameness? Why do we assign differences to the surface world and assert that deep down we are the same? What is the danger in thinking deep down we are different? For some cogent explication on these issues, I turn to a philosopher from India, Sri Aurobindo, who grounds the "Ideal of Human Unity" in the concept of "Diversity in Oneness," and the idea of "Oneness" is taken from Hindu cosmology/philosophy—that the Brahman, the absolute, formless, divine energy, must take diverse forms in its varied manifestations. Metaphysically, when these diverse forms converge into the "One," the differences are not erased but retained to show how the *one* can become *many*. Sri Aurobindo explains:

> But uniformity is not the law of life. Life exists by diversity; it insists that every group, every being shall be, even while one with all the rest in its universality, yet by some principle or ordered detail of variation unique. The over-centralization, which is the condition of a working uniformity, is not the healthy method of life. Order is indeed the law of life, but not artificial regulation.
>
> *(1997, p. 490)*

Culture is always heterogeneous; it cannot be any other way. In order to orchestrate the diverse elements, the popular slogan and demand is "unity in diversity," but Aurobindo and Bakhtin are likely to flip the equation and call for "diversity in unity" to retain the primacy of differences. Aurobindo argues that the self finds its genuine voice, its true freedom, and its strength and power in a world of differences: "the truest order is that which is founded on the greatest possible liberty; for liberty is at once the condition of vigorous variation and the condition of self-finding" (p. 490).

For Aurobindo, homogeneity amounts to cessation of life because the "pulse of life" could be measured only by the "richness of the diversities" it creates, and recognizing the life force of diversity allows one to engage with the dissonant other without any fear of disorder, confusion, or strife. Aurobindo points out that while diversity is essential for vigor and vitality of life, unity is necessary for order and stability; unity must be achieved, but not the kind grounded on uniformity. Aurobindo explains the reasons behind the pull of "deep down, we are the same":

> While the life power in man demands diversity, his reason favors uniformity. It prefers it because uniformity gives him a strong sense and ready illusion of unity in place of the real oneness at which it is so much more difficult to arrive. It prefers it, secondly, because uniformity makes easy for him the otherwise difficult business of law, order and regimentation.

> It prefers it too because the impulse of mind is to make every considerable diversity an excuse for strife and separation and therefore uniformity seems to him the one secure and easy way to unification.
>
> *(pp. 401–402)*

Erasing differences is a clever ploy; it allows dominant groups in a culture to pull other groups into their orbit and to define unity on their terms and create a façade of harmony. Interestingly, it is also a convenient escape, a timid act, because of unwillingness to deal with real reasons behind social disharmony and to create an illusion of unity. Under these circumstances, there is no room for empowerment of individuals; there is only gross abuse of power.

Aurobindo's call is for appreciation of uniqueness—uniqueness of individual acts, uniqueness of cultural practices, uniqueness of the call and need of the hour, and uniqueness of various avatars of God—over a hastily and temporarily glued unity that disregards uniqueness. To appreciate internal freedom and interior truth, one must highlight uniqueness. For Bakhtin also, the plenitude of differences in the world is so immense and that coupled with the solipsism that the individual cannot possibly transcend, leaves us with only partial glimpses of truth, and even that is subject to constant change. The validity of truth, according to Bakhtin, is in the "unity of the actual and answerably act-performing consciousness" (TPA, p. 38), and it is in this act that the individual leaves his signature, thereby taking ownership and fulfilling ethical responsibility and eventually gaining and affirming power. Bakhtin writes that "It is unfortunate misunderstanding (a legacy of rationalism) to think that truth can only be the truth that is composed of universal moments" (p. 37); this abstract universality, he says, is divorced from concrete individuality—the truth of the moment—and that is why Bakhtin asks us to set aside *unity* (as in universal moments) and focus instead on *uniqueness* (unrepeatable, individual, and faithful to actual time and space). Individual accountability perhaps is the best defense against dogma.

It is precisely because of the emphasis placed on individual responsibility and involvement that Bakhtin was drawn to "a *sense* of faith"—an attitude toward a Higher Power over plain faith—as "specific faith in orthodoxy" (PDP, p. 294). In his lecture on "Grounded Peace," Bakhtin (2001) states that the "task of philosophy of religion" is to understand how "prayer, ritual, hope" gain validity, for these concepts, along with confession and repentance, are aspects of "feeling for faith" rather than codified aspects of religion. A feeling for faith is diversified and inconclusive, while religion with its do's and don'ts is fixed and conclusive; as Emerson observes, " a "feeling for (or groping toward) faith is restless, engaged, at risk, conscious of being on the boundary with another and different substance" (2001, p. 188). The restless search, guided by committed feelings for faith, has the capacity to grow and diversify, and this builds a genuine regard for the other, who is likely to have a differing feeling for faith. That is why Bakhtin insists that "Philosophy of religion, inasmuch as it posits problems, must, initially, pose dogma itself as a problem, that is nondogmatically" (2001, pp. 207–208).

Bakhtin's call to "pose dogma itself as a problem" by the "philosophy of religion" could very well be extended to "philosophy of life" in general because dogma shows its ugly face in virtually all areas of life. Ironically, dogma itself comes in many forms in so many spheres of life, and detecting and questioning it is so vital to maintaining mental health in a world of differences. Religion is not the exclusive domain of dogma, although that is where its shows its most virulent form, and that is where it is most glaringly visible. In a healthy pluralistic society, governing bodies must give freedom for religions, and religion must sanction freedom for its practitioners, and practitioners must use freedom wisely and responsibly, and if certain members of a society want freedom from religion, then society must accommodate that too. We must recognize that in addition to religious dogmas, there are political dogmas, philosophical dogmas, ideological dogmas, theoretical and methodological dogmas, dogmas of mental health diagnosis, and many more. The list could be inexhaustible. It seems that no area of life is spared of dogma, and vigilance and concerted effort is needed to detect and confront it.

Consider the work of Vincent Crapanzano (2000)—*Serving the Word*—in which he juxtaposes the Bible and the Constitution to show the streak of rigid literalism in interpreting these texts. Instead of allowing for creative and refreshing interpretation of the text that responds to concrete concerns, Crapanzano points out that inflexible and monologic biblical scholars and constitutional experts resort to various rhetorical devices to restrict the range of possible meanings. In order to exercise their authority, words are pulled out of their meaningful context and their subjective interpretation—loaded with vested interest—is presented as the "divine law" or the "nation's law." Both claim that they are "serving the word" in the authoritative text and any variation in interpretation is dismissed as unfaithful or, worse, blasphemous to the sacred word, be it in the scripture or in the constitution.

The monologic context of literalism can be shattered or weakened only when there is a recognition of multiple temporalities at play in the interpretive act—the time of the text (when it was composed) and the time when the text is read—and this dialogic interplay between the "world" and the "law" represented in the text enters the real-life time-space only to be further enriched. Crapanzano rightly observes that literalism in the pulpit and on the bench is a very troubling trend in American life. Contrary to the claims made by those engaging in literal reading of a text, that their goal is to safeguard the text, they are in fact weakening or rendering the text dead and irrelevant to contemporary life. About the life of a text, Bakhtin writes, "The work and the world represented in it enter the real world and enrich it, and the real world enters the work and its world as part of the process of its creation, as well as part of its subsequent life, in a continual renewing of the work through the creative perception of listeners and readers"

(FTCN, p. 254). Bakhtin cautions that the world represented in the text and the world grappling with the text are not to be fused, nor are we to assume the boundaries are "absolute and impermeable" because such an assumption would lead to "oversimplified, dogmatic splitting of hairs"; he goes on to say that one must not "confuse the listener or reader of multiple and varied periods, recreating and renewing the text, with the passive listener or reader of one's own time (which leads to dogmatism in interpretation and evaluation)" (p. 253). In sum, in the dialogic world of differences, the commentator, the text, and the listeners gain potential to grow and acquire the will to power.

Brainstorming or Brainwashing in Group Decision Making?

A common practice in almost every institution is to periodically call for a "brainstorming" session to figure out a creative solution to a sticky problem. In theory, the principle is to invite the participants to freely think aloud and express their divergent viewpoints in the dialogic space and debate the merits and shortcomings of each viewpoint to arrive at a suitable solution. In principle, this assemblage of multiple voices has all the markings of a Bakhtinian dialogue in action. But what happens in reality? Practically, anybody who is employed, regardless of their position in the institutional hierarchy knows all too well that very often the "brainstorming" sessions fall short of the proclaimed ideals. Why do groups fail and what would make them succeed? In their popular book *Wiser* (2015), Cass R. Sunstein, a legal scholar and a former government official, and Reid Hastie, a professor of behavioral science in a business school, conduct a series of studies to identify the factors that contribute to the failure and success of group decision making. Interestingly, the examples they draw from a wide range of organizations—from the government to Google to the CIA—resonate well with Bakhtinian principles and, more important, validate the leitmotif of this book—*differences* (divergent viewpoints) when well orchestrated in a *dialogue* lead to the *development* (finding creative approaches) of an institution and its members. The authors observe that very often groups fail because, in practice, they move far away from brainstorming and get close to brainwashing, thus never allowing a dialogue to begin. The reasons are many; first, given the hierarchical nature of institutional structure, the employees, despite their direct knowledge of ground realities, hesitate to express their observations and thoughts freely for fear of repercussions, or they falsely assume that the authorities might have additional information that they are not privy to. Second, the social pressure to conform is immense in a group situation. These conditions create room only for chorus agreement, and Sunstein and Hastie identify the problems that emerge from this homogenous condition. The authors point out that instead of correcting errors of other members in a group, they amplify errors. Third, groups suffer from cascade effects—members blindly follow what the first speaker or dominant member said. The fourth problem that the authors point out is most critical to our increasingly polarized society—homogeneity leads to greater polarization, meaning members end up embracing more extreme version of ideas and ideals than what they started out with. For instance, if individuals had a mild leaning toward conservative political ideas, they may become more extreme and militant after being reinforced by others who share their political views. This is the classic case of seeking an alibi for your views that Bakhtin so vociferously opposed, and, it is clear, for a good reason. When individuals deliberated with people with differing political views, the extremism was toned down. Last, there was no cognitive gain when groups spoke in one voice because they focused on shared information, what everyone knew, rather than new information.

The takeaways of this study on institutions for our individual psychological concerns are many: agreement and absence of dissent leads not to the correction of errors, but amplification of errors and subsequent acceptance of errors. Second, it promotes a herd mentality rather than a freethinking individual. Third, intra-psychic dialogue of competing viewpoints and a pluralistic society with myriad philosophies is the best bet against militancy, fundamentalism, and violence. Last, for the mind to grow, new information and new insight are needed, and that can come only from exposure to competing ideas and theories and by lending your ears to multiple voices in society. Sunstein and Hastie arrived at the same conclusion:

> One of the particular advantages of diversity and dissent is that they promote two things that institutions need: creativity and innovation. When minority voices are heard, well-functioning groups are likely to be jolted out of their routines, and fresh solutions, even a high degree of innovation, can follow. When dissent and diversity are present and levels of participation are high, groups are likely to do a lot better.
>
> *(2015, p. 104)*

Living and moving in a world of differences—different personalities, different philosophies, different beliefs, and so on—does not in any way weaken the integrity and unity of the individual or the institution. In a monologic world truth is disembodied, impersonal, decontextualized, and de-historicized. Bakhtin insists that a unified truth, a well-integrated individual, and institutions promoting innovation are found not in a repressive monologic world, but in an open dialogic world:

> It should be pointed out that the single and unified consciousness is by no means an inevitable consequence of the concept of a unified truth. It is quite possible to imagine and postulate a unified truth that requires a plurality of consciousnesses, one that cannot in principle be fitted into the bounds of a single consciousness, one that is, so to speak, by its very

nature *full of event potential* and is born at a point of contact among various consciousnesses.

(PDP, p. 81)

When Sunstein and Hastie (2015) demonstrate that diversity and dissent make individuals smarter and institutions stronger, they offer real-world proof for what Bakhtin calls "event potential" in a pluralistic world, and for Nietzsche, this is the "will to power" that "interprets" because in the world of differences "it defines limits, determines degrees," and recognizes "variations of power" (#643). In such a world, nuanced thinking develops and thoughtful choices can be made.

Interior Truth and Internal Freedom *under* the Open Sky *on* an Uneven Earth

The vastness and illimitable nature of the open sky must surely beckon to the *spirit* that aspires to roam freely, but it must periodically yield, at least momentarily, to the rhythmic closure brought by the soul—coming from the other—operating in an uneven world. The open sky stands as an emblem to all that is ideal, infinite, abstract, and it is the desire, while the uneven earth is the reality, the finite, and the concrete. But the ideal, as Bakhtin would say, must intersect with the real to gain validity—ethical validity, aesthetic validity, and scientific validity—and it is at this intersection that dialogic truth, dialogic freedom, and also, I would add, dialogic development (central argument of this book) emerge.

Throughout Bakhtin's works, we hear his concerns with events on the "uneven earth," but he does not dismiss the "open sky" either; he insists on "the actual architectonic of the actually experienced world of life—the world of participant and deed performing consciousness" (TPA, p. 73). Bakhtin objects to a stand-alone, floating in the sky, so to speak, of "some sort of special *theoretical ought*"; instead, he reflects, "I must think veridically; veridicality or being-true is the ought of thinking" (p. 4). For Bakhtin, it is all about "grounded peace," "lived reality," "answerable acts"—all of them earthbound—and not ideas and ideals depicted in floating syllables of the sky. He points out that the "abstract value judgment by disembodied theoretical consciousness" can only speak of a generic individual, any individual, akin to Piagetian epistemic subject, but "incapable of engendering a concrete deed that is not *fortuitously* unique" (p. 78); for Bakhtin, the world is full of infinitely diversified particulars and disregarding them is unacceptable to him. Furthermore, he adds that abstract theoretical consciousness "can engender only a value-judgment about a deed *post factum* as an exemplar of a deed" (ibid.), but this abstract deed was once performed in a specific time and place, and to pluck it out of its specific context and present it as an independent entity in the open sky would be an incomplete picture.

Silence pervades the open sky and the uneven earth is unarguably noisy. What, then, is the role of silence in a dialogue? When is silence inert? What kind of silence or rather under what circumstances can silence ignite the mind and stir the imagination? Spiritual practices recognize the energizing power of meditative silence—one that connects you to interior truth and catalyzes liberation—that unfettered feeling, the internal liberation. In an interesting quatrain Rabindranath Tagore writes about the nature of exchange:

> "What language is thine, O sea?"
> "The language of eternal question."
> "What language is thy answer, O sky?"
> "The language of eternal silence."
>
> *(2002a, Stray Birds, #12, p. 288)*

Is silence a suitable response to a question? Does that constitute participation in a dialogue or a refusal? Is it a snub or consent, or an opportunity for the questioner to figure out the answer? To find some possible explanations, we find a suitable situation in the parable "The Grand Inquisitor" in Dostoevsky's famous work *The Brothers Karamazov*. After listening silently to all the accusations made by the grand inquisitor, Christ kisses him and leaves without saying a word. In the novel, Ivan narrates the parable to his brother Alyosha, to express his disdain for organized religion and question the existence of a personal and benevolent God. After hearing the story, like Christ, Alyosha kisses Ivan and leaves. Did the Grand Inquisitor and Ivan get a fair hearing? Was the silent response meant to leave them alone to figure out their thoughts and actions? In other words, was silence needed for potential transformation? Caryl Emerson interprets: "Christ did not see fit to bestow a verbal response in the Inquisitor's confession—but that confession could only have occurred in His presence," and, more important, "the mournful love that permeates Christ's silent 'listening act' is indispensable for full and honest unfolding of this inspired quest for self-acquittal" (2001, p. 187). On the transformative power of silence, Rabindranath Tagore puts it nicely in one line: "God's silence ripens man's thoughts into speech" (2002a, Stray Birds, #314, p. 326). Similarly, in a therapeutic situation, the silent inter-listening of the therapist has enormous healing potential for the client. In many situations in our social life, the confessor, tacitly or otherwise, demands silence as a response, for he or she wants to release interior truth uninterrupted to achieve internal freedom. Very often, a hardworking, sincere student who has done poorly in an exam walks into my office to explain why he/she did poorly, and the reasons could be many—difficult situation and/or inadequate preparation—and all I have to do is nod my head, and often even before I say, "I understand," they say, "Thank you," and walk out. They just want to be heard. Bakhtin asserts: "For the word (and, consequently, for a human being) there is nothing more terrible than a *lack of response*" (1986, p. 127). I concur with Emerson (2001) that "not being heard" is an affront to dialogue, but being left alone to sort out the inner turmoil is beneficial as it creates space for intra-psychic dialogue. Furthermore, utterances and confessions are addressed not only to other concrete individuals, but, according to Bakhtin, there is always the presence of another third party—the *Superaddressee*—be it God, conscience, humanity, and so on, and hence the silence allows the message to reach the third party. Emerging from this compassionate and generative silence is the will to power and hence incredibly empowering so that one may exercise the freedom to choose.

But we cannot disregard another dimension; silence can be and often is exploited on this uneven earth. For a demagogue, God's silence is a convenient condition for him to continue his acts of deception. Besides, rabid monologists, in addition to the many delusions they live in, may think, again deluding themselves, that by the sheer volume of their voice, they managed to silence the others and even feel triumphant. In this situation, there is neither any regard for interior or exterior truth, nor any internal freedom in a true sense. There is only a false illusion of freedom and victory.

Freedom finds its multifarious expression in the collected works of Bakhtin with distinct tone and dimension. One is the freedom of laughter in the carnival space and time. It is a collective gaiety. It is primordial and it is not directed toward anybody, but refers to the absurdities of reality. There is no room for the uniqueness of self in the carnival space. The "I" just dissolves into the collective—participating in the collective feasting and demanding justice for all. It is a serious play. Bakhtin insists that "Only dogmatic and authoritarian cultures are one-sidedly serious" (FNM 70–71, p. 134). Besides, Bakhtin adds, "Violence does not know laughter" (ibid.). Spontaneous laughter cannot be forced; individuals freely join the laughing chorus only when the ridiculous becomes glaringly visible, not when a group is targeted in a mean-spirited manner; but at the same time no one is spared, including authority figures. Bakhtin insists, "It is impossible to implant laughter or festivities" (FNM 70–71, p. 135). In full freedom, individuals laugh and willingly participate in festivities.

Furthermore, carnival laughter, as I have discussed in detail in the earlier chapter on "Carnivalization of Consciousness," is faithful to the interior truth, with very little concern for polish and décor; instead, it retains coarseness in the service of truth and freedom. The abnormal sense of self-importance—the exaggerated sense of "I"—its exclusivity and uniqueness, which occurs in the non-carnival space, is suspended temporarily to enter the carnival space to be part of collective humanity. I would argue that the "will to power" is to carnivalize consciousness periodically and the strength of a culture is determined by the carnival space it sanctions. Bakhtin writes:

> Everything that is truly great must include an element of laughter. Otherwise it becomes threatening, terrible, or pompous; in any case, it is limited. Laughter lifts the barrier and clears the path.
>
> *(FNM 70–71, p. 135)*

Some truths are accessible only to laughter and laughter alone gives the feeling of unbridled freedom.

Truth, freedom, and justice take on different dimensions outside the carnival space—truth that is dialogic and context-dependent and freedom that comes with ethical obligations—and here self and other retain their uniqueness and exclusivity.

Because each individual always occupies a unique position in space and time, Bakhtin insists, a philosophy of life must "include the theoretical world within the unity of life-in-process-of-becoming" (TPA, p. 13)—the abstract principles of the open sky—must gain validity in the concrete life on the uneven earth, with all its necessities, contingencies, and obligations. Therefore, any claims to truth, freedom, justice, and other philosophical constructs must be constructed on uniqueness, outsideness, and boundedness of real life, as Bakhtin cautions on the dangers of disregarding them:

> Aesthetic seeing is justified, as long as it does not go beyond its own bounds. But in so far it pretends being a philosophical seeing of unitary and once-occurrent Being in its event-ness, aesthetic seeing is inevitably doomed to passing off an abstractly isolated part as the actual whole.
> *(TPA, p. 17)*

Making any claims by pretending "to go beyond its own bounds" is flawed on many levels, according to Bakhtin. It constitutes trespassing into the domain of the other. Besides, at a practical level, you cannot simultaneously see from the position you occupy and from the position the other occupies. Humans don't enjoy omnipresence. Therefore, you need to rely on the other, the different other, to get a broader perspective. Aesthetic vision demands outsideness and multiple consciousnesses, and therefore "going beyond its own bounds" would compromise aesthetics. Bakhtin's early philosophical works concentrate mainly on plurality of consciousness, uniqueness of the position we occupy, manifestation of the abstract in the concrete world to gain validity, and these ideas set the stage for his later works to present a comprehensive account of the innumerable possibilities in the world of differences.

Even a sincere intent to help another individual suffering from emotional turmoil, according to Bakhtin, necessitates the recognition and understanding of the uniqueness of self and the other. Without the benevolent demarcation, help does not reach the troubled individual. Only by acknowledging the unique position you occupy can you offer sincere counsel that has the potential to heal because you are different and you are outside. Helping someone because it makes you feel good is still self-centered and the counsel is not geared specifically for the other who is in pain. Bakhtin refers to such an approach where you seek glory and significance in the lives of others as "parasitism"—an invasion of the consciousness of the other—so much so that the world of differences that is supposed to offer creative solutions fails to achieve that goal. In the vocabulary of clinical psychologists, it is the danger of counter-transference in the treatment process. Bakhtin puts it nicely:

> Aesthetic empathizing into the participant of an event is not yet the attainment of a full comprehension of the event. Even if I know a given person thoroughly, and I also know myself, I still have to grasp the truth of our interrelationship, the truth of the unitary and unique event which links us and in which we are participants.
>
> *(TPA, p. 17)*

For Bakhtin, giving and receiving, be it help, love, a gift, or anything else, requires graciousness—giving due regard to the other without diminishing the significance of self—and hence giving and receiving are ideally conjoined. In order to be munificent, I must be mindful of the vulnerabilities of the other, and in order to receive graciously, I must trust the goodwill of the other, even as I feel vulnerable. But de-hyphenating giving and receiving and making them unidirectional, according to Bakhtin, is a symptom of a frightened and insecure mind that acts blindly in its own closed world of certainty. Bakhtin describes the timid mind as "the people who are afraid of accepting a favor, afraid of becoming obligated; what we are dealing with here is precisely the *fear* of receiving a gift, and thereby obligating oneself too much" (2001, p. 220). It is easy to put on a veneer of confidence and bravado and think all answers to life's predicaments can be found within, but this does not lead to transformation and development; while vulnerability, at least initially and momentarily is the immediate feeling in opening yourself up to the other, but it eventually has the potential to transform and catalyze development. I want to emphasize "potential" because opening yourself up to the other does not guarantee fresh perspective, but the possibility opens up. Even if the potential is not realized, opening yourself up to the other frees you from fear. Now, that is a psychological gain.

When we study the entire Bakhtinian oeuvre carefully, we find that he maintains that delicate balance between the necessity of the other and the integrity of the self without compromising the freedom of either party, and we find this principle expressed in every human relation (author–hero, God–devotee, and other social relations), in every domain of human functioning (cognition, emotions, ethics, language, and so on), and in every human activity (artistic and everyday life). The cornucopia of differences in the world gives us the freedom to choose and construct selfhood. The artist chooses from the available "surplus of meanings" to bring disparate elements to make them into a consummated whole. The self, operating amidst the triadic equation of *I-for-myself*, *I-for-others*, and *Others-for-me*, is able to freely select from the emerging images and yet yield to others to do their provisional final touches, in the same way an author eventually defers to his own created hero and his readers so that they may make their contribution to the semantic sphere. For a work of art to be alive, all aspects and parties involved must be full of life and fully free.

> It is one thing to be active in relation to a dead thing, to a voiceless material that can be molded and formed as one wishes, and another thing to be active *in relation* to someone else's autonomous consciousness.
>
> *(PDP, p. 285)*

What applies to art also applies to life in practically every domain; as Bakhtin asserts, "I cannot manage without another, I cannot become myself without another; I must find myself in another by finding another in myself (in mutual reflection and mutual acceptance)" (1984b, p. 287). Bakhtin is not referring to the energizing silence or solitude, where there is the presence of others in the intra-psychic sphere; nor is he referring to a simple presence of others—a gathering of individuals where each one is carrying out a monologue with total disregard for the other. Bakhtin makes room for fullness in solitude and energy in meditative silence and acknowledges the possibility of emptiness and loneliness in a crowd. Whether in solitude or in social situations, Bakhtin asks us to recognize that "A person has no internal sovereign territory, he is wholly and always on the boundary; looking inside himself, he looks *into the eyes of another* or *with the eyes of another*" (PDP, p. 287). One could very well engage in a social conversation and *not* look into the eyes of the other or with the eyes of the other, and when that happens there is an experience of inner loneliness. Bakhtin makes an even stronger case: "Separation, dissociation, and enclosure within the self as the main reason for the loss of one's self" (PDP, p. 287). There is no promise or potential in the monologic world that is unyielding, unproductive, and terrifyingly lifeless.

The open-ended world of differences holds incredible promise and potential for the individual to reassess his or her actions, rebuild broken relationships, and reclaim valuables that are lost or ignored, and these possibilities contribute immensely to transformation and development, and that is why Emerson (2001) rightly identified "plenitude as a form of hope." The closed monologic world/consciousness is always in search of definitive conclusions offering no hope for change and growth; thereby disempowering the individual, whereas the dialogic world resists any kind of *"conclusive conclusion"*—for there is always the carnival space to open up all provisional endings, to point toward the future; as Bakhtin asserts, *"nothing conclusive has yet taken place in the world, the ultimate word of the world and about the world has not yet been spoken, the world is open and free, everything is still in the future and will always be in the future"* (PDP, p. 166). Development relies on the future for moving forward. Even the past—individual and cultural—has hope. In this book, we are dealing with human development from the standpoint of sociohistorical epistemology, and hence need to recognize that development is not solely an individual affair; cultural growth is equally essential. It would be helpful if cultures took note of Bakhtin's bold proclamation, interestingly made in one of his last works: "Nothing is absolutely dead: every meaning will have its coming festival. The problem of *great time*" (TMHS, p. 170). Perhaps it is time to make collective effort to reclaim valuable meanings of the past buried in the perennial stream of *Great Time* and prepare for their homecoming festival.

In one of his most fascinating works, but unfortunately not as popular as it deserves to be, Lev Vygotsky (1971) showed just as much concern to *The Psychology of Art* as he did to *The Art of Psychology*. But Vygotsky was an equally committed scientist, exploring the mysteries of the mind. Interestingly, it seems a creative approach is not built on an either/or model, and therefore the study of consciousness is both a science and an art, and, perhaps, that is why Toulmin's (1978) reference to Vygotsky as "the Mozart of Psychology" seems befitting. Bakhtin admired Dostoevsky for the convergence of science and art in his vision and method. The hardcore scientific community, Bakhtin says, has been far more cognizant of the probabilities and multiplicities that govern the universe and have figured out a way to take them into account, while the humanities and social sciences have rarely displayed such sophistication.

> The scientific consciousness has long since grown accustomed to the Einsteinian world with its multiplicity of systems of measurement, etc. But in the realm of *artistic* cognition people sometimes continue to demand a very crude and very primitive definitiveness, one that quite obviously could not be true.
>
> (PDP, p. 272)

Therefore, dialogic vision and method is not a fanciful idea; it is in fact closer to the truth about the human world and hence unarguably scientific. It is also artistic because it allows for a new form of visualization—one that simultaneously captures reality and shows innumerable possibilities—so that we may get glimpses of "new sides of the human being and his life" (PDP, p. 270). This kind of artistic angle cannot be the exclusive domain of literary writers; those of us in the human sciences also can make rightful claim to this domain. Perhaps, what is needed is a special kind of *"polyphonic artistic thinking"* to orchestrate the immense diversity in our social world so that we may gain better insights into the *"thinking human consciousness and the dialogic sphere of its existence"* (PDP, p. 270), and this is something that monologic position is incapable of grasping.

We live in a world where close encounter with other cultures is an immediate reality, and the pressing concern is ways to promote intercommunal, interreligious, and inter-lingual dialogue and, more important, intra-psychic dialogue of competing ideas and ideals, so that cultures and individuals alike may grow, develop, and achieve harmony. In this globalized world, we are always operating at the confluence of cultures and in the parliament of languages, where meanings must be negotiated and the other must be accommodated. Diversity in ideas, faith, customs, and in practically every area of life is the greatest gift a culture can offer, for it enables one to forge a new vision of globalization, not of the marketplace (which has already happened anyway), but of the consciousness. Human life is packed with the need for love, innumerable failures, regrets, fears, and the reality one faces is death, disease, calamities, and occasionally miracles. Some events are our own making and many more are due to factors beyond our comprehension. Fate, chance, and luck may be workings of some unknown powers, but entering into a dialogue with them is still an assertion of human power and intellect.

The plenitude of differences give us the will to power, the freedom to choose, the hope for reconstruction, and the capacity to love the other, not because the other is like the self, but because the other is different from the self. Operating in a world of infinitely differentiated specifics, we come across innumerable possibilities even as we recognize the trappings of language, time, and space, and it is in this dynamic field we may find new ways of relating to each other in this amazingly pluralistic world.

Freedom, vastness, and limitlessness seem like the property of the open sky, but I like to think that these very constructs can be experienced on this uneven earth too. But that requires effort—to respond dialogically to the world of differences and move forward to develop, so that we may eventually claim the carnivalesque license to mock at the skies and proclaim that *"we have them too"*—a hard earned gift—a life full of possibilities . . .

REFERENCES

Bakhtin, M. M. (1981) *The Dialogic Imagination: Four Essays* (C. Emerson and M. Holquist, Trans.). M. Holquist (Ed.) Austin: University of Texas Press.
Bakhtin, M. M. (1984a) *Rabelais and His World* (H. Iswolsky, Trans.). Bloomington: Indiana University Press.
Bakhtin, M. M. (1984b) *Problems of Dostoevsky's Poetics* (C. Emerson, Trans. and Ed.). Minneapolis: University of Minnesota Press.
Bakhtin, M. M. (1986) *Speech Genres and Other Late Essays* (V. W. McGee, Trans.). C. Emerson and M. Holquist (Eds.) Austin: University of Texas Press.
Bakhtin, M. M. (1990) *Art and Answerability: Early Philosophical Essays by M. M. Bakhtin* (V. Liapunov, Trans.). M. Holquist and V. Liapunov (Eds.) Austin: University of Texas Press.
Bakhtin, M. M. (1993) *Toward a Philosophy of the Act* (V. Liapunov, Trans.). V. Liapunov and M. Holquist (Eds.) Austin: University of Texas Press.
Bakhtin, M. M. (2001) Appendix: M. M. Bakhtin's Lectures and Comments of 1924–1925. In *Bakhtin and Religion: A Feeling for Faith* (S. M. Felch and P. J. Contino, Eds.) Evanston: Northwestern University Press.
Bakhtin, M. M. and Medvedev, P. N. (1985) *The Formal Method in Literary Scholarship: A Critical Introduction to Sociological Poetics* (A. J. Wehrle, Trans.). Cambridge, MA: Harvard University Press.
Bandlamudi, L. (1994) Dialogics of Understanding Self/Culture. *ETHOS*. Vol. 22(4): 460–493.
Bandlamudi, L. (1999) Developmental Discourse as an Author/Hero Relationship. *Culture & Psychology*. Vol. 5(1): 41–65.
Bandlamudi, L. (2010) *Dialogics of Self, The Mahabharata and Culture: The History of Understanding and Understanding of History*. London: Anthem Press.
Barresi, J. (2002) From "the Thought is the Thinker" to "the Voice is the Speaker": William James and the Dialogical Self. *Theory & Psychology*. Vol. 12(2): 237–250.
Baudrillard, J. (1994) *Simulacra and Simulation* (S. F. Glaser, Trans.). Ann Arbor: The University of Michigan Press.
Bauman, Z. (2007) *Consuming Life*. Malden, MA: Polity Press.

Bocharov, S. (1994) Conversations with Bakhtin. *PMLA*. Vol. 109(5) (October 1994): 1009–1024.

Burkitt, I. (2010) Dialogues with Self and Others: Communication, Miscommunication, and the Dialogical Unconscious. *Theory & Psychology*. Vol. 20: 305–321.

Carey, John. (2003) Introduction. In The Joke and Its Relation to the Unconscious by Sigmund Freud (J. Crick, Trans.). New York: Penguin Classics.

Clark, K. and Holquist, M. (1984) *Mikhail Bakhtin*. Cambridge, MA: Harvard University Press.

Crapanzano, V. (1992) *Hermes' Dilemma and Hamlet's Desire: On the Epistemology of Interpretation*. Cambridge, MA: Harvard University Press.

Crapanzano, V. (2000) *Serving the Word: Literalism in America from the Pulpit to the Bench*. New York: New Press.

Cresswell, J. (2011) Being Faithful: Bakhtin and a Potential Postmodern Psychology of Self. *Culture & Psychology*. Vol. 17: 473–490.

Cresswell, J. and Baerveldt, C. (2011) Bakhtin's Realism and Embodiment: Towards a Revision of the Dialogical Self. *Culture & Psychology*. Vol. 17: 263–277.

Csikszentmihalyi, M. (1993) *The Evolving Self: A Psychology for the Third Millennium*. New York: Harper Collins.

Danziger, K. (1990) *Constructing the Subject: Historical Origins of Psychological Research*. Cambridge: Cambridge University Press.

Dewey, J. (1958) *Art as Experience*. New York: Minton, Balch & Company.

Emerson, C. (1989) The Tolstoy Connection in Bakhtin. In *Rethinking Bakhtin: Extensions and Challenges* (G.S. Morson and C. Emerson, Eds.) Evanston, IL: Northwestern University Press.

Emerson, C. (1996) Keeping the Self Intact during the Culture Wars: A Centennial Essay for Mikhail Bakhtin. *New Literary History*. Vol. 27(1): 107–126.

Emerson, C. (1997) *The First Hundred Years of Mikhail Bakhtin*. Princeton, NJ: Princeton University Press.

Emerson, C. (2001) Afterword: Plenitude as a Form of Hope. In *Bakhtin and Religion: A Feeling for Faith* (S.M. Felch and P.J. Contino, Eds.) Evanston, IL: Northwestern University Press.

Erdinast-Vulcan, D. (2013) *Between Philosophy and Literature: Bakhtin and the Question of the Subject*. Stanford, CA: Stanford University Press.

Erikson, E.H. (1959) *Identity and the Life Cycle*. New York: International University Press, Inc.

Fox Keller, E. (1983) *A Feeling for the Organism: The Life and Work of Barbara McClintock*. New York: W.H. Freeman and Company.

Frankfurt, H.G. (2005) *On Bullshit*. Princeton, NJ: Princeton University Press.

Freud, S. (2003) *The Joke and Its Relation to the Unconscious* (J. Crick, Trans.). New York: Penguin Classics.

Fukuyama, F. (1989) *The End of History*. Online: www.wesjones.com/eoh.htm (accessed May 1, 2008).

Gardner, H. (1993) *Creating Minds*. New York: Basic Books.

Gianturco, E. (1990) Introduction. In *On the Study Methods of Our Time*. Giambattista Vico. Ithaca, NY: Cornell University Press.

Good, P. (2002) *Language for Those Who Have Nothing: Mikhail Bakhtin and the Landscape of Psychiatry*. New York: Kluwer Academic Publishers.

Hegel, G.W.F. (1857/2010) *Introduction to the Philosophy of History* (J. Sibree, Trans.). Digireads.com book.

Hermans, H.J.M. and Kempen, H.J.G. (1993) *The Dialogical Self: Meaning as Movement.* San Diego, CA: Academic Press, Inc.
Holquist, M. (1983) Answering as Authoring: Mikhail Bakhtin's Trans-Linguistics. *Critical Inquiry.* Vol. 10(2): 307–319.
hooks, b. (1990) *Yearning: Race, Gender, and Cultural Politics.* Boston, MA: South End Press.
Huntington, S. P. (1993) The Clash of Civilizations. *Council on Foreign Relations Inc.* Online: www.alamut.com/subj/economics/misc/clash.html (accessed May 22, 2007).
Ivanov, V. V. (1991) The Dominant of Bakhtin's Philosophy: Dialogue and Carnival. Paper presented at *Fifth International Bakhtin Conference.* Manchester, University of Manchester. July 15–19.
James, W. (1890/1900) *The Principles of Psychology* (Vol. 1). London: Macmillan.
James, W. (1920) *Psychology: Briefer Course.* New York: Henry Holt and Company.
Karnad, G. (1994) *Three Plays: Nāga-Mandala; Hayavadana; Tughlaq.* Delhi: Oxford University Press.
Kessen, W. (1979) The American Child and Other Cultural Inventions. *American Psychologist.* Vol. 34(10): 815–820.
Leontiev, A. N. (1971) Introduction. In *The Psychology of Art.* L. S. Vygotsky. Cambridge, MA: The MIT Press.
Lotman, Y. M. (1990) *Universe of the Mind: A Semiotic Theory of Culture.* Bloomington: Indiana University Press.
Lotman, Y. M. and Uspenskii, B. A. (1985) Binary Models in the Dynamics of Russian Culture (to the End of the Eighteenth Century). In *The Semiotics of Russian Cultural History: Essays by Lotman, Ginsburg, Uspenskii.* (A. D. Nakhimovsky and A. S. Nakhimovsky, Eds.) Ithaca, NY: Cornell University Press.
Lukács, G. (1971) *The Theory of the Novel: A Historico-philosophical Essay on the Forms of Great Epic Literature.* Cambridge, MA: The MIT Press.
Maslow, A. H. (1976) *The Farther Reaches of Human Nature.* New York: Penguin Books.
Mead, G. H. (1934) *Mind, Self and Society.* Chicago, IL: University of Chicago Press.
Mill, J. S. (1985) *On Liberty.* Middlesex: Penguin Books.
Monier-Williams, M. (1899) *Sanskrit English Dictionary.* New Delhi: Munshiram Manoharlal Publishers Pvt. Ltd.
Morson, G. S. and Emerson, C. (1990) *Mikhail Bakhtin: Creation of Prosaics.* Stanford, CA: Stanford University Press.
Nandy, A. (2001) *An Ambiguous Journey to the City: The Village and Other Odd Ruins of the Self in the Indian Imagination.* New Delhi: Oxford University Press.
Nietzsche, F. (1961) *Thus Spoke Zarathustra: A Book for Everyone and No One.* London: Penguin Books.
Nietzsche, F. (1967) *The Will to Power.* New York: Vintage Books.
Nietzsche, F. (1989) *Beyond Good and Evil.* New York: Vintage Books.
Pepper, S. C. (1942) *World Hypotheses: A Study in Evidence.* Berkeley: University of California Press.
Plato (1945) *The Republic of Plato.* Translated with Introduction and Notes by Francis MacDonald Cornford. London: Oxford University Press.
Rogers, C. (1969) *Freedom to Learn.* Ohio: Charles E. Merrill Publishing Company.
Rousseau, J. J. (1979) *Emile.* Introduction, Translation and Notes by Allan Bloom. New York: Basic Books.
Schuman, S. (2014) *Freedom and Dialogue in a Polarized World.* Newark: University of Delaware Press.

Scribner, S. (1985) Vygotsky's Uses of History. In *Culture, Communication and Cognition: Vygotskian Perspectives* (J. Wertsch, Ed.) Cambridge: Cambridge University Press.
Shotter, J. (2011) *Getting It: Withness-Thinking and the Dialogical . . . in Practice*. New York: Hampton Press, Inc.
Siegel, L. 1987. *Laughing Matters: Comic Tradition in India*. Chicago, IL: University of Chicago Press.
Somadeva. (1994) *Tales from The Kathāsaritsāgara*. New Delhi: Penguin Classics.
Spivak, G. C. (1991) *Time and Timing: Law and History*. In *Chronotypes* (J. Bender and D. E. Wellbery, Eds.) Stanford, CA: Stanford University Press.
Spivak, G. C. (1994) Can the Subaltern Speak? In *Colonial Discourse and Post-Colonial Theory* (P. Williams and L. Chrisman, Eds.) New York: Columbia University Press.
Sri Aurobindo. (1997) *The Human Cycle; The Ideal of Human Unity; War and Self-Determination*. Pondicherry: Sri Aurobindo Ashram.
Sri Aurobindo. (1999) *Collected Poems*. Pondicherry: Sri Aurobindo Ashram.
Sullivan, P. (2007) Examining the Self–Other Dialogue through "Spirit" and "Soul." *Culture & Psychology*. Vol. 13: 105–128.
Sullivan, P. (2012) *Qualitative Data Analysis: Using a Dialogical Approach*. London: Sage.
Sullivan, P. and McCarthy, J. (2005) A Dialogical Approach to Experience-based Inquiry. *Theory & Psychology*. Vol. 15(5): 621–638.
Sullivan, P. and McCarthy, J. (2009) An Experiential Account of the Psychology of Art. *Psychology of Aesthetics, Creativity and the Arts*. Vol. 3(3): 181–187.
Sunstein, C. R. and Hastie, R. (2015) *Wiser: Getting Beyond Groupthink to Make Groups Smarter*. Boston, MA: Harvard Business Review Press.
Tagore, R. (1971) *Gitanjali*. New York: Macmillan Publishing Company.
Tagore, R. (2002a) *Collected Poems and Plays of Rabindranath Tagore*. New Delhi: Rupa.
Tagore, R. (2002b) *Creative Unity*. New Delhi: Rupa.
Tagore, R. (2002c) *Personality*. New Delhi: Rupa.
Toulmin, S. (1978) The Mozart of Psychology. *The New York Review of Books*. September 28.
Unni, N. P. (Editor and Translator). 1998. *Natyasastra* (Vols. 1–4) Delhi: Nag Publishers.
Vasudeva, S. (Editor and Translator) 2005. *Three Satires by Bhallata, Kshemendra & Nila-Kantha*. Clay Sanskrit Library. New York: New York University Press.
Vico, G. (1744/1984) *The New Science of Giambattista Vico*. T. G. Bergin and M. H. Fisch (Trans.). Ithaca, NY: Cornell University Press.
Vico, G. (1990) *On the Study Methods of Our Time*. E. Gianturco (Trans.). Ithaca, NY: Cornell University Press.
Volosinov, V. N. (1986) *Marxism and the Philosophy of Language*. L. Matejka and I. R. Titunik (Trans.) Cambridge, MA: Harvard University Press.
Vygotsky, L. S. (1971) *The Psychology of Art*. Cambridge: The MIT Press.
Vygotsky, L. S. (1978) *Mind in Society: The Development of Higher Psychological Processes*. Cambridge, MA: Harvard University Press.
Vygotsky, L. S. (1987) *The Collected Works of L. S. Vygotsky. Vol. 1. Problems of General Psychology*. R. W. Rieber and A. S. Carton (Eds.) New York: Plenum Press.
Vygotsky, L. S. (1989) Concrete Human Psychology. *Soviet Psychology*. Vol. 27(2): 51–64.
Vygotsky, L. S. (1990) Imagination and Creativity in the Adolescent. *Soviet Psychology*. Vol. 29(1): 73–88.
Weinberger, D. (2007) *Everything Is Miscellaneous: The Power of New Digital Disorder*. New York: Henry Holt and Company.
Wittgenstein, L. (1980) *Remarks on the Philosophy of Psychology*. Vol. II. Chicago, IL: University of Chicago Press.

INDEX

Abhinavagupta 66, 69
aboutness method 110–11
abstract objectivism 113
abstract time 27
Acharya Somadeva 77
adventure novel 10, 20–3, 38
adventure time 20–1
adventurous-heroic type 57–9
advocatory speech 30, 32–3
aesthetic activity 53–4
aesthetic consciousness 57–9
aesthetic contemplation 52
aesthetics: objective-analytical method of 44; problems with experimental aesthetics 42–4
analytic form 25
Apology of Socrates (Plato) 27
Apuleius 20
architectonics 11, 40–1, 95
Aristotle 25, 33
art: essence and function of 43; as expression 42; life and 40–1; psychology and 46–7
Art as Experience (Dewey) 46
Aurobindo, Ghosh (Sri) 122–3
Author and Hero in Aesthetic Activity (Bakhtin) 49
authoring 91–3, 101, 104

Bakhtin Circle 49
Bakhtin, Mikhail: on aesthetic activity 40–3; on aesthetics 48–54; architectonics of 11, 40–1, 95; on authoring the self 104; on carnival genre 76; on carnival laughter 67–71, 75–6; on carnival space 64, 79–82; on death 104; dialogical self theory of 89–90; discussion of soul 89, 99–101; discussion on expressive aesthetics 98–9; discussions on empathy and sympathy 97–8; on Dostoevsky's artistic imagination 36; on ethical conduct 96; on human relations 54–62; on laughter 65, 69, 72; on life of a text 125–6; observations about culture of marketplace 72–5; on parody 65; on religion 124–5; on scientific method 107–8; on spirit of inquiry 111–12; study of novelistic forms 14–39; suffering from osteomyelitis 78–9, 95; on use of chronotopes 16–17; on use of genres 15–16
Baldwin, James 8
Baudrillard, Jean 31, 32
Bauman, Zygmunt 31
Beyond Good and Evil (Nietzsche) 83–4
biographical consciousness 57–9
biographical novel 10, 25–6
biographical time 27
birth 59
Boccaccio, Giovanni 78
Bocharov, Sergey 49
bodies 78
brainstorming 126–8
The Brothers Karamazov (Dostoyevsky) 129

Index

carnival 11–12, 64–5
carnival genre 76
carnivalized consciousness 79–85
carnival language 75–6, 78–9, 82–5
carnival laughter 67–8, 70–2, 84, 130
carnival space 64, 79–82
Cervantes, Miguel de 78
"the child" 7
childhood 7
childrearing practices 8
children: narratives on development and tales about 7–9; Vygotsky's stories of 37
chronotopes: of adventure novel 21; in biographical novel 25; of biography and autobiography 26; boundaries of analysis 117; concept of 10, 16–17; genres and 117; images of self distorted by other 94; in *Platonic* novels 29; real-life chronotopes 30; in rhetorical biography 30–2; in Vygotskian worldview 37
Cicero, Marcus Tullius 34
clan 33
Clark, K. 1, 78
clinical psychology 98
cognitive acts 53
cognitive development 34
The Colbert Report 82
Colbert, Stephen 82
communication systems 113–14
compliments 31
consciousness: aesthetic consciousness 57–9; biographical consciousness 57–9; carnivalized consciousness 11, 79–85; dangers of arresting 109–10; genres and 116–17; in Greek romance novel 20; language development and 34–5; novelistic genres and 10; plurality of 89; scientific consciousness 134
conscious zone 45
counter-transference 132
Crapanzano, Vincent 105–6, 119, 125
Creating Minds (Gardner) 46
creativity 11
crisis: in adventure novels 20–3; in *Platonic* novels 27–8
Csikszentmihalyi, Mihaly 11, 46–7
culture 6–7, 60–1, 102, 122, 134–5

The Daily Show 82
Danziger, Kurt 24, 106
Darwin, Charles 7
death 59–60, 104

Descartes, Rene 73, 110
developing subject 17–19
development: in adventure novels 20–3, 38; in biographical novel 25–6; in biography and autobiography 26–7, 33–5; in Greek romance novels 19–20; in novelistic genres 17–19; in *Platonic* novels 27–9; psychosexual theory of 45–6; role of dialogue in 5–7; in Roman autobiography 33; in sociohistorical novel 35–8; theories about 8–9; in travel novels 24–5; typologies of novels as models of 38–9; in Vygotskian worldview 37
developmental narratives 7–9, 12
Dewey, John 11, 46–7
dialogical self 89–91
dialogic method: artistic dimension of 134; for human sciences 105–20; scientific method and 108–12; use of 12–13
dialogism 13, 106–8, 120
dialogue 5–7, 103, 112, 115, 120
difference: brainstorming and 126–8; dialogue and 4–5; sameness and 123
digital public square 30–2
dogma 13, 124–5
Dostoevsky, Fyodor M. 10; artistic imagination of 35–6; biographical novels and 25; development and 5; hearing ear of 52; polyphonic novels of 89, 122; role of silence in parable of 129; theological concerns of 49–50; underground man of 101; use of carnival motifs 78, 82
drawing-room rhetoric 34

Einstein, Alfred 46
Einstein's Theory of Relativity 16
Eliot, T.S. 46
Emerson, Caryl 3, 60, 94, 101, 129
Emile (Rousseau) 7, 122
empathy 57, 97–9
encomia 29–31
energia form 25
Enlightenment period 28
epic 17–19
"epistemic child" 7, 28, 37
epistemography 29
Erikson, Erik 26
essentialist approach 44
ethical conduct 96
everyday time 21

experimental aesthetics 43
expressive aesthetics 97–9

Facebook 30
faith 124–5
fatalism 20
flow 46–7
folklore 76
foreign cultures 61, 102–4
form 99
Formalism 42
freedom 122, 130
Freud, Sigmund 8, 11, 44–6, 68–9
Fridman, I. N. 3

game stage 89
Gandhi, Mohandas K. 46
Gardner, Howard 11, 46
genre 15–16, 116–17
Gianturco, F. 110–11
giving 132
Goethe, Johann W. 5, 35, 37, 52–3
The Golden Ass (Apuleius) 21
Good, Peter 98
Graham, Martha 46
Greek romance novel 10, 19–20
group decision making 126–8

Hamlet (Shakespeare) 42
Hastie, Reid 126–8
Hayavadana (Karnad) 77
healing 97–9
Hegel, Georg W. F. 29
Hermans, Hubert 89–90
hero: in adventure novels 20–3; in Greek romance novels 20–3; in novels 17–19; in *Platonic* novels 27–8
heroine 20
heteroglossia 65
Hindu cosmology/philosophy 76, 122
Hippocratic novel 70
historical method 111
historical time 21–3
history 6–7, 17, 29
Holquist, M. 1, 78, 88
hooks, bell 94
humanist psychology 25–6
human sciences 25, 107

ideal time 27
I-I system 113–14
immigrants 61, 102
India 47–8, 76–8, 104

information overload 32
inquiry 111–12
internal chronotopes 30
I-s/he system 113–14

James, William 88, 109
The Joke and Its Relation to the Unconscious (Freud) 68

Kant, Immanuel 48, 93
Karnad, Girish 77
Kathāsaritsāgara (Somadeva) 77
Keller, Evelyn Fox 52–3
Kempen, H. J. G. 89–90
Kessen, William 8
Kohlberg, Lawrence 58
Kshemendra 63

language: art and 44; carnival language 75–6, 78, 82–5; differences in 5; novelistic genres and 15; use in dialogic method 112–15
language development 34–5
The Last Supper (Leonardo da Vinci) 98
laughter: carnival laughter 64, 67–8, 70–2, 84; features of 67–8; freedom and 130; nature of 65–6; philosophical dimensions of 69–70
Leonardo da Vinci 98
Leontiev, A. N. 41
letters 34
On Liberty (Mill) 122
literalism 125
Locke, John 7
Lord Shiva 94
Lotman, Y. M. 113–14
love 56
Lukács, George 26

The Mahabharata 24, 103, 114, 116
Mann, Thomas 77
Maslow, Abraham 25–6
mass media 85
McCarthy, John 115
McClintock, Barbara 53–4
Mead, George Herbert 88–9
meaning 32
Medvedev, P. N. 3, 16, 43, 116
metamorphosis 21
Mill, John Stuart 122
Mind, Self and Society (Mead) 88
monologic understanding 102
Morson, G. S. 101

144 Index

Müller-Freienfels, Richard 44
multiculturalism 61
multilayered/multifaceted understanding 102

Nandy, Ashis 104
natural sciences 25, 107
Natya Sastra (Sage Bharata) 47–8, 69
Nietzsche, Frederick 50, 83–4, 128
novels: adventure novel 10, 20–3; biographical novel 10, 25–6, 33–5; developing subject and 17–19; as developmental narratives 12; the epic and 17–19; Greek romance novel 10, 19–20; Hippocratic novel 70; of historical emergence 36; polyphonic novel 89; rhetorical biography 10–11, 27–32; Roman autobiography 11, 33–5; sociohistorical novel 35–8; travel novel 10, 23–5; types of 10–11; typologies as models of human development 38–9
numerical data 117–18

objective-analytical method 44
objective reasoning method 28
open sky 128–35
the other 54–62, 93–7, 122

pain 97–9
parody 65–6
Petronius 20
Phaedo (Plato) 27
photographs 93
Piaget, Jean 7, 9, 28–9, 37, 128
Picasso, Pablo 46
Plato 27, 122
Platonic novels 27–8
play stage 89
Plutarch 33
polyphonic novel 89
positivist psychology 23–4
The Principles of Psychology (James) 88
"prophesy" 18
Proust, Marcel 14
psychiatry 98
psychoanalysis 45
psychology: art and 46–7; clinical psychology 98; humanist psychology 25–6; ideas, concepts, and imageries of the self in 88–91; investigative practices and their resistance to dialogicality in 106–8; positivist psychology 23–4; stimulus-response model in 109

The Psychology of Art (Vygotsky) 41, 134
psychosexual theory of development 45–6
public feasting 74
publicity 30
public square 30–2
Pushkin, Alexander S. 30

quantitative statistical data 117–18
question and answer relationship 111

Rabelais, François 3, 70, 73, 76, 78, 82, 85
reality 116–17
real-life chronotopes 30
reason 28
rebirth 20–3
receiving 132
relational-bilateral understanding 102
relational-unilateral understanding 102
religion 124–5
Renaissance period 69
The Republic (Plato) 122
researchers 105–6, 119–20
rhetorical biography 10–11, 27–32
Rogers, Carl 26
Roman autobiography 11, 33
Rousseau, Jean Jacques 7, 111, 122

Sage Bharata 48, 69
satirico-ironic language 33–4
Satyricon (Petronius) 20
Schuman, Sharon 122
scientific consciousness 134
scientific method 25, 106–8
Scribner, Sylvia 37
seeker 27–8
the self: authoring 91–3, 101, 104; creative composition of 54–62; dialogical self 89–91; freedom and 122; ideas, concepts, and imageries in psychology 88–91; self-other relationship 57–9
self-actualization 25–6
self-development 12
selfhood: model of 12; theory of novelistic 35; variables in theorem for 30
selfies 87, 93
self-other relationship 57–9
self-representation 30–2
Serving the Word (Crapanzano) 125
Shakespeare, William 37, 42
Shotter, John 109
silence 5, 128–30
Simulacra and Simulation (Baudrillard) 32

simulation 31–2
slavery 94
social-quotidian type 57–9
sociohistorical novel 35–8
soliloquys 34
soul 89, 99–101
speech 34–5
spirit and soul relationship 103
Spivak, Gayatri 17, 29, 94
staged self 29–32
stage theory 29
Stewart, Jon 82
stimulus-response model 109
stoic autobiography 34
Stravinsky, Igor 46
street talk 11
subaltern 94
subconscious zone 45
suffering 131–2
Sullivan, Paul 115
Sunstein, Cass R. 126–8
survivor's tales 23
sympathetic co-experience 57
sympathy 97–9

Tagore, Rabindranath 103–4, 129
thinking 34–5

tickling 69–70
time: in adventure novels 20–3; chronotopes and 117; in Hegel's philosophy of history 29; operation of 17; in Piaget's genetic epistemology 29; in *Platonic* novels 27; seeing and reading 37; stage theory 29
Toulmin, S. 134
transcendental aesthetics 48
The Transposed Heads (Mann) 77
travel novel 10, 23–5
triadic equation of self and other 30, 54–5, 95–6, 132
truth 124

uneven earth 128–35
uniqueness 124

Vico, Giambattista 110–11
visualization 134
Volosinov, V. N. 3, 113
Vygotsky, Lev 34–7, 41–5, 82, 85, 88, 134

Watson, James 8
witness-thinking 109–12

Zone of Proximal Development 37